Understanding Innovation

Series editors
Christoph Meinel
Potsdam, Germany

Larry Leifer
Stanford, USA

More information about this series at http://www.springer.com/series/8802

Steven Ney • Christoph Meinel

Putting Design Thinking to Work

How Large Organizations Can Embrace
Messy Institutions to Tackle Wicked Problems

Steven Ney
T-Systems International
Berlin, Germany

Christoph Meinel
Hasso Plattner Institute
University of Potsdam
Potsdam, Germany

ISSN 2197-5752 ISSN 2197-5760 (electronic)
Understanding Innovation
ISBN 978-3-030-19608-0 ISBN 978-3-030-19609-7 (eBook)
https://doi.org/10.1007/978-3-030-19609-7

© Springer Nature Switzerland AG 2019
This work is subject to copyright. All rights are reserved by the Publisher, whether the whole or part of the material is concerned, specifically the rights of translation, reprinting, reuse of illustrations, recitation, broadcasting, reproduction on microfilms or in any other physical way, and transmission or information storage and retrieval, electronic adaptation, computer software, or by similar or dissimilar methodology now known or hereafter developed.
The use of general descriptive names, registered names, trademarks, service marks, etc. in this publication does not imply, even in the absence of a specific statement, that such names are exempt from the relevant protective laws and regulations and therefore free for general use.
The publisher, the authors, and the editors are safe to assume that the advice and information in this book are believed to be true and accurate at the date of publication. Neither the publisher nor the authors or the editors give a warranty, express or implied, with respect to the material contained herein or for any errors or omissions that may have been made. The publisher remains neutral with regard to jurisdictional claims in published maps and institutional affiliations.

This Springer imprint is published by the registered company Springer Nature Switzerland AG.
The registered company address is: Gewerbestrasse 11, 6330 Cham, Switzerland

Contents

1	**Introduction**	1
	What is Design Thinking?	2
	Innovating in Diverse and Autonomous Teams	5
	Creating Room(s) for Innovation	7
	Mobilising Creative Potential: The Design Thinking Process	9
	Brief Overview of the Book	15
	References	18
2	**Innovation, Wicked Problems and Design Thinking**	21
	Why People Want Design Thinking: Innovation and Organisational Survival	22
	Innovation in Businesses	22
	Innovation in the Economy	24
	Shelter from the Storm: Fads and Fashions in Management	25
	Why People May Need Design Thinking	27
	Innovation in the Public Sector: Value as Problem-Solving	27
	Wicked Problems	31
	Knowledge, Frames and Paradigms	33
	Solving Wicked Problems: Integrative Thinking and Clumsy Solutions	34
	Design Thinking, Integrative Thinking and Clumsy Solutions	36
	Conclusion	40
	References	41
3	**Clumsy Solutions, Messy Institutions and Cultural Change**	43
	Wicked Problems, Innovation and Large Organisations	44
	Reasons for Organisational Failure	44
	Transformation and Organisational Viability	46
	More In-Built Failure	51

	From Ambidextrous to Multi-Dextrous Organisations	54
	Messy Institutions	63
	Four Roads to Clumsiness	63
	Four Sets of Strengths and Weaknesses	66
	Messy Institutions and Design Thinking	68
	Conclusion	69
	References	71
4	**Creating Social Spaces for Exploration**	73
	Space, Deliberation and Mini-Publics	74
	Carving New Organisational Spaces Out of Institutional Silos	76
	Expanding and Narrowing Strategic Options for Organisations	79
	Individual Discomforts, Professional Grievances	80
	Three Patterns of Resistance: Disruption, Agenda-Setting and Manipulation	82
	Lessons Learnt	85
	Design Thinking Causes Alienation Too	86
	Senior Management Support May Not Be Enough	86
	Design Thinking Spaces Need Protection at Operational Level	87
	New Management of Interfaces	87
	Conclusion	88
	References	90
5	**Hunting, Gathering and Taking It Home: Bringing New Perspectives and Perceptions into Organisations**	93
	Hunting, Gathering and Taking It Home: Strengthening Diversity in Teams and Giving Users a Voice in the Design Process	94
	Mobilising Diversity	96
	Teasing Out Diversity Within Teams	96
	Hunting and Gathering: Incorporating User Voices in Design Processes	97
	The Benefits of a Rich Pool of Ideas	99
	Confronting Assumptions	99
	Designing Better Outputs	100
	The Difficulties of Setting Up a Richer Pool of Ideas (And an Open Question)	101
	Marginalisation and Exclusion	101
	Lacking Skills	102
	Misuse and Misunderstanding	103
	How Diverse Is Diversity?	104
	Lessons Learnt	104
	Acknowledge Shifts of Accountability and Legitimacy	105
	Enable Continuous Learning	106
	Balance Exploration and Exploitation in Methods	107
	Ensure a Requisite Variety of Voices	108
	Conclusion	108
	References	110

6 Design Thinking and Messy Practices ... 113
Messy Design Thinking ... 114
   Output-Oriented Practices ... 115
   Inclusion-Oriented Practices ... 120
   Process-Oriented Practices ... 123
   Chance-Oriented Practices ... 125
Strengths and Weaknesses of Contending Practices ... 126
   Avoiding Dilettantism ... 126
   Preventing Paralysis ... 128
   Reigning in Expertise ... 128
Pluralist Practices in Large Organisations ... 130
   Output-Oriented Practices ... 130
   Inclusion-Oriented Practices ... 132
   Process-Oriented and Chance-Oriented Practices ... 133
Messiness in Practice: Impacts of Messy Practices on Large
Organisations ... 134
   Output- and Inclusion-Oriented Practices as an Antidote
   to Prevailing Process Orientation ... 135
   Dilettantism: Undesired Impacts of Output-Oriented Practices ... 138
   Paralysis and Intolerance ... 139
Lessons Learnt ... 140
   Design Thinking Practices Are 'Messy', But Concentrate on Output
   and Inclusion ... 140
   Design Thinking Programmes at the HPI Schools of Design Thinking
   Are Probably More 'Messy' Than the Design Thinking Initiatives
   in the Large Organisations Covered in the Studies ... 141
   Design Thinking Initiatives in Large Organisations Tend to Be
   Embedded in Predominantly Hierarchical Institutional Contexts ... 141
   There May Be a Trade-Off Between Delivering Innovation
   and Bringing About Cultural Change Within the Wider
   Organisation ... 142
Conclusion ... 142
References ... 144

7 Leadership, Design Thinking and Messy Institutions ... 147
Networks of T-Shaped People: Autonomous, Transversal
and Pluralist ... 147
   Design Thinkers Are Autonomous and Responsible ... 148
   Networks of T-Shaped People Cut Across Organisational
   Boundaries ... 149
   Networks of T-Shaped People Are Pluralist and Diverse ... 150
Leadership Challenges and Opportunities ... 151
   Enabling Collaboration ... 151
   Making Sense of Ambiguity ... 154
   Encouraging Constructive Conflict ... 157

	Engaging with Design Thinking................................	161
	Experiencing Design Thinking............................	161
	Hands-on Management..................................	162
	Tailoring Design Thinking...............................	163
	Conclusion..	165
	References..	166
8	**Conclusion**...	169
	The Conceptual Framework: Wicked Problems, Innovation and Messy Institutions..	169
	Design Thinking in Practice..................................	174
	What Worked?..	175
	What Didn't Work.....................................	179
	New Ideas and Insights.................................	183
	Open Questions..	187
	How Best to Gauge and Operationalise Messiness.............	187
	How to Best Protect Design Thinking Teams in Large Organisations?.......................................	188
	How to Ensure That Design Thinking's Structures, Ideas and Practices Diffuse Through the Organisation?.............	189
	References..	191

Chapter 1
Introduction

Human-centered design drives the success of many start-ups across the globe. Among the many different approaches to human-centred design, one particular framework—conceived at Stanford University in California and developed at the Hasso-Plattner-Institute (HPI) in Potsdam—has received a lot of attention in the past decade: 'Design Thinking'. Its radical focus on users and their needs, its tactics for leveraging the potential of transdisciplinary teams, as well as its iterative evolution of ideas have enabled design thinkers to find effective responses to complex and uncertain problems. Indeed, Design Thinking helps people tackle the types of thorny challenges that confound tried-and-tested problem-solving stratagems. The emphasis on small teams has made human-centred design a natural choice for entrepreneurial start-ups in fields ranging from IT to development aid.

This success has generated a great deal of interest beyond the world of entrepreneurial start-ups. Increasingly, people who face complex challenges in large organisations, be it in the public or private sector, are wondering whether the methods and mindsets of Design Thinking could help them deal with the thorny challenges that simply do not seem to go away. This is why organisations from a wide spectrum of fields are investing considerable resources to learn to be as nimble and flexible as start-ups.

But what does it mean for a large and established organisation to take on Design Thinking?

The following chapters will endeavour to answer precisely this question. Design Thinking is attractive to large organisations because it seems to be a toolbox that promises problem-solving, innovation and success. That said, evidence from both practical experience and design research also suggests that there is considerably more to Design Thinking than a set of tools for innovation. In addition to methods, Design Thinking entails mindsets and practices that may sit rather awkwardly in the way large organisations usually go about their business. Indeed, some argue that if people want to use Design Thinking to successfully tackle complex problems, this will necessitate fundamental changes in how they work and collaborate. Adopting Design Thinking, then, may very well be the first step on a journey that profoundly transforms organisational structures, values and practices. Whether Design Thinking can live up to this promise, then, seems to depend on whether and how organisations digest the socio-cultural changes implied by human-centred design.

This book, then, is about what happens when large organisations introduce the methods and mindsets of Design Thinking. More precisely, this book examines the impact on the structures, values and practices of an organisation—in short, its organisational culture—when people decide to clear the chairs out of meeting rooms, put white board foil up on the walls, and hand their colleagues felt-tip pens to fill their coloured sticky notes.

Before addressing these issues, it may make sense to recap what we know about Design Thinking.

What is Design Thinking?

As design thinkers, we sometimes dread being asked what it is we do for a living. This is because design thinking is a surprisingly slippery concept. The term has come to mean very different things to very different people. In general, commentators (Kimbell 2011; Hassi and Laakso 2011; Johansson-Sköldberg et al. 2013) like to point to two conversations about 'Design Thinking'. One conversation takes place between designers and people studying the practice of design. In this conversation, which has been going on since the 1960s, the term 'Design Thinking' denotes an object of study (Buchanan 1992; Cross 2011). Here, 'Design Thinking' is a thing that sets designers apart from other professionals such as, say, lawyers or engineers. This thing called 'Design Thinking' is a terrain to be explored, gauged, and charted: for designers and design researchers, 'Design Thinking'—sometimes also referred to as 'designerly thinking' (Cross 2006)—is a vessel to be filled with meaning by systematic inquiry and research. Since this is mostly a conversation among academics, it tends to follow the rules that govern the production of scientific knowledge (Johansson-Sköldberg et al. 2013).

Another conversation is underway in the much larger field of 'management'. It is younger, more pluralist, and considerably less decorous (Cooper et al. 2009; Hassi and Laakso 2011). While academics certainly participate in this debate, they are not the only or even most important actors. This lively and sometimes raucous conversation features voices from businesses, individual entrepreneurs, civil society organisations (CSOs), consultants as well as a myriad of other practitioners. For them, Design Thinking is an array of mindsets, methods and practices to help people in all walks of life become more productive, creative and innovative (Liedtka and Bennett 2013). Tim Brown, CEO of one of the agencies that pioneered Design Thinking as a method for innovation—IDEO—, tells us that Design Thinking is

> ...a discipline that uses the designer's sensibility and methods to match people's needs with what is technologically feasible and what a viable business strategy can convert into customer value and market opportunity (Brown 2008, p. 86).

What distinguishes these two conversations? On the one hand, designers and design researchers are interested in understanding what a 'designer's sensibility and methods' are and how the designer wields them. On the other hand, the conversation in the management community is about making use of the precepts and tools of designers to help anyone generate novel and innovative ideas. Indeed, Jan Liedtka and her colleagues (2013) argue that today's business problems—and by extension all other types of challenges—can only yield to creative responses (see also Ney and Verweij 2015). They understand the methods and mindsets of Design Thinking to be the technology for building a "...bridge to take us from current reality to a new future". To them, Design Thinking

> ...may look more pedestrian than miraculous, but it is capable of reliably producing new and better ways of creatively solving a host of organisational problems. Best of all, we believe that it is teachable to managers and scalable throughout the organisation (Liedtka and Bennett 2013, p. 2)

A key difference between the conversations, then, is about whether and where to draw a line between designers and other professionals. Design researchers look for the things that make up the unique creativity of designers, thereby distinguishing those who can legitimately be called designers and those who cannot. In contrast, pundits in the management discourse seem to be softening or dissolving the boundaries between designers and others by insisting that Design Thinking (*qua* method and mindset) can help anyone become creative. Design thinking as a method, gives anyone what David Kelley, the founder of IDEO and a pioneer of Design Thinking methodology, calls 'creative confidence' (Kelley and Kelley 2013).

In terms of these two conversations, what is this book about? Over the past decade and a half, many large organisations have adopted Design Thinking as a way of bringing about innovation. In the following chapters, then, we take a close look at what happens to and in large organisations that embrace Design Thinking as *a collection of methods, mindsets and practices for solving problems*. The book critically discusses the implications of blurring the boundaries between designers and other professionals in large organisations.

How, then, does this notion of Design Thinking help people become more innovative? Nailing down Design Thinking is difficult because it is a living and highly decentralised practice. Design Thinking has evolved in many different organisational and socio-cultural contexts. Unlike, say, sociology or physics, Design Thinking practices develop without the benefits of the rigorous rules of academic scrutiny. This is why, different practitioners and theorists focus on and develop different aspects of Design Thinking. The result has been a wide—often somewhat bewildering—variety of practices, methods and approaches that all (rightfully) call themselves Design Thinking.

Perhaps this explains why definitions of Design Thinking (as a method) tend to enumerate the aspects and elements that make up Design Thinking. Robert Curedale

(2013) provides a definition, worth quoting at length, that nicely summarises this perspective:

> Design Thinking is a methodology or approach to designing that should help you be more consistently innovative. It involves methods that enable empathy with people, it focuses on people. It is a collaborative methodology that involves iterative prototyping. It involves a series of divergent and convergent phases. It combines analytical and creative thinking approaches. It involves a toolkit of methods that can be applied to different styles of problems by different types of people. Anyone can use Design Thinking. It can be fun (Curedale 2013, p. 14).

Here, Curedale outlines some of the key components of Design Thinking. They include

- Innovation
- The use of empathy
- The focus on people, i.e. users and stakeholders
- An emphasis on collaboration
- A plurality of modes of thinking; both divergent and convergent thinking as well as analytical and creative;
- A wide range of potential applications
- Emphasis on fun

As with anything worthwhile, Design Thinking does not easily reduce to one or another element. Many people believe Design Thinking consists of tools to enable innovation. While this is true, there is far more to Design Thinking. Others see Design Thinking as a method to encourage collaboration in heterogeneous teams. Again, this is most definitely true but does not describe Design Thinking as a whole. Others still understand Design Thinking as problem-solving through design (Dorst 2015). And while it would be difficult to deny both the influence of design and the focus on problem-solving, this alone does not do justice to the holistic nature of Design Thinking.

In a very real sense, then, Design Thinking is all these things albeit perhaps not always at the same time. But this is just like the social scientists' stock answer that things are "terribly complex"—true, but frustrating. How, then, do these elements come together to give people 'creative confidence'?

When we speak of Design Thinking at the HPI D-School, we generally refer to the dynamic interplay of three basic elements (see Fig. 1.1). First are *diverse and heterogeneous teams*. Second, Design Thinking consists of the *Design Thinking process*. Third, Design Thinking takes place in *innovation spaces*. Each of these elements is valuable and important in and of itself. Commentators have a long pointed to the benefits of heterogeneous and transdisciplinary working arrangements. Similarly, few would dispute the value of design processes in innovation work. The same is true for the impact of spatial arrangements on creativity and productivity. And yet, none of these individual elements alone constitutes Design Thinking: instead, it is the dynamic interaction of these elements that creates Design Thinking.

We will discuss these elements in turn.

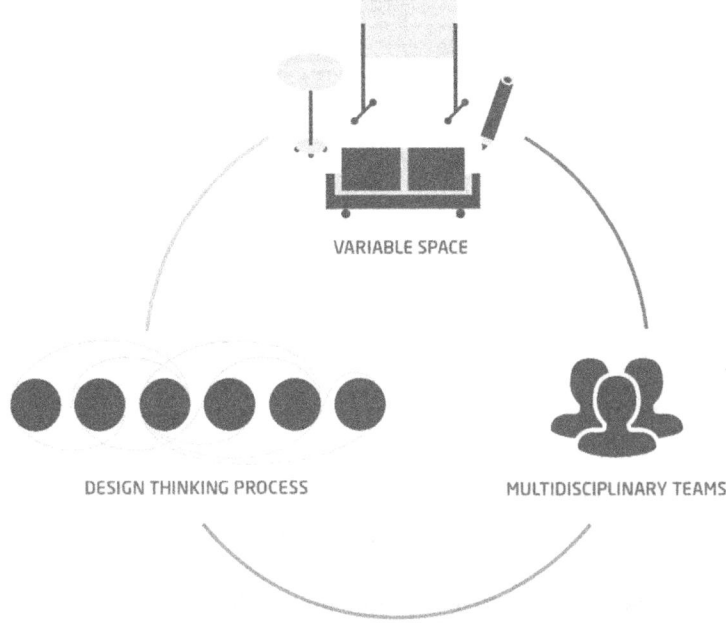

Fig. 1.1 The three elements of Design Thinking. Source: © HPI Academy 2018

Innovating in Diverse and Autonomous Teams

What drives innovation? Conventionally, we like to see innovations as the work of larger-than-life hero entrepreneurs. Today, we look up to characters such as the late Steve Jobs almost as people of a previous age venerated saints. We admire their vision. We marvel at their fortitude that allows them to persevere against stiff opposition. We wonder at their knack to make out the call of opportunity when most of us hear nothing but white noise. On this view, innovation—particularly the type that lets pundits speak breathlessly of 'disruption'—is beyond the reach of mere mortals.

Of course, we design thinkers publicly pay homage to the contemporary saints of innovation. Yet for us, teams, not individuals, drive innovation. Here, "good ideas that work" Mulgan et al. 2007) emerge from a concerted effort of small and pluralist teams. This is why these teams are at the heart of Design Thinking.

Typically, Design Thinking teams consist of 4 to 8 individuals. Despite ongoing research into team composition (Plattner et al. 2012, 2014), there are no hard and fast rules concerning the size of Design Thinking teams. However, experience of running student and executive education programmes at the HPI School of Design Thinking and the HPI Academy in Potsdam suggests that different team sizes suit different purposes. For actual project work, teams of about five seem to be best. This allows for some divergence between team members without it becoming too unwieldy. Similarly, an odd number of team members prevents deadlock when teams call

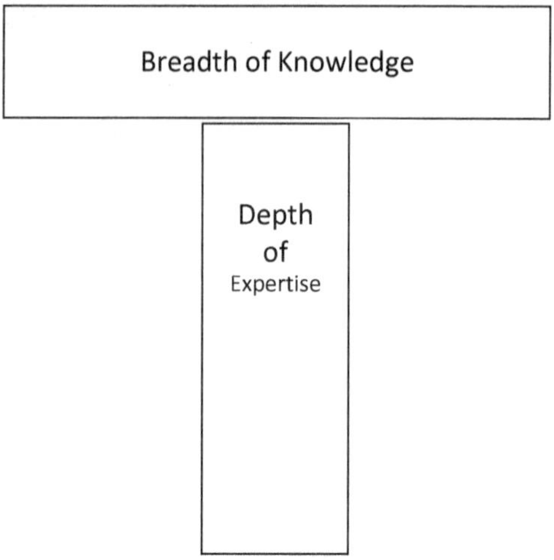

Fig. 1.2 T-shaped people

```
┌─────────────────────────────────┐
│       Breadth of Knowledge      │
└─────────────────────────────────┘
            ┌──────────┐
            │  Depth   │
            │    of    │
            │ Expertise│
            │          │
            │          │
            │          │
            └──────────┘
```

a vote. Conceptual or preparatory work—that is work on the Design Thinking process itself—tends to run smoothly with about three persons. It would seem that Design Thinking coaches need others for inspiration. But it also seems true that too many coaches tend to spoil the workshop, so to speak. Last, for teaching and training purposes team sizes can vary from 4 to 8. In this context, it is important that individuals experience teamwork: too small a team makes the training feel like a tutorial, too large a team makes it difficult to include all members in the activities.

Regardless of the size, Design Thinking teams ideally consist of a wide plurality of members. In particular, Design Thinking teams feature a diversity of so-called 'T-shaped people' (see Fig. 1.2). The T-Shape denotes that individuals bring two separate but nonetheless essential sets of skills to the team. The stem of the 'T' describes an individual's expertise and specialist knowledge. At universities, for example, this typically refers to a specific disciplinary background such as microbiology, ethnography or computer science. In less academic environments, the stem may describe a specialization or function within an organization: say, human resources, finance or production. In turn, the bar of the 'T' tells us something about the individual that connects them with others: a love for literature, a talent for painting, a passion for outside sports or the ability to tell a good (or bad) joke.

Innovation, we argue, comes about when a team of T-shaped people trains its range of capabilities on a design challenge. The creative potential of this team, we believe, lies in the confrontation between contending perspectives that team members bring to the group. Unlocking this potential, in turn, means bringing about this confrontation in form of a lively deliberation between the 'T-Shaped' people. This suggests that innovation is all about mobilizing different types of knowledge, insight and experience (Chaps. 1 and 2 look at this in more detail) (Verweij et al. 2006). Rather than solipsistic cogitation of the (largely mythical) hero innovator or the mono-disciplinary conversations in the isolated ivory towers of academia, new ideas in Design Thinking result from the tension that occurs when individuals with divergent perspectives collectively grapple with a complex challenge.

Putting this plurality of knowledge, insight and experience to good use means that teams need to be free to explore the design challenge as they see fit. In short, effective teams govern themselves. Self-governance enables teams to follow wherever the insights gleaned from user-research take them. It is this open-ended process of exploration that creates opportunities for breakthrough innovations. For this reason, Design Thinking teams have no default or given organisational structure. Instead, teams themselves decide on the structures and processes they need to manage their projects. Furthermore, these structures and processes can (and very frequently do) change over the course of a project.

Similarly, Design Thinking teams do not distinguish individual members in terms of formal distinctions. Teams feature no predetermined division of labour: the team negotiates and re-negotiates all roles and functions. The stem of each team member's 'T-Shape', that is the individual specialization or expertise of each member, may suggest that certain members take the lead in specific phases of the project. For example, the team's ethnographer or sociologist may want to oversee the user research phase. Yet, even this does not necessarily follow: given the injunction to 'take a beginner's mind set', members of Design Thinking teams may want to explore issues, methods or problems outside their immediate field of expertise. This also means that leadership and decision-making processes evolve continuously throughout Design Thinking project.

Pluralist and autonomous teams, then, are the motor of innovation in Design Thinking. Innovation occurs when teams autonomously mobilize the diversity of knowledge, of insights, and of experience. However, self-governance requires an adequate social and physical space. In turn, realising the potential of Design Thinking teams requires a process to help galvanise the creative potential of diversity.

Let us first turn to space.

Creating Room(s) for Innovation

Space matters. It reinforces and reproduces fundamental organisational arrangements by promoting (or prohibiting) specific patterns of behaviour. This is particularly true of the workplace. Oak-panelled board-rooms with hardwood oval tables and seating arrangements that place the chairperson at the head of the table signify the difference in importance of those who meet there. Likewise, the small cubicles typical of large open-plan offices may tell employees that they are all equal. That said, they also discourage interaction, let alone collaboration, between these employees.

How can space support self-governing and autonomous Design Thinking teams? The core feature of Design Thinking spaces is that they are variable and easily adjustable to the needs of the team. These needs emerge from, on the one hand, by the ebbing and flowing of the Design Thinking process itself (see next section) and, on the other, by the specific conditions of teams at any given point in time.

Variability implies that teams can easily transform spaces to support different types of activities. What, then, are the basic patterns of behaviour that spaces need to support?

First, Design Thinking spaces need to encourage, facilitate and enable teamwork. This means, Samuel Tschepe (2017) argues, that Design Thinking spaces need to be *open and accessible*. At a minimum, a Design Thinking space, its resources and amenities need to be accessible to all members of the Design Thinking team at all times. What is more, Design Thinking spaces need to enable teams to work together: common work areas need to be able to host all team members at once. Significantly, they need to do this without creating distinctions (spatial or otherwise) between the team members. For this reason, many Design Thinking practitioners have developed furniture—specifically tables and white boards—that enable teams of 5–8 individuals to operate in the same space at the same time. Team-work also implies that the outputs and fruits of the team's labour—be it the preliminary cogitations, the results of the synthesis or the results from testing—be accessible to everyone. Design Thinking teams require vertical surfaces: by 'posting' data, insights, ideas or user feedback (typically with the help of sticky notes) onto a white board, black board, wall or a window, this information immediately becomes available to everyone. In this way, team spaces also become the collective memory of the team. Not only does the Design Thinking space show the outputs and outcomes of a team's efforts, it also documents the process and progress of the project.

Yet, while Design Thinking teams mobilise the creative potential of pluralist teams, this does not mean that there is no individual work. At times, then, individual team members may need to work on their own, for example when setting up user or expert interviews, when reading and processing articles or when doing online research. Similarly, when teams are working on a more involved prototype, different smaller sub-teams may want to work on different parts of the prototype. In either case, the space needs to support the teams in setting up effective (if temporary) individual work-spaces.

Second, Design Thinking spaces need to support and encourage the spirit of rapid experimentation and prototyping. For Tschepe (2017), this means that spaces need to be "stimulating". Materials within easy reach of everyone encourage teams to transform their ideas into tangible prototypes. These materials can range from simple paper, glue, paints and cardboard to more sophisticated materials such as Lego, Arduino or a 3D printer. But Design Thinking teams do not exclusively prototype products or artefacts. In fact, Design Thinking is all about creating experiences. Prototypes of services—if they are to be experienceable for users—often recreate the situations in which these services occur. This implies teams must be able to recreate real-life contexts in creative spaces. For one, furnishings within the space need to be sufficiently versatile (Tschepe 2017) to allow for rapid modelling of a real-life situation. Furthermore, Design Thinking spaces ideally also ought to provide teams with the equipment for effective role-playing, such as costumes and props.

In order to support the self-governance of Design Thinking teams, these materials and the spatial transformations must be readily accessible to all team members at any time. Whenever the team feels it need to build a prototype of a product idea or needs to rearrange the workspace to resemble, say, an ATM, an effective Design Thinking space should make this possible with the least of effort. In practice, this means that furniture needs to be mobile as well as versatile. For example, all the tables, whiteboards and (the obligatory red) couches at the HPI School of Design Thinking in Potsdam are on wheels. What is more, the Design Thinking space contains foam cubes that teams use to easily (re)-build simple structures such as counters, bars, waiting rooms, etc.

Third, just as the somewhat hectic activity of prototyping is an essential aspect of Design Thinking, so too is the need for teams to withdraw, reflect and recuperate. Design Thinking spaces, then, must allow teams as well as individuals to shield themselves from the outside world. For teams, particularly those that are either reflecting on data or on their own performance and practices, work spaces need to provide a way of neutralising outside influences. At the HPI D-School in other Design Thinking, spaces provide a quiet room for teams that require seclusion during a particularly tricky phase. Similarly, individual team members occasionally need to withdraw from team-work. For this reason, the more sophisticated Design Thinking spaces provide nooks and crannies that allow individuals to take some time out from the bustle of team work. Often, these spaces allow individuals to retreat from sight completely.

Design Thinking spaces, then, support exploration by allowing teams to switch back and forth between these contrasting work modes. In this way, Design Thinking spaces empower teams to follow their own judgement. Since the furnishings and equipment keep the costs of rearranging the space to an absolute minimum, so too are the costs of misjudgement. This, then, encourages teams to try things out and experiment.

But how do Design Thinking teams mobilise their creative potential in these spaces?

Mobilising Creative Potential: The Design Thinking Process

The Design Thinking process helps teams activate their creative potential and apply it to a design challenge. In essence, the Design Thinking process sends teams on a journey of exploration and learning. Here, teams progress along their journey—or learn—by critically confronting their assumptions with the perspectives and experiences of users. Teams will do this in different ways: at times they observe and research, at other times they reflect and synthesise, at still other times they make things and test them. Here, learning takes place in iterative loops. Knowledge generated in the Design Thinking process remains contested and contestable: for

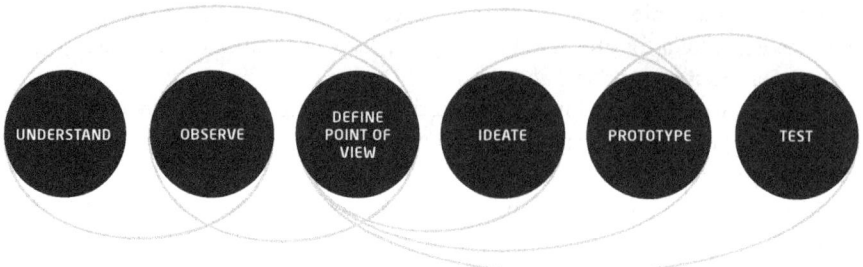

Fig. 1.3 The design thinking process. © HPI Academy 2018

Design Thinking teams, the insights that emerge from research or testing are little more than informed assumptions to be critically examined by juxtaposing them to experiences of users.

For teaching purposes, the HPI D-School divides this process into six phases (Fig. 1.3). Box 1.1 provides a brief overview of the individual phases. The first three phases (Understand, Observe and Synthesize) make up the 'problem space'. Here, Design Thinking teams focus on exploring and reframing the problem, challenge or issue from a human-centred perspective. The last three stages (Ideation, Prototyping, Testing) comprise the "solution space". During these stages, the team develops solutions for reframed problems.

What is missing from Fig. 1.3 is the design challenge. For all Design Thinking exercises—whether they are training runs or fully-fledged projects—the design challenge marks the starting point of the team's journey. As the name implies, the design challenge throws down the gauntlet for Design Thinking teams. It outlines, usually in general terms, an issue area, a user group as well as the wider organisational or social context in which the challenge exists. Design challenges are not conventional task descriptions or project briefs. They do not imply a fixed list of to do's or a backlog of tasks. Rather, design challenges are the initial impetus for an open-ended journey of discovery. Instead of a map and an itinerary, then, a design challenge furnishes a team with a license or a charter for exploration.

Once the team embarks on its journey, the Design Thinking process becomes their compass—it is the only real orientation they have. Then underlying assumption is that either the issue area is largely uncharted or that the existing charts of the problem terrain are unreliable. The Design Thinking process helps the teams make sense of this contested and unknown terrain.

Reframing Design Challenges: The Problem Space

After setting out, the Design Thinking teams enter the 'problem space'. Here, teams explore design challenges in two ways. First, teams analyse and critically reflect on the challenge in terms of the diversity within the Design Thinking team itself. It is here—usually in the Understand phase—that teams discuss and share what they know and, more importantly, what they think they know about the design challenge. This means looking closely at both their understanding of the issue area as well as the user group. During this discussion, the team creates a first rough map of their (largely unquestioned) assumptions about the challenge. This is also when the team identifies the gaps in their knowledge and devises a research strategy for closing these gaps. Significantly, the team needs to map the salient aspects of the challenge and decide which to pursue during research with users and stakeholders. This could be an aspect that interests or fascinates the team; it could be a perceived gap in the knowledge; it could be a paradox or dilemma; it could be a mystery on open question.

Second, and more importantly, the learning journey demands that teams contrast their knowledge and assumptions with the perceptions and experiences of users. Design thinking teams do this by empathising with users and stakeholders. Relying on the methods of the qualitative social sciences—in particular ethnography—Design Thinking teams examine how the abstract issues implied in the design challenge impinge upon users' lives. For example, user research about a design challenge on urban traffic congestion may uncover that, for young women, congestion means being more vulnerable to unwanted physical attention in crowded busses and trains. Unlike social scientists, Design Thinking teams are not in the business of generating scientific explanations of observed behaviour. Instead, Design Thinking teams look for inspiration; an insight need not be robust, it needs to inspire. An insight—which can be a previously unidentified user need, a new or surprising causality as well as a contradiction, paradox or dilemma—can inspire a team if it opens up new ways of looking at and making sense of the design challenge.

Examining generic design challenges in terms of the real-life problems of users creates new vantage points for the team from which to understand the issue. For example, looking at public transport from the point of view of a pregnant mother with a toddler at her hand opens up an entirely different vista on the underground system. This view is likely to be at odds with a conventional engineering perspective or the efficiency-maximising perspectives of economists. Similarly, viewing drinking behaviour at the weekend through the eyes of a young adult reveller may reveal very different insights than those offered by traditional public health experts. Empathy, then, helps Design Thinking teams reframe the design challenge. They remodel a generic or abstract issue—say, poverty, demographic ageing or the digital transformation—into a concrete problem with which real people struggle every day.

Reframing and recasting requires a considerable degree of interpretation. During the 'Synthesis' phase, teams use their fieldwork data to make inferences about users' needs and emotions. Typically, teams here try to challenge their own assumptions and look beyond the immediate. Some design theorists, most notably Jon Kolko (2010), argue the 'magic of design', that is the part in which the new and innovative comes into the world, requires 'abductive reasoning'. This is risky: there are no guarantees that the team's interpretations are in any way 'accurate'. So, constructing insights about users from data is always a bit of a gamble. But these inferences and interpretations help teams shift their perspective. This recasting or realignment of design challenges, then, opens up new solution spaces.

Solving Problems Through Innovation: The Solution Space

The latter part of the Design Thinking process is about populating solution spaces with ideas. Here, Design Thinking teams draw on the methods and approaches of the engineering sciences, economics and business studies. In the solution space, Design Thinking teams aim at coming up with as many potential solutions as possible (given resources and time available for the project). This usually takes place during "Ideation Phase" in which teams deploy a battery of brainstorming techniques to create options and choices for further exploration.

In the solution space, teams explore ideas by making them tangible so that users can experience them. This serves two interrelated purposes. First, it allows teams to flesh out and develop their ideas. By building simple but workable prototypes teams can arrive at a common understanding of what these ideas may mean. Furthermore, it also shifts the perspective to different, far less intellectual mode of idea generation, something called 'thinking with your hands'. Second, and more importantly, prototypes help teams gather meaningful feedback from users and stakeholders. Just like insights in the problem space, ideas and solutions are never complete or beyond contestation. Indeed, teams understand ideas and prototypes as propositions about appropriate responses to the design challenge. Thus, prototypes of ideas do not need to be perfect; rather, they need to allow users to experience the underlying idea.

For this reason, Design Thinking teams always return to users and stakeholders to test their prototypes. The objective here is to learn. Testing is supposed to bring to light the flaws and misconceptions that invariably occur during synthesis. Recall that synthesis is all about interpretation and taking risks. By encouraging users and stakeholders to interact with and critically examine prototypes, teams are resolving their bets while the stakes are still low. Over and above the reality check, testing sets up Design Thinking teams for the next iteration of the Design Thinking process. It helps teams to identify new problems, tasks and challenges.

This, then, opens up a new problem space for teams to explore.

Round and Round It Goes: Iteration

The linear depiction of the Design Thinking process in Fig. 1.3 is somewhat misleading. Design thinking is an iterative and cyclical undertaking. Indeed, iteration is at the core of Design Thinking. It is not a fall-back option if the user tests did not produce glowing reviews.[1] As teams repeatedly cycle through the Design

---

[1] Indeed, some coaches send teams back out into the field if they return with predominantly positive feedback: the team, they quite rightly argue, obviously did not properly test the prototype.

What is Design Thinking?

Fig. 1.4 The IBM design thinking process. Source: IBM Design (https://www.ibm.com/design/thinking/loop)

Thinking process, they learn more about users, their needs and their life-worlds. Moreover, teams also learn about their solutions and prototypes. By constantly framing and reframing design challenges, teams build and refine more effective responses to the design challenge.

Iteration means that Design Thinking teams can afford to take risks. Every decision along this exploratory journey—whether they are about the field work strategy, the interpretation of the data, the construction of the key insights, the choice of ideas, assembling of the prototype or the design of the testing scenario—is necessarily based on untested assumptions. The complex nature of issues addressed in design challenges means that teams will never have the luxury of unambiguous knowledge: if they did, then the design challenge is probably not suited for Design Thinking (more about this in Chap. 2). Moving forward in the Design Thinking process, then, means taking risks. These risks, however, become learning opportunities if the 'failure' of an idea or prototype sets up a new, more interesting problem space.

Far from linear, then, the Design Thinking process is constantly ebbing and flowing. Design thinking teams set up assumptions, confront them with the realities of users, only to set up new (and hopefully better) propositions which, in turn, these are tested with users, and on and on it goes. This ebbing and flowing is about creating options, taking risks by interpreting these options to then to move the process onward by making a choice. Theorists and practitioners often refer to this movement as 'flaring and focusing'. When teams create options and alternatives (i.e. during Understand, Observe, and Testing phases) the process 'flares'. When teams take (risky) decisions (Ideation, Synthesis and Prototyping), the process encourages teams to 'focus'. The designers and design thinkers of IBM probably capture this back-and-forth best: for them, the Design Thinking process is an endless circular movement between the three basic activities of observing, reflecting, and making (see Fig. 1.4).

In sum, the Design Thinking process helps a team mobilise its inherent diversity, set up and confront assumptions with data from users and focus this new but still contestable-knowledge on the design challenge.

Box 1.1 The Phases of Design Thinking Process
Understand

This phase is a preliminary exploration of the design challenge. Here, team members set out to become experts in the issue or problem to be tackled. To do this, they may consult existing research or knowledge on the topic. They may also contact and interview experts in the field. Most importantly, however, the understand phase is about articulating the different (and quite possibly conflicting) perceptions and assumptions about the design challenge that each member brings to the team. This, then, is the basis for preparing the empathy work in the next phase.

Observe

During the Observe-Phase, the team goes into the field to build empathy with users and stakeholders. Here, the team generates data by engaging with users (through interviews), by observing users (through participant observation) and immersing themselves in users' lifeworld (by trying to relive users' experiences). Although the design team uses the tools and methods of qualitative social and ethnographic research, it is not conducting scientific research. Design teams use these methods to unearth ideas, approaches and insights that are supposed to inspire design. They are not trying to fashion an explanation for observed individual behaviour or collective action.

Point-of-View

Defining a point-of-view requires engaging in creative synthesis. This, in turn, calls for reframing the design challenge in order to open up new conceptual spaces for innovation. The aim of this phase is to extract new meanings from or make new sense of the insights generated in empathy work. Here, the team brings its trans-disciplinarity to bear on the design challenge. In practice, design teams collate and make visible their research findings, systematically search for insights that may help construct new meanings and cast these insights into a reframed perspective, a so-called Point-of-View, of the design challenge.

Ideation

Ideation aims to generate as many innovative responses to the design challenge as possible. In practice, the design team deploys a range of brainstorming techniques to respond to so-called "How-Might-We" and "How-To" questions. These questions, in turn, are based on the Point-of-View derived from the synthesis phase. Brainstorming follows a set of rules designed to encourage the generation of many different ideas, of wild ideas as well as ideas that emerge from team collaboration. At the end of this phase, the design team chooses one of the ideas to take forward in the process.

Prototyping

The prototyping phase brings the design team's ideas to life. The objective here is to create a rough model of the idea or ideas so that users can experience

(continued)

Box 1.1 (continued)
the team's solution. Prototyping makes ideas more tangible and, thereby, allows the team to test the idea with users and stakeholders. While in the early stages of a project, design teams are encouraged to create low resolution prototypes that allow users to experience specific aspects of the idea, these prototypes become increasingly sophisticated as the project cycles through different iterations. In many respects, prototyping is an extension of ideation: here, team members "think with their hands". The process of making an idea more tangible and experienceable also very effectively reveals problems and shortcomings of the proposed solution.

Testing

In the testing phase, the design team takes the prototypes into the field to confront users and stakeholders. Here, the team sets out to test with users the underlying principles or hypotheses of their proposed solutions. The insights gleaned through testing feeds back into and set up the next iteration of the design thinking process. In a very real sense, testing relies on many of the techniques of observation.

Iteration

Iteration is not really a phase at all. Here, the team deciphers the feedback from testing and decides how best to move the project forward. In particular, the team will need to identify learnings and draw the necessary consequences from the data gathered during testing. This means teams need to decide where in the DT process to cycle back to. Does the feedback suggest that more fieldwork is necessary? Or should the team revisit the existing fieldwork data? Will the team work on new ideas? Does the feedback suggest improvements to the prototypes? Or does the team need to think of different testing scenarios for existing prototypes?

Brief Overview of the Book

This book is about what happens in and to large organisations when they implement the methods and mindsets of Design Thinking. Finding out and assessing what happens in these organisations will involve doing two things over the course of the following chapters. First, in Chaps. 2 and 3, we put forward a conceptual framework to help us make sense of how Design Thinking affects large institutions. In particular, this conceptual framework enables us to identify and evaluate the impacts of Design Thinking on the *institutional cultures* of large organisations. Second, the book then applies this framework to actual programmes for implementing Design Thinking in large organisations. In Chaps. 4, 5 and 6, then, we take an in-depth and critical look at the way implementation programmes installed Design Thinking in large private- and public-sector institutions in Europe, the US and South East Asia.

In order to set up the conceptual framework, Chap. 2 explores the relationship between the challenges contemporary organisations face today, innovation, and Design Thinking. People in large organisations are interested in Design Thinking because it promises to deliver innovation. Today, organisational stakeholders agree that innovation is the key to institutional survival: innovation, particularly so-called 'breakthrough innovation', keeps you ahead of the game. But how do innovations emerge from Design Thinking? We argue that Design Thinking can sustain organisations—large or small in the private or public sector—because its methods and mindsets help solve the complex and uncertain challenges we face today. These challenges, also called 'wicked problems' (Rittel and Webber 1973), have an uncanny way of evading tried-and-tested solutions (Ney 2009). In an increasingly complex and uncertain world, responses to wicked problems emerge from the interplay of different professional and disciplinary perspectives. We suggest, then, to think of innovations as those solutions that successfully and creatively bring together the different insights from a range of disciplines, perspectives and professions. This, we contend, is exactly what Design Thinking enables teams to do: it helps mobilise wide range of disciplines, professions and perspectives for tackling wicked problems.

Chapter 3 asks what all this means for large organisations. At present, prevalent cultures in sizeable institutions are not set up to tackle wicked problems. On the contrary, it would seem that organisations are more effective at what the veteran organisational theorist James March (1991) refers to as the *exploitation* of existing knowledge rather than the *exploration* of new knowledge. Since survival requires both exploitation and exploration, large organisations will need to find ways of engaging in and learning from both modes of operation: in short, they need to become 'ambidextrous' (O'Reilly and Tushman 2013). Design Thinking, we argue, is an effective way for showing large organisations how to skilfully use their 'other hand'. Indeed, Roger Martin (2009a) contends that 'Design Thinking' brings about ambidexterity: it enables organisations to pursue innovations in terms of the two contending institutional logics of reliability (required for exploitation) and validity (required for exploration).

Building on Roger Martin's work (Martin 2009a, b), Chap. 3 develops a conceptual framework that relates Design Thinking to required cultural changes in large organisations. Drawing on insights from social anthropology (Douglas 1987), the chapter suggests that we think of organisations as viable combinations of social relations, ideas and practices. For cultural change to be sustainable, it needs to take place in these three organisational dimensions. First, change processes needs to set up spaces—physical, but predominantly social—within organisations that promote experimentation and learning. Second, cultural transformation will need to make a wide diversity of ideas and perceptions available to Design Thinking teams. This involves mobilising the inherent diversity of ideas within large organisations as well as 'hunting and gathering' for inspiration in the world beyond the institution (Plattner et al. 2012, 2014). Last, the process of cultural change needs to provide effective practices for synthesising innovations from the messy diversity of ideas and perceptions. This approach also argues that tackling wicked problems requires the mobilisation of a wider range of institutional logics than the exploration/exploitation (March 1991) or the validity/reliability (Martin 2009b) dichotomies may suggest. Indeed, finding effective responses to wicked problems may call for what we call 'multi-dextrous' or 'messy' institutions.

In the subsequent chapters, we apply this framework to re-analyse cases in which large organisations implemented the methods and mindsets of Design Thinking. In particular, the chapters scrutinise whether and how these programmes set up exploration spaces (Chap. 4), populated these spaces with a 'messy' diversity of ideas (Chap. 5) and installed requisite variety Design Thinking practices (Chap. 6). Each of the chapters looks at the conceptual background, discusses whether and how the programmes studied brought about this change and identifies the key lessons learned from these cases in large organisations. Specifically, each chapter reviews how methods and approaches of Design Thinking have been adapted to and have evolved in different organisational settings.

In Chap. 4, we look at the way implementation programmes set up *spaces* aimed at promoting exploration (or, to use Martin's terms, validity) in large, mostly hierarchical organisations. Framing exploration spaces in terms of social networks within and across organisations, the chapter shows how the creation of transdisciplinary and trans-boundary Design Thinking teams carved new institutional spaces out of hierarchical and vertically structured institutions. Based on the analysis of case studies, the chapter outlines the lessons learned from these implementation experiences in large organisations.

In Design Thinking, innovations emerge from the mobilisation of a *plurality of approaches, skills and perspectives*. This is why exploration spaces in large organisations need large reservoirs of variegated (and even contending) ideas and approaches. Chapter 5, then, looks at how best to generate and manage these pools of contending ideas, frames and perspectives. In particular, the chapter reviews two ways of ensuring a plurality of views for exploration. First, the chapter explores the contribution of multi-disciplinary teams to these reservoirs of ideas. The chapter discusses how multi-disciplinary project teams generate pluralism both at the level of perceptions and frames as well as at the level of methods and practices. Second, the chapter also shows how methods of qualitative social science and ethnography enable design teams to 'hunt and gather' insights from users (Plattner et al. 2012). Like Chap. 4, this chapter draws lessons from the analysis of the implementation cases.

Chapter 6 explores the implementation of Design Thinking *practices* in large organisations. Establishing exploration spaces as well as hunting and gathering for insights set up the framework for innovation. Yet, innovation also needs an effective set of practices for mobilising diversity of design teams to transform insights into innovation. Specifically, the chapter looks at the extent to which the implementation of Design Thinking has created spaces in large organisations that are or approximate 'messy institutions' (Ney and Verweij 2015). These are organisational spaces that put problem-solving methods from different and often contending organisational cultures at the disposal of design teams. The chapter shows how *output-oriented practices* drive the process of innovation by encouraging pragmatism and experimentation. *Inclusion-oriented processes* ensure that all voices and approaches—even the outliers and extreme users—get a fair hearing in the innovation process. *Process-oriented practices*, in turn, provide the rules that enable the process to stay on track and produce outputs based on the best available knowledge. Last *chance-oriented practices* introduce an element of serendipity designed to accustom Design Thinking teams to failure. Using cases of large organisations that have introduced Design Thinking, the chapter critically scrutinises the extent to which a plurality of practices has supported and promoted the creative reframing of wicked problems. Just like the previous two chapters, we outline the critical lessons learned from implementing the plural practices that shape innovation.

Chapter 7 takes a step back from fray of cultural change to contemplate how these transformations are likely to impact on *management and organisational strategy*. This chapter discusses the leadership challenges that emerge from the cultural transformations associated with Design Thinking. It looks at the impacts of Design Thinking on organizational structures, organizational actors as well as the way people interact with these new structures. Based on this analysis, the chapter identifies three central management challenges: enabling collaboration among more autonomous Design Thinking teams, making-sense of and dealing with increased ambiguity and uncertainty, as well as promoting critical, yet constructive conflict. The chapter also provides an overview over the preconditions for leaders to effectively face these management challenges.

The conclusion in Chap. 8 wraps up the argument, summarises the learnings and outlines possible future developments.

It is now time to develop a conceptual framework that can explain the impacts of Design Thinking on large organisations and help us analyse real life Design Thinking initiatives.

References

Brown, T. (2008). Design thinking. *Harvard Business Review, 86*(6), 84–95.
Buchanan, R. (1992). Wicked problems in design thinking. *Design Issues, 8*(2), 5–21.
Cooper, R., Junginger, S., & Lockwood, T. (2009). Design thinking and design management: A research and practice perspective. *Design Management Review, 20*(2), 46–55.
Cross, N. (2006). *Designerly ways of knowing*. London: Springer.
Cross, N. (2011). *Design thinking: Understanding how designers think and work*. New York: Bloomsbury Academic.
Curedale, R. (2013). *Design research methods: 150 ways to inform design*. Topanga, CA: Design Community College Inc.
Dorst, K. (2015). *Frame innovation*. Boston, MA: MIT Press.
Douglas, M. (1987). *How institutions think*. London: Routledge and Kegan Paul.
Hassi, L., & Laakso, M. (2011). *Conceptions of design thinking in the management discourse*. European Academy of Design Biannual Conference, Porto, Portugal
Johansson-Sköldberg, U., Woodilla, J., & Çetinkaya, M. (2013). Design thinking: Past, present and possible futures. *Creativity and Innovation Management, 22*(2), 121–146.

References

Kelley, T., & Kelley, D. (2013). *Creative confidence: Unleashing the creative potential within us all*. New York: Crown Business.

Kimbell, L. (2011). Rethinking design thinking: Part I. *Design and Culture, 3*(3), 285–306.

Kolko, J. (2010). *Exposing the magic of design: A practitioner's guide to the methods and theory of synthesis*. Oxford: Oxford University Press.

Liedtka, J., & Bennett, K. B. (2013). *Solving problems with design thinking: 10 stories of what works*. New York: Columbia University Press.

March, J. G. (1991). Exploration and exploitation in organizational learning. *Organization Science, 2*(1), 71–87.

Martin, R. L. (2009a). *The design of business: Why design thinking is the next competitive advantage*. Boston, MA: Harvard Business Press.

Martin, R. L. (2009b). *The opposable mind: Winning through integrative thinking*. Boston, MA: Harvard Business Press.

Mulgan, G., Tucker, S., Ali, R., & Sanders, B. (2007). *Social innovation: What it is, why it matters and how it can be accelerated*. Oxford: Skoll Centre for Social Entrepreneurship.

Ney, S. (2009). *Resolving messy policy issues*. London: Earthscan.

Ney, S., & Verweij, M. (2015). Messy institutions for wicked problems: How to generate clumsy solutions? *Environment and Planning C: Government and Policy, 33*(6), 1679–1696.

O'Reilly, C., & Tushman, M. (2013). Organizational ambidexterity: Past, present and future. *The Academy of Management Perspectives, 27*(4), 324–338. https://doi.org/10.5465/amp.2013.0025.

Plattner, H., Meinel, C., & Leifer, L. (2012). *Design thinking research: Measuring performance in context*. Berlin: Springer Science & Business Media.

Plattner, H., Meinel, C., & Leifer, L. J. (2014). *Design thinking research: Building innovators*. Cham: Springer.

Rittel, H., & Webber, M. (1973). Dilemmas in a general theory of planning. *Policy Sciences, 4*, 155–169.

Tschepe, S. (2017). Mindset? Process? Method? A comprehensive descriptive model for design thinking. Retrieved May 2, 2017, from https://medium.com/swlh/mindset-process-method-a-comprehensive-descriptive-model-for-design-thinking-27a501bf80cf

Verweij, M., Douglas, M., Ellis, R., Engel, C., Hendriks, F., Lohmann, S., Ney, S., Rayner, S., & Thompson, M. (2006). Clumsy solutions for a complex world: The case of climate change. *Public Administration, 84*(4), 817–843.

Chapter 2
Innovation, Wicked Problems and Design Thinking

Interest in Design Thinking has grown significantly in the past decade. Judging from the number of articles in magazines, websites and blogs, it is probably fair to speak of an explosion of attention to Design Thinking. Indeed, commentators such as Jon Kolko see Design Thinking 'coming of age' (Kolko 2010). Among other things, this has meant that large organisations in both the private and public sectors have become increasingly interested in Design Thinking. In short, Design Thinking has become a buzz word, a word to conjure with.

Does that mean that Design Thinking, to paraphrase Victor Hugo, is an idea whose time has come? Or, as some seem to suspect, is Design Thinking little more than a flash in the pan?

This as well as the next chapter addresses these questions by taking to look at why people—and particularly people in large organisations—may *want* to know about Design Thinking. Broadly, we argue, the perceived relationship between markets, innovation and organisational survival fuels the growing interest in Design Thinking. People seem to believe that Design Thinking stimulates innovation which, in turn, will give their organisations an advantage in increasingly competitive global markets. Here, Design Thinking is little more than a strategic tool.

However, we argue, there is more to Design Thinking than creating a competitive edge for businesses. Significantly, Design Thinking helps people deal with complex and messy problems; Design Thinking enables small (but diverse) teams to pull together a plurality of experiences and ideas of users to forge effective responses to complex problems. This, we argue, is why people in large organisations may *need* to know about Design Thinking.

Why People Want Design Thinking: Innovation and Organisational Survival

Today innovation has become synonymous with success. Perhaps more poignantly, the inability to innovate seems to have become the reason why businesses and other organisations fail. Oddly, these are businesses that seem to be doing everything right in terms of management strategy, production, marketing and, worryingly, even R&D. And yet, these well-run and erstwhile successful businesses can trip up and fail in a remarkably short period of time.

The management literature as well as the popular (business) mind is full of tales of how large and commercially powerful companies failed when they left innovation to others. A well-known story tells us how nimble innovatosrs of personal computers felled the computing giant IBM. Or how Kodak—the undisputed world leader in the photography industry—was relegated to the side-lines by their inability (and unwillingness) to seize the opportunities of digital photography. A more recent but no less popular story is how Apple's iPhone undermined Nokia's dominance in the global mobile phone market.

Often, incredibly, these firms are beaten with rods of their own making. Kodak invented and patented digital cameras but failed to deploy this to their advantage. Peter Drucker, probably the most subtle of management gurus, shows out how transistor technology invented in the US in the 1950s languished in technological limbo and commercial obscurity until Japanese companies, most notably Sony, used this very same technology to conquer and ultimately dominate the home entertainment market (Drucker 1985).

Much of this is driven by developments in technology (Christensen 2000). This is certainly the case for some of the classic examples, such as the way relatively cheap quartz-based digital devices replaced—almost overnight—high precision mechanical scales in scientific research. But it is by no means always technology that reduces powerful enterprises to little more than spectators in markets they thought they controlled. New ways of conducting business or delivering a particular service can also disturb what seemed like calm seas (Yu and Hang 2010). For example, the *Uber* web-service is currently threatening the highly regulated and often monopolist taxi-trade in many countries,

How, then, does innovation—recombining existing means of production in ways that generates new value—create the kinds of turbulences that can sink formerly sturdy vessels of business?

Innovation in Businesses

At the level of businesses and firms—what economists like to call the 'micro-level'—Clayton Christensen's work at the Harvard Business School has significantly shaped the contemporary debate about innovation (Christensen 2000).

Successful organisations, he contends, consistently misjudge opportunities for innovation. This is why even (or especially) successful enterprises fail.

His argument is as simple as it is elegant. Innovation, he tells us, comes in two basic guises. One type of innovation, that he calls "sustaining innovation", improves or fine-tunes "...the performance of established products, along the dimensions of performance that mainstream customers in major markets have historically valued" (Christensen 2000, p. 179). The other type, the so-called "disruptive innovation", "...bring to market a very different value proposition than had been available previously" (Christensen 2000, p. 179). Often, Christensen continues, the potential of these new products, services or business models is not immediately apparent, particularly to incumbent market leaders. These innovations tend to be simpler, less sophisticated and seem to appeal to customers at the margins of the market (Christensen 2000). Yet, once customers understand and embrace these innovations, they reshape markets much to the detriment of incumbent companies.

At worst, incumbents perish when "...despite its inferior performance on focal attributes valued by existing customers, the new product displaces the mainstream product in the mainstream market" (Yu and Hang 2010, p. 437). Christensen has called this process, or rather the outcome of this process, "disruption". This term has become rather popular (if not universally accepted, see (Lepore 2014)); indeed, given the evolutionary flavour of Christensen's theory, one may justifiably speak of a "meme" (Dawkins 2006).

Disruptive innovations, Christensen continues, present managers of incumbent firms with a tricky problem. For reasons we will discuss in depth in the following chapter, successful market leadership fosters perceptions and practices that militate against recognising or, if identified, acting on the emergence of disruptive innovations. Seen from the vantage point of maintaining market leadership with established products and services, disruptive innovations, Christensen argues, do not look terribly attractive or even viable (Christensen and Overdorf 2000). But even if managers in incumbent companies were to recognise a disruptive innovation for what it is, existing practices required to deliver their successful products and services make it very difficult for firms to act on that knowledge (Drucker 1985; Christensen and Overdorf 2000; Christensen 2000). And while research suggests that disruption does not inevitably lead to the demise of erstwhile market leaders (witness Nokia or US Steel) (Yu and Hang 2010; Lepore 2014), this does not relieve the pressure created by what Christensen calls the "innovator's dilemma". On the contrary, the fact that large and established firms could possibly weather the turbulences of disruptive innovations (then again, they may not) does little to render options for decision-making processes any clearer.

On this view, then, innovation is the key to the survival of businesses in what seems to be an evolutionary process. Here, innovation, a bit like Charles Darwin's natural selection, is a double-edged sword capable of generating wealth and progress even as it inflicts hardship (on incumbents) and turbulence (on markets).

Innovation in the Economy

The idea of innovation as a simultaneously destabilising and stimulating force has considerable pedigree. The idea goes back (at least) to the writings of the Austrian economist Josef Schumpeter. An economist active in the inter-war period of the twentieth century, Schumpeter asked the big questions of his time. Are the turbulent boom-and-bust cycles not evidence of the irreconcilable contradictions within capitalism that Karl Marx had identified? Is capitalism doomed? Will socialism prevail?

Schumpeter thought not.[1] But, unlike most of his contemporaries, Schumpeter sought to explain the socio-economic dynamics of capitalism that Marx had identified as the "iron tendency for profits to fall". As "one of the more intelligent critics of Marx" (Hobsbawm 2012, p. 12), Schumpeter set out to reconcile two potentially contradictory observations: the turbulent and at times rather harsh socio-economic realities of capitalism and the unequivocal success of that very system in generating unprecedented wealth and social progress. After all, Schumpeter argued, capitalism had expanded the access to goods and services to an ever-increasing proportion of the population.

For Schumpeter, the explanation was innovation. Unlike much of the economic thought of his time (and, arguably, even today), Schumpeter wanted to understand economic transformations. For him, the driving force of transformation and change in capitalism was the entrepreneur who "...is concerned not with the *administration* of existing industrial plant and equipment but with the incessant *creation* of new plant and equipment, embodying new technologies that revolutionise existing industrial structures" (Schumpeter 1947, p. 198) (original emphasis). Innovations bring about what Schumpeter called the 'creative response' or 'structural adaptation' in economies and economic sectors. Creative responses do not merely adjust existing markets within known parameters. Rather, structural adaptation creates an entirely new technological, economic and socio-institutional basis for production and exchange. The creative response to competitive pressures, Schumpeter argued, not only elude prediction by mere extrapolation and inference of what is known, they change "social and economic situations for good..." (Schumpeter 1947, p. 201). But in addition to being creative (in the sense of generating something new), these processes also rudely sweep aside the old. This is why Schumpeter argues that innovating entrepreneurs unleash "gales of creative destruction". These gales bring about changes "...from which there is no bridge to those situations that might have emerged in its absence" (Schumpeter 1947, p. 210). While these creative adaptations are the source of considerable hardship and vicissitudes—particularly for those whose livelihood has been 'creatively destroyed'—they are also the motor for the unprecedented growth of wealth and prosperity.

But the turbulence generated by creative destruction—as the oxymoron suggests—simultaneously gives rise to new ways of creating value. Most of this value, Schumpeter argues, initially accrues to the entrepreneur in the form of

---

[1]Despite being rather gloomy about the long-term prospects of capitalism (Schumpeter 2013).

so-called 'super-normal profits'. Not only does the prospect of what Schumpeter calls 'entrepreneurial profits' encourage entrepreneurs with similar 'productive talents' (Baumol 1990), it attracts other businesses into the new markets that innovations have created. These businesses are looking to secure a slice of the entrepreneurial pie. In this way, then, new markets settle into a steady groove in which competitors tinker with their products, services or business models to protect (or expand) their market share. Until, of course, another innovation comes along that unleashes the next 'gale of creative destruction'. And, Schumpeter argues, this is bound to happen in capitalism. Productive entrepreneurs, attracted by the prospects of wealth that accrue to successful innovators, are constantly seeking to 'revolutionise' the means of production (to use a Marxian term). This is why businesses find themselves in a "perennial gale of creative destruction".[2]

Shelter from the Storm: Fads and Fashions in Management

From the vantage point of academic economists, safely ensconced in the ivory tower, the failure of established and successful businesses is not only an inevitable but ultimately desirable aspect of economic evolution. This, of course, is of little comfort to the managers or owners of businesses caught in Schumpeter's perennial gale of creative destruction. Who would argue that a cyclone viewed from outer space is not impressive and, in some senses, beautiful. It is, however, rather more difficult to appreciate this beauty when one is blown this way and that by gale force winds. The advisable—and indeed rational—course of action here is to take shelter. And this, Andrej Huczynski (1993) suggests, is precisely what managers do to survive Schumpeter's 'perennial gales of creative destruction'.

Since the stakes in the innovation game are high, anything that will let you hedge your bets to mitigate the risks is welcome. This, Andrej Huczynski argues, explains the phenomenon of 'management fads' (Huczynski 1993, 2012). Huczynski points to the cyclical rise and fall in popularity of contending prescriptions for managing a business or organisation. These approaches or, as Huczynski calls them, 'management ideas' are part of one of six different families of ideas (see Box 2.1). The knowledge in these families is akin to "...an intellectual bank from which the producers of management techniques make withdrawals in order to produce what ultimately may become the next management fashion" (Huczynski 1993, p. 445).

---

[2]So in a way, Schumpeter concedes that Marx was right. The boom-and-bust of business cycles, the contraction and expansion of economies as well as the flourishing and decaying are an inextricable part of the dynamic evolution of capitalism. Where Marx went wrong, however, is that these business cycles are dysfunctional and move unerringly towards the fulfilment of some implicit historical telos, namely the advent of a socialist millennium.

> **Box 2.1 Families of Management Fads**
>
> Bureaucracy
> Scientific Management
> Administrative Management
> Human Relations
> Neo-human relations
> Guru Theory
>
> Source: Huczynski (1993)

What drives the cycle of management fads is a somewhat cynical strategic game between the consumers and the suppliers of management ideas. Huczynski identifies a range of environmental, individual and organisational reasons why consumers of management ideas, that is managers, want access to these management ideas. As Huczynski so elegantly shows, most of these reasons are strategic in nature. Managers may want to use 'new' management ideas to move up the career ladder faster or further, preferably both. Or they may recruit new management ideas into fighting a rear-guard action. Or they have become part of what R. J. Mayer delightfully calls the "Panacea Conspiracy" (Huczynski 2012). Here managers, trained in highly specialised fields, not only lack the requisite generalist management skills but also have neither time nor real inclination to acquire these capabilities for which they are now being paid. To mask this ignorance, the manager turns to the management equivalent of snake-oil: a quick fix for what everyone involved in the 'panacea conspiracy' knows to be a long-term and complex problem.

At the same time, Huczynski identifies a set of suppliers—that is consultants—who are happy to fuel the fashion cycles in management ideas. By repackaging and rebranding existing concepts from the reservoir of management knowledge, suppliers ensure 'planned obsolescence' of their fads. Similarly, suppliers of management ideas seem to offer busy managers and executive respite from the onerous and time-consuming task of searching for suitable management techniques (Huczynski 2012).

So people may *want* Design Thinking—and its perceived innovative capacity—for strategic reasons. They may want their business to survive and excel by out-innovating competitors. Individual managers may want Design Thinking to help them secure their jobs or advance in the organisation or advance their careers. In the sense that it helps us weather the perennial gales of creative destruction, the methods and mindsets of Design Thinking have the makings of a management fad. And if Design Thinking is little more than a way to secure the short-term careers of managers, it would rightly deserve to join terms such as 'synergy' in management fad limbo.

We, however, believe otherwise.

Why People May Need Design Thinking

The survival of a business, then, is why people *want* innovation. It is also why they pay good money to people who promise to bestow innovative capabilities. And yet, despite being entirely understandable, this strategic view obscures another, to our mind more fundamental aspect of innovation in general and Design Thinking in particular.

The survival of an organisation is not an end in itself. Peter Drucker once wrote that the mission of a business was not to maximise profits. For Drucker, profit is little more than a device of micro-economic theory, a minimum operational requirement; without profit, no enterprise—be it in the private, public or citizen sector—can pursue its mission. The mission itself, however, is to 'create a customer' with products and services that fulfil peoples' needs (Drucker 1985).

So how do organisations fulfil people's needs to create customers?

In order, then, to be able to look beyond the evolutionary pressures of organisational survival, it may be instructive to look at the role of innovation in sectors where institutional survival is far less directly related to commercial viability: the public and citizen sectors.

Innovation in the Public Sector: Value as Problem-Solving

Many people would not immediately point to the public sector and civil society as places of innovation and entrepreneurship. To a large extent, this is due to the self-portrayal and perceptions of civil servants and public service providers themselves. As we have seen, innovation means change, transformation and reform. But the value of change and transformation in societal and governmental institutions is not immediately obvious to everyone. Indeed, many would rightly argue that these institutions ought to be guarantors of stability and continuity. People have not always had the stomach for innovation in the public sector and civil society. And for good reason: historically, political, social or religious innovations often unleashed 'gales of destruction' that have been neither creative nor productive (Baumol 1990).

And yet, remarkable innovations have emerged from the public sector and civil society (Mulgan and Albury 2003). Innovations here include the principles of modern nursing outlined by Florence Nightingale (Bornstein 2004), the postage stamp invented by William Dockwra in the seventeenth century and developed in the nineteenth century by Rowland Hill (Bornstein 2004), social insurance systems (developed by civil servants under Prussia's 'Iron Chancellor' Otto von Bismarck), or social housing (developed in a number of places, most prominently Vienna, in the inter-war years of the twentieth century) to name but a few. More recently, ideas such as micro-credits (pioneered by the economist and Nobel Laureate Muhamad Yunus) or crowd funding not only have made a tremendous impact on the lives of people, they have profoundly changed the way we look at and act upon certain issues. At a broader, more abstract level, conceptual innovations—such as the idea of sustainable development—have had a significant impact on the way we understand our relationship with nature.

Like in business, innovation exerts evolutionary pressures on institutions in the public sector and civil society. Unlike the private sector, this pressure is articulated by and works through a myriad of institutional channels. Despite decades of *New Public Management* (NPM) reforms aimed at introducing market-type competition into public sector and social service provision (Pollitt 1990, 2003; Hood 1991), innovation impinges on these sectors in a different as well as somewhat differentiated way. Sectors in which NPM reforms have created so-called quasi-markets for public contracts, many Civil Society Organisations (CSO) and private service providers now face stiffer competitive environments than they have in the past. It may not be a coincidence, then, that CSOs and public sector organisations in these newly competitive environments are looking to Design Thinking for inspiration (see Chaps. 3, 4 and 5). For other regions in the institutional landscape of the public and citizen sectors—for example policy-making and administration—innovation poses less of an immediate threat to institutional survival.[3]

How, then, can we describe innovations in the public sector and civil society? And what role do they play in the development of these sectors?

The definition of social and public sector innovations is, like so many emerging concepts, contested. Some thinkers perceive social and public sector innovation to be analogous to innovations in the private sector. Here, disruptive and game-changing social innovation generates social change (Dees 1998; Martin and Osberg 2007; Shapiro 2013). Innovations are products and services that empower individuals to lead independent lives. Whether locked in absolute poverty, illiteracy, or political oppression, social innovations help target populations throw off their shackles. Analogous to Josef Schumpeter's entrepreneurs in markets, social entrepreneurs are in the business of 'creative destruction' (Dees 1998; Martin and Osberg 2007). Like in markets, 'breakthrough innovations' in government and the public sector revolutionise ways of producing public goods and, by the same token, make older practices obsolete (Sahni et al. 2013).

Others, in turn, understand innovation in the public and citizen sectors to be a multifaceted thing. At the most general level, Geoff Mulgan defines social (and public sector) innovations as simply "good ideas that work" (Mulgan and Albury 2003; Mulgan et al. 2007). These good ideas or successful innovations, Mulgan and Albury contend, are

> ...the creation and implementation of new processes, products, services and methods of delivery which result in significant improvements in outcomes efficiency, effectiveness or quality (Mulgan and Albury 2003).

---

[3]And yet, curiously, these institutions are also interested in Design Thinking.

Yet, good ideas come in different shapes and forms. Mulgan and Albury identify three different types of policy and social innovation: incremental (improvements to the existing), radical (new services, products or delivery) and systemic innovation (major socio-institutional transformation, such as the National Health Service in the UK) (Mulgan and Albury 2003). Not all innovations, then, need to be game changers.

Others still suggest that innovation in the public sector and civil society has little to do with actual products and services. Instead, these thinkers and practitioners focus on the social organisation of the production and distribution of goods and services: the so-called social enterprises. Unlike the 'hero social entrepreneurs', social enterprises aim to bring about social change by providing radically different models of conducting business. In essence, social enterprises not only aim to claw back social space colonised and despoiled by the market and its business practices but also aim to provide a real, democratic and human alternative to market participation. What is needed, so the argument goes, is an economic system that generates solidarity and social capital instead of stratifying and polarising societies. For this reason, social enterprises need to create social spaces in which equity and fairness rule (Borzaga and Defourny 2001).

Box 2.2 provides some examples of innovation in the public and citizen sectors.

Box 2.2 Innovation in the Public and Citizen Sectors
The impact of innovations in the public sector and civil society can be as profound as in the private sector. Geoff Mulgan argues that, contrary to popular contemporary belief, the public sector has historically been a source of innovations with wide-reaching consequences. Examples are systems of social security, particularly public systems of health care provision. In conjunction with improvements in sanitation of the late nineteenth century, public health care systems have been responsible for the spectacular rise in life-expectancy in developed countries of Europe, Asia and the Americas (predominantly Canada).

The OECD and the World Bank (OECD and World Bank 2018) identifies three areas in which public sectors the world over have introduced innovations to service delivery in the past decades. First, the OECD points to innovations that expand access to public services. By creating what the OECD refers to "single access points", innovations in both the digital realm as well as the real world have made it easier for citizens to access public services. Innovations such as one-stop-shops, which integrate public service delivery capabilities of different public authorities and agencies, or digital e-governance portals, are helping citizen not only to claim their rights but also to fulfil their civic obligations. A good example here is the VERA, the National Citizen Health Portal in Iceland. This web-based application allows the citizens of Iceland to access their digital health data as well as all e-Health services. This virtual

(continued)

Box 2.2 (continued)

one-stop shop enables citizens to securely access their data, communicate with health professionals, make eBookings and enter data they wish to share with health professionals at any level of the heath system in Iceland (OECD and World Bank 2018).

Second, public sector innovation processes have increasingly involved citizens in public service design. Not only, the OECD and the World Bank argue, does this lead to a more nuanced understanding of stakeholder needs, citizen participation also creates ownership for and identification with public sector innovations. In addition, the insights and ideas from citizens also contribute to the innovation process. For example, in 2016–2017, the Australian Central Government piloted a smart parking scheme in the country's capital, Canberra. Using infrared parking bay sensors, street-signs displaying parking availability in real time, as well as a dedicated smart phone app, the innovation aimed to reduce wasted time and vehicle emissions. However, this particular focus and smart parking technology had emerged from a consultation exercise with citizens and other stakeholders. Furthermore, the SIMPLEX + programme in Portugal emerged from extensive public consultation, citizen participation and co-creation. The programme comprises 255 measures to de-bureaucratise existing regulation and replace it with smarter, more adaptive approaches. The core of this programme consists of an innovative citizen consultation and co-creation process that mobilised about 2600 citizens in face-to-face consultations and 1400 submissions across the country (OECD and World Bank 2018).

Third, public sector innovations are helping to better target and tailor public services more closely to citizen needs. This, the OECD points out, applies both to the way services are designed to better respond to citizen needs as well as to how public sector communicaton adapts to user behaviour. For example, the Immigration, Refugee and Citizenship Canada (IRCC) are prototyping a wide range of new solutions for tailoring and better targeting immigration services for refugees new to Canada. In particular, these 60 odd small-scale prototypes were developed with the help of a Design Thinking approach, were tested rapidly and, for those showing promise, iterated (OECD and World Bank 2018).

Source: OECD and World Bank (2018)

Despite their differences, these approaches to public sector and social innovation focus on social problems. For the social entrepreneurship approach, breakthrough innovations are ideas that do away with structures and practices that trap the poor and disadvantaged in "suboptimal equilibria" (Martin and Osberg 2007). It is social problems—such as illiteracy, poor access to health care or barriers to education—that generate "suboptimal equilibria". Similarly, a 'good idea works' for Mulgan if it in some way enhances or extends capabilities to tackle social problems, either directly or indirectly. The social enterprise approach attacks social problems obliquely or, if you will, holistically. Social problems, so the argument goes, result from inequitable and unjust relations. By creating viable egalitarian alternatives to oppressive economic and social organisations, social enterprises attack the root cause of all social problems.

This is not to say that people in the public and citizen sectors are driven solely by high-minded public ethics while people in firms and enterprises are cynically self-centred.[4] The point here is that innovation is not primarily desirable because it secures organisational survival. Rather, innovation is desirable—and therefore makes organisations viable—because it can provide solutions.

Solutions to what, though?

Wicked Problems

The problems that organisations face today, whether in the private, public or citizen sectors, are so-called 'wicked problems'. The notion of a 'wicked problem' is not new. The two engineers Melwyn Webber and Ernst Rittel used the term in the early 1970s to describe challenges that seemed to confound urban planners at the time. In contrast to what they called 'tame problems', 'wicked problems' seemed oddly immune to resolution by tried-and-tested approaches. Contemporary examples of wicked problems include issues such as climate change, most non-communicable diseases such as diabetes, or, in the world of business, Mergers & Acquisitions as well as the dealing with and regulating the global financial system. Large organisations—both in the private and public sector—have found it remarkably difficult to deal with wicked problems. In their seminal paper, Rittel and Webber outline ten characteristics of wicked problems (see Box 2.3) (Rittel and Webber 1973). In essence, however, 'wicked problems' are highly complex and fundamentally uncertain.

Box 2.3 Characteristics of Wicked Problems

- Wicked problems have no stopping rule
- Solutions to wicked problems are not true-or-false but good-or-bad
- Every solution to a wicked problem is a 'one-shot' operation; because there is no opportunity to learn by trial-and-error, every attempt counts significantly

(continued)

---

[4]For all its considerable weaknesses, the Public Choice literature, most famously Anthony Downs' 'Inside Bureaucracy', has conclusively shown that public and citizen sector organisations are subject to very similar utility-maximising and rent-seeking behaviour that defines economic actors.

> **Box 2.3** (continued)
> - Wicked problems do not have enumerable (or exhaustively describable) set of potential solutions, nor is there a well-described set of permissible operations that may be incorporated into the plan
> - Every wicked problem is essentially unique
> - Every wicked problem can be considered to be a symptom of another wicked problem
> - The existence of a discrepancy representing a wicked problem can be explained in numerous ways. The choice of explanation determines the nature of the problems's resolution
> - The planner (or policy-maker) has no right to be wrong
>
> Source: Rittel and Webber (1973)

Complexity means that activities in one social sphere may have unintended and entirely unpredictable consequences in another sphere, possibly at some remove from the issue at hand. This is why it may be the education of girls—rather than just improving the quality and supply of food—that may be the key to fighting malnutrition in some parts of the world (Ney 2009). Complexity not only creates unpredictable and counter-intuitive connections between existing issues, wicked problems also feature opaque entanglements through time. What was an effective method with demonstrable results yesterday, say health care provision, may no longer work despite or probably precisely because of its previous success. A good example here is demographic ageing. Arguably, some of the causes of demographic ageing, in developing and developed countries alike, are rooted in the spectacular success of sanitation and public health care provision of the past century.

Uncertainty, in turn, does not simply mean the absence of data or knowledge. On the contrary, one of the key frustrations with wicked problems is that there seems to be an abundance of facts and data that, however, does not provide much authoritative guidance about what 'we should do next' (Fox and Miller 1995). Take climate change. The Intergovernmental Panel on Climate Change (IPCC), the authoritative voice of science in all climate change matters, produces reams of data and scientific analysis in its so-called Assessment Reports, in its fifth edition at the time of writing. And yet, sadly, it does not feel as if we were perceptibly closer to solving or even tackling the climate change issue. This is not because, as some might argue, the IPCC produces poor science. It is because scientific knowledge—objective and dispassionate facts—about wicked problems never unambiguously points to or prescribes a specific course of action. In this context, wickedness means an increase in the *ambiguity* of knowledge.

How, then, do we know what to do about these wicked problems?

Knowledge, Frames and Paradigms

Contrary to common wisdom, facts actually do not speak for themselves. If they were people, facts would be painfully shy; they would mumble and stammer, speaking in impenetrable dialects. Understanding what facts and data mean for solving the wicked problems is never automatic, it always requires some form of application to the particular context and situation. In other words, uncertainty means that making sense of data requires some degree of interpretation. This, in turn, implies sifting through, prioritising and selecting the most salient of the data.

But how do we know which of the data are salient and which are irrelevant? Fundamental uncertainty means that we do not know for sure and are unlikely to ever find out. Instead, we rely on things known as 'frames' to guide our judgement about what is important and what is safe to ignore (Fleck et al. 1935; Douglas 1987; Rein and Schön 1994). Frames are the systematic sets of ideas and values that help us explain the natural and social world around us.[5] Donald Schön and Martin Rein tell us that using these frames is

> …a way of selecting, organising, interpreting, and making sense of a complex reality to provide guideposts for knowing, analysing, persuading, and acting. A frame is a perspective from which an amorphous, ill defined, problematic situation can be made sense of and acted on (Rein and Schön 1994, p. 146).

Frames equip individuals with the criteria for selecting what is important, relevant or salient out of the wealth of experiences, events, observations, sensations or data at their disposal. Frames also provide people with the means of assembling these salient but selective bits of knowledge into plausible and credible accounts of what is going on. In this way, individuals can make sense out of an "otherwise anarchic stream of event" (Rayner 1991).

These frames or paradigms do not emerge from thin air. Instead, frames or as the biologist and physician Ludwik Fleck called them, thought-styles (*Denkstile*) are inextricably linked to the communities that generate and sustain them (Fleck et al. 1935; Douglas 1987). For Fleck himself, interested as he was in understanding the evolution of scientific knowledge, thought-styles emerge from groups of researchers and scientists that work on similar problems within a shared institutional context and normative outlook. He called these groups "thought-collectives" (*Denkkollektive*). More recently, scholars of the policy process refer to 'discourse coalitions' (Hajer 1993), 'epistemic communities' (Adler and Haas 1992) or 'advocacy coalition' (Sabatier and Jenkins-Smith 1993) to describe the types of communities—populated with a wide variety of actors—that coalesce around these frames or thought-styles. On this view, then, criteria for what is and what is not salient or relevant reflects what is important to or what defines the community or thought-collective.

While frames help us generate important insight, they provide us with inherently selective accounts of wicked problems. Selectivity and focus also mean that

---

[5] Another, probably more commonly used term for a frame is 'world-view'.

accounts and knowledge they create are inevitably incomplete. Making sense of the world necessarily relegates some things to the conceptual sidelines even as it places other aspects into focus. However, since the problems are complex, small changes in seemingly unrelated factors—such as the famous flapping of a butterfly's wings—can have momentous but largely unforeseen impacts on the issue in question. These, then, are the so-called 'unanticipated impacts' of strategies or policies. For example, the unanticipated impact of post-war health and social policies in Europe has been to erode the financial sustainability of many social protection systems due to demographic ageing. Unanticipated effects are the things that happen due to conceptual blind-spots of frames: quite literally, unanticipated effects are the things people in organisation did not and, in a very real sense, could not see coming (Weick and Sutcliffe 2015). On this view, then, knowledge is always ambiguous and, more importantly, contested.

It would seem, then, as if are caught in a double-bind. Relying on frames for solving wicked problems leaves us vulnerable to nasty surprises that risk derailing these solutions. Yet, at the same time, it is only through frames—precisely because of their selectivity—that we can make any kind of sense of wicked problems in the first place.

Solving Wicked Problems: Integrative Thinking and Clumsy Solutions

So, what are we to do? Is the best we can hope for a temporary respite from wicked problems as our partial solutions inevitably unravel at the flap of a butterfly's wing? Are we forever doomed to failure accompanied by increasing levels of conflict, anxiety and acrimony?

It is more than a little ironic that the things about our contemporary world that seem to exacerbate uncertainty and complexity also hold the key to finding effective responses to wicked problems. Globalisation and the social changes it has brought about have made the world a more diverse place. This is not only true in a merely demographic sense. The past decades have seen vast improvements in health care and education. People today are healthier and better educated than they were 50 or 100 years ago. Admittedly, these trends are probably most striking in the developed countries of the so-called Global North. And yet people in developing countries have also experienced and profited from the growth of education, health and communication. One result of globalisation has been the development and spread of a range of alternative life-styles and life-plans. This growing pluralism of the way people choose to live together has also led to a more crowded and boisterous market place for ideas and potential solutions.

Of course, it's not quite as easy as all that. The expansion of ideas has in itself brought about uncertainty about how best to judge the value of these ideas. Whereas for a long time, we seemed to believe that science and technology could solve our problems (and religion before that), more recently we have become more critical of the role of science is society. Without wanting to join the worryingly large ranks of people that deny science and technology have any value, the past decades have also shown that scientific and technological development does not provide all the answers either (c.f.Latour 2005). This is particularly true for wicked problems.

We are moving on new paths with a wider choice of vehicles. However, having to choose from larger number of pathways with no authoritative map or obvious way of distinguishing good from bad paths significantly increase the risk of getting lost. And, as anyone who has got lost on a family holiday will know, a lack of orientation begets conflict. Arguments about the way to the camping site ("I told you, you should have asked for the way") are rarely constructive and can rapidly degenerate into a rather nasty row featuring mutual recrimination.

A cursory glance at public debates about wicked problems will reveal that diversity and pluralism implies tension and conflict. Whether it concerns typically inflammatory issues—such as immigration, poverty or the crime—or whether it concerns seemingly technical topics—such as cyber-security, pension reform or child-care—debate is steeped in conflict and features irrepressible tensions. In many cases, particularly on issues such as, say, immigration, pluralist positions are so polarised as to render any public debate little more than a shouting match (see Chap. 7). In businesses, these conflicts are less public but feature the same acrimony. While conflicts in the public sphere lead to paralysis (Ney 2009), fundamental disputes about corporate strategy are often resolved by management fiat. But resolute decision-making in the face of many clamouring voices is not always the same as good judgement: indeed, the literature is littered with cases of resolute but catastrophic decision-making in sectors ranging from banking (Weick and Sutcliffe 2015) to consumer electronics and IT (Drucker 1985, 2007) to space exploration (Collingridge 1992). In either case, pluralism and diversity seem to be more of a distraction than a boon.

And yet, it is this plurality of ideas and concepts, with all its uncertainties, risks and dead-ends, that is the key to tackling wicked problems. While controversy can leads to paralysis, ignoring the diversity of ideas and approaches is not an alternative. Not asking locals (or Google) for the way to the hotel is likely to cause us to choose the wrong route. At best, we will waste our valuable holiday-time. By the same token, not making use of the rich and diverse reservoir of ideas and potential solutions leaves inherently partial solutions to wicked problems wide open to failure (see Chap. 3). This is true for solutions devised by firms and enterprises, public sector organisations or organisations in the citizen sector.

In the past, the theories that inform decision-making about wicked problems were of little real help. On the whole, they provided us with two equally unattractive (and unviable) alternatives. Either we find a way to reduce competing framings of wicked problems to a single 'rational' or 'objective' frame (or, if this proved to be difficult, to dismiss this framing as 'irrational' and therefore wrong). Or, we accept—indeed even embrace and celebrate —that the constant interplay of an endless multitude of different frames subvert any attempt of extracting meaning from reality.

Neither position is terribly helpful for people facing real problems in business, government or civil society. In fact, there is increasing evidence to suggest that people solve wicked problems by building on and integrating contending, frame-based but necessarily selective accounts of wicked problems. Roger Martin calls this process "integrative thinking". He locates this ability in individuals who "...have the predisposition to hold two diametrically opposing ideas in their heads. And then...they're able to produce a synthesis that is superior to either opposing ideas" (Martin 2009, p. 6). In his book, Martin recounts stories of how business leaders in sectors as varied as circus and finance have neither boiled their options down to the most 'rational' nor have they given up solving the problem. Key to practicing this skill—and Martin seems to think integrative thinking is something that can be learned—is a fundamental awareness that there are more than one way to frame wicked problems. What is more, Martin argues that successful integrative thinkers know, more often than not at an informal level, that much of our knowledge about wicked problems emerges from fundamentally incomplete and selective models of reality. However, they also know that solutions to wicked problems are unlikely emerge from any single frame. Instead integrative thinkers realise that solving wicked problems means creatively and flexibly combining the insights from a range of different models, incomplete and imperfect as they may be. For integrative thinkers, solving wicked problems is not about discovering the one 'true' answer. Rather, it is about negotiating multiple and plural truths about wicked problems. This process is also called 'reframing' (Dorst 2015; Kolko 2010).

'Integrative thinking', then, is a strategy for effectively dealing with the inherent ambiguity of knowledge. It implies that addressing wicked problems involves bringing conflicting frames and their contending solutions to bear on the issue in question. The trick here is to identify and integrate the valuable insights that emerge from each frame without succumbing to the inherent blindspots of these frames. In other words, instead of asking which frame is 'correct' or, worse, investing time and energy in trying to prove that one's particular frame is the best path to truth, tackling wicked problems involves creatively combining contending solutions from different frames.[6]

Design Thinking, Integrative Thinking and Clumsy Solutions

One of the reasons for the growing interest in Design Thinking is that it enables people to use 'integrative thinking' to assemble effective responses to wicked problems. At the heart of what designers do—the thing that seems to make design

---

[6]These types of responses have come to be known as 'clumsy solutions' (Verweij et al. 2006). They are called 'clumsy' solutions because they somewhat inelegantly incorporate what look like incompatible approaches and contending rationalities. We shall have more to say about the nature of these solutions in the following chapter.

so distinctive—is the recognition of the contingent and inherently contested nature of frames and mental models (Kolko 2010; Buchanan 1992). Design, these thinkers tell us (somewhat indignantly), is not merely or even primarily about aesthetics (Cross 2011). Making things attractive, desirable or pretty may be a welcome side-effect of design (or, if you will, a not entirely unanticipated impact of design). However, limiting design to the aesthetic or, as Richard Buchanan calls it, the 'decorative', spectacularly misses the point of design (Cross 2011; Dorst 2015). The real value of design, so the argument goes, is the ability of designers to practice what Donald Schön calls 'frame reflection'. Designers seem to understand that frames, paradigms and mental models are inherently selective, incomplete and, therefore, malleable. The practice of design, based on something Nigel Cross has called 'designerly thinking', enables designers to tackle wicked problems by moving across different frames and paradigms (Buchanan 1992). Buchanan calls this process 'repositioning'. Here, designers use what Buchanan calls 'placements' that "...allows the designer to position and reposition the problems and issues at hand" (Buchanan 1992, p. 17). In essence, placements help designers and others question dominant framings by throwing the social constructed nature of these mental models into sharp relief.

But unlike post-modern theorists, designers are not content to simply de-construct contested the meanings of wicked problems and leave it at that. For designers, de-construction also implies re-construction. This process of re-construction—which the design researcher Jon Kolko calls synthesis—draws new meanings of wicked problems from the friction and tensions created by contending frames (Kolko 2010). Reframing wicked problems in this way opens up new solution spaces to designers. This is precisely the way Robert Verganti understands the role of design in 'breakthrough innovations' (Verganti 2009): design, he argues, is about making new sense of things (p.22). For Verganti, radical and breakthrough innovations are also always "radical innovations of meaning". Just like radical technological change revolutionises the means of production, to use a phrase of the nineteenth century, or, to use a more contemporary term, a specific technological regime, the 'radical innovation of meaning' overthrows what Verganti calls a "socio-cultural regime or paradigm" (or, in our parlance, a frame). Like Martin, Verganti seems to understand innovation in terms of overcoming existing sets of meanings. In this sense, then, designers 'reframe' wicked problems to open up new solution spaces. For Kolko, this process repositioning and synthesis makes up the "magic of design" (Kolko 2010).

This is what it means to think like a designer (or to practice Design Thinking). Thinking like a designer involves knowing (or at least pretending for a little while) that all frames are fundamentally contestable, incomplete and, therefore, plastic. (Recall that this is also the precondition for effective 'integrative thinking'.) Thinking like a designer also entails creating new meanings by repositioning and synthesising contending frames. It is also an effective strategy for dealing with the *complexity of wicked problems* and the attendant ambiguity of knowledge.

It is no coincidence that synthesis is at the centre of the Design Thinking process (see Fig. 2.1 below). Synthesis is the pivotal point of the process. It links the part of

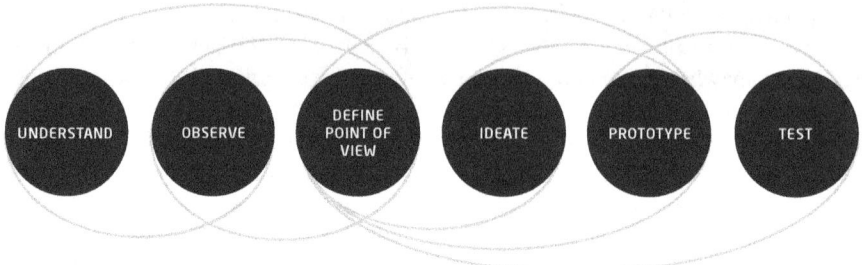

Fig. 2.1 The design thinking process

the process concerned with critical inquiry and empathy with the part that concentrates on inventing and developing solutions. Synthesis is the phase in which design teams reframe and reposition wicked problems in terms of user and stakeholder insights. This is where teams apply abductive logic to integrate different, often conflicting, accounts and narratives about the wicked problem at hand. This activity makes innovation possible: reframing enables teams to think about and understand wicked problems in new and unforeseen ways. Reframing, in turn, allows us to quite literally, think the 'unthinkable'. Box 2.4 provides some examples of successful reframes from the world of social innovation. By repositioning frames, Design Thinking teams open up new spaces for innovative solutions.

Designers not only open up new spaces, they also populate them with possible solutions. More than that, though, designers give these solutions a tangible form. Designers know that the 'new meanings' they generate through creative synthesis are no less ambiguous and uncertain than any other solution. These meanings are little more than propositions or bets about possible solutions to wicked problems. Making solutions tangible in terms of prototypical artefacts not only allows designers to cogitate in a different mode ('thinking with their hands'), they also enable users and stakeholders to interact with and test possible responses to wicked problems. This, then, is an approach for tackling the *inherent uncertainty of wicked problems*.

The methods, practices and mindsets of Design Thinking allow teams of non-designers to engage in this type of reflexive synthesis. Transdisciplinary teams ensure that a variety of contending frames are available and can brought to bear on the design challenge. What is more, the structure of and interaction within the team encourages members to perceive their preferred frames and perceptual lenses as inherently fallible and contestable. A wide range of methods sees to it that teams position and reposition insights from user research within and across a range of contending frames. Moreover, the Design Thinking process also provides practices for devising solutions and rendering them tangible (Chap. 6 looks at these practices in more depth). We can call this process of collective creative synthesis *team-based integrative thinking*.

> **Box 2.4 Reframing Issues for Social Innovation**
> The heart of most path-breaking innovations is a compelling reframe of the problem. It is this recasting of problems—problems that experts and pundits believe to know very well—that opens up spaces and vistas for new ideas.
>
> The revolutionary innovation of micro-credit—pioneered by Mohammad Yunus—revolves around a shift in the perception of the poorest members of society in Bangladesh. Micro-credits provide small amounts of funds to people who would never qualify for commercial bank loans because they live in absolute, crushing poverty. Instead of being able plying their trades (of which these poverty-stricken people were more than capable), they were left at the mercy of usurious loan-sharks. Illiteracy compounded their already precarious market position. Yunus' idea of providing very modest amounts of money (in the region of $20–100) to enable the poor—specifically poor women—to purchase supplies for their trades (e.g. tailoring or basket weaving) centres on a radical reframe of this group. Rather than casting poor, predominantly illiterate women in Bangladesh as victims—as did most of development aid either explicitly or implicitly—Yunus suggested we understand this group as potential micro-entrepreneurs (Yunus 1998, 2007).
>
> A similar reframe drives the social innovation of street newspapers sold by homeless people. These publications, such as the Big Issue sold in major UK cities, provides the homeless with an independent source of income while sleeping rough. Often involving homeless in the production of content, these newspapers allow homeless people to keep a part of the cover price. Most major European cities now feature one or more of these homeless newspapers. Not unlike the idea of micro-credits, the concept of homeless newspapers refuses to assume that homeless people are exclusively victims. Again, the underlying logic of these newspapers is that the rather individualist and entrepreneurial tendencies that homeless people exhibit is an untapped resource. Or, more precisely, existing entrepreneurial opportunities are incapable of tapping the entrepreneurial skills and instincts of some homeless people (Big Issue Foundation 2018).
>
> Source: Big Issue Foundation (2018)

This, then, is why people and organisations may *need* Design Thinking. People may want Design Thinking because it promises the types of 'breakthrough' innovation that provide organisations with some shelter in the 'perennial gale of creative destruction'. But there is more to Design Thinking (and, by extension, breakthrough innovations). People may need Design Thinking because its mindsets and practices offer a way to come to grips with the highly complex and uncertain challenges—or wicked problems—that we face today. Design thinking can help us tackle wicked problems by distilling the 'magic of design' (Kolko 2010). By making the craft of repositioning and reframing available to non-designers, Design Thinking empowers people to develop clumsy solutions using team-based integrative thinking.

Conclusion

This chapter has taken a look at why Design Thinking has become so attractive to people in large organisations. At first sight, the answer seems obvious: Design Thinking helps generate the types of breakthrough innovations that have become key to organizational survival. Today, enterprises that do not (or cannot) innovate will, sooner or later, fall prey so-called 'disruptive innovations' that reconfigure entire business environments. As we have seen, even well managed and successful companies are not immune to the turbulence that the 'perennial gales of creative destruction' inflict on markets. In fact, for reasons we discuss in the next chapter, well-run and successful companies are particularly susceptible to the evolutionary pressures generated by breakthrough innovations.

At this level, then, the demand for Design Thinking is driven by organizational survival. The determination to stay in business also fuels the search for means to survive Schumpeter's perennial gales of creative destruction. As we have seen, this desire to weather the storms of innovation feeds the cycles of management fads. Some pundits are already heralding the demise of Design Thinking as it falls out of favour, as all fads inevitably must, with the managers—both the desperate and the ambitious—looking for ways to stay ahead of the competition.

Yet, there is considerably more to Design Thinking than a means for aspiring managers to climb the greasy pole. Design thinking can help people in large organisations tackle the wicked problems they face. Since these challenges are highly complex and uncertain, organisations have little choice but to rely on frames that generate knowledge about wicked problems that is selective, emergent and incomplete. To complicate matters, a wide range of different frames is potentially applicable to complex and uncertain problems. Any solutions based on these inherently selective paradigms are likely to reflect the strengths—but also the shortcomings—of each frame, paradigm or mental model. This is why wicked challenges—such as global trade, ageing, the environment, poverty or big data—have proven remarkably immune to the prescriptions that have emerged from individual frames, disciplines or paradigms. Thus, getting to grips with complex challenges in business, government or civil society requires ways of bringing this plurality of contending frames to bear on wicked problems. More than that, facing up to wicked challenges means integrating insights into new and innovative solutions. In this sense,

Design thinking enables teams in organisations to do just this. As we have seen, the repositioning and reframing of wicked problems—or creative synthesis—is central to the design practice (Buchanan 1992; Kolko 2010; Cross 2011). It allows designers to open up new solution spaces for wicked problems (Dorst 2015). The methods and mindsets of Design Thinking make the practice of reframing available for non-designers. If done properly, this is a space in which the insights of contending frames and paradigms are available for sustainable solutions. At the same time this space allows design teams to recognise and avoid blind-spots and in-built weaknesses. By enabling what we have called *team-based integrative thinking*, Design Thinking enables teams to tackle and (re)solve wicked problems for customers, clients and citizens.

Yet this begs further questions. Why do large organisations find dealing with wicked problems and integrative thinking so difficult? What does the process of integration and synthesis actually entail for these organisations? How can we ensure that Design Thinking processes successfully solve wicked problems? How does the implementation of Design Thinking practices affect large organisations?

We turn to these questions in the following chapter.

References

Adler, E., & Haas, P. (1992). Conclusion: Epistemic communities, world order, and the creation of a reflective research program. *International Organisation, 46*(1), 367–389.
Baumol, W. J. (1990). Entrepreneurship, productive, unproductive and destructive. *Journal of Political Economy, 98*(5), 893–921.
Big Issue Foundation. (2018). *History and achievements*. Retrieved February 2, 2018, from https://www.bigissue.org.uk/about-us/history-and-achievements
Bornstein, D. (2004). *How to change the world: Social entrepreneurs and the power of new ideas*. Oxford, UK: Oxford University Press.
Borzaga, C., & Defourny, J. (2001). *The emergence of social enterprise*. London: Taylor & Francis.
Buchanan, R. (1992). Wicked problems in design thinking. *Design Issues, 8*(2), 5–21.
Christensen, C. M. (2000). *The innovator's dilemma: When new technologies cause great firms to fail*. New York: HarperBusiness.
Christensen, C. M., & Overdorf, M. (2000). Meeting the challenge of disruptive change. *Harvard Business Review, 78*(2), 66–77.
Collingridge, D. (1992). *The management of scale: Big organisations, big decisions, big mistakes*. London: Routledge.
Cross, N. (2011). *Design thinking: Understanding how designers think and work*. New York: Bloomsbury Academic.
Dawkins, R. (2006). *The selfish gene*. New York: Oxford University Press.
Dees, G. (1998). *The meaning of social entrepreneurship: From philanthropy to commerce*. Norfolk, N.C.: Center for Advancement of Social Entrepreneurship.
Dorst, K. (2015). *Frame innovation*. Boston, MA: MIT Press.
Douglas, M. (1987). *How institutions think*. London: Routledge and Kegan Paul.
Drucker, P. F. (1985). *Innovation and entrepreneurship*. London: Butterworth-Heinemann.
Drucker, P. F. (2007). *The essential Drucker* (Classic Drucker Collection Edition) London: Butterworth-Heinemann.
Fleck, L., Schäfer, L., & Schnelle, T. (1935). *Entstehung und Entwicklung einer wissenschaftlichen Tatsache*. Basel: Schwabe.
Fox, C. J., & Miller, H. T. (1995). *Postmodern public administration: Towards discourse*. Thousand Oaks, CA: Sage.
Hajer, M. A. (1993). Discourse coalitions and the institutionalisation of practice. In F. Fischer & J. Forester (Eds.), *The argumentative turn in policy analysis and planning*. Durham, NC: Duke University Press.
Hobsbawm, E. J. (2012). *How to change the world: Tales of Marx and Marxism*. London: Abacus.
Hood, C. (1991). A public management for all seasons? *Public Administration, 69*, 3–29.
Huczynski, A. (2012). *Management gurus*. London: Routledge.
Huczynski, A. A. (1993). Explaining the succession of management fads. *International Journal of Human Resource Management, 4*(2), 443–463.

Kolko, J. (2010). *Exposing the magic of design: A practitioner's guide to the methods and theory of synthesis*. Oxford: Oxford University Press.

Latour, B. (2005, September). Reassembling the social-an introduction to actor-network-theory (pp. 316). Oxford: Oxford University Press. Foreword by Bruno Latour.

Lepore, J. (2014). The disruption machine: What the gospel of innovation gets wrong. *The New Yorker*.

Martin, R. L. (2009). *The opposable mind: Winning through integrative thinking*. Boston, MA: Harvard Business Press.

Martin, R. L., & Osberg, S. (2007). Social entrepreneurship: The case for definition. *Stanford Social Innovation Review*, 29–39.

Mulgan, G., & Albury, D. (2003). *Innovation in the public sector*. London: The Cabinet Office Strategy Unit.

Mulgan, G., Tucker, S., Ali, R., & Sanders, B. (2007). *Social innovation: What it is, why it matters and how it can be accelerated*. Oxford: Skoll Centre for Social Entrepreneurship.

Ney, S. (2009). *Resolving messy policy issues*. London: Earthscan.

Organisation for Economic Cooperation and Development and The World Bank. (2018). *The innovation policy platform*. Retrieved February 19, 2018, from https://www.innovationpolicyplatform.org

Pollitt, C. (1990). *Managerialism and the public services: The Anglo-American experience*. Oxford: Blackwell.

Pollitt, C. (2003). The essential public manager. In P. Christopher (Ed.), *The essential public manager* (pp. 26–51). Maidenhead: Open University Press.

Rayner, S. (1991). A cultural perspective on the structure and implementation of global environmental agreements. *Evaluation Review, 15*(1), 75–102.

Rein, M., & Schön, D. (1994). *Frame reflection: Towards the resolution of intractable policy controversies*. New York: Basic Books.

Rittel, H., & Webber, M. (1973). Dilemmas in a general theory of planning. *Policy Sciences, 4*, 155–169.

Sabatier, P. A., & Jenkins-Smith, H. (1993). *Policy change and learning: An advocacy coalition approach*. Boulder, CO: Westview Press.

Sahni, N., Wessel, M., & Christensen, C. (2013). Unleashing breakthrough innovation in government. *Stanford Social Innovation Review*. Summer.

Schumpeter, J. (1947). The creative response in economic history. *Journal of Economic History, 7*(2), 149–159.

Schumpeter, J. A. (2013). *Capitalism, socialism and democracy*. London: Routledge.

Shapiro, R. A. (2013). *The real problem solvers: Social entrepreneurs in America*. Stanford, CA: Stanford Business Books.

Verganti, R. (2009). *Design-driven innovation: Changing the rules of competition by radically innovating what things mean*. Boston, MA: Harvard Business Press.

Verweij, M., Douglas, M., Ellis, R., Engel, C., Hendriks, F., Lohmann, S., Ney, S., Rayner, S., & Thompson, M. (2006). Clumsy solutions for a complex world: The case of climate change. *Public Administration, 84*(4), 817–843.

Weick, K. E. A., & Sutcliffe, K. M. (2015). *Managing the unexpected: Sustained performance in a complex world* (3rd ed.). Hoboken, NJ: Wiley.

Yu, D., & Hang, C. C. (2010). A reflective review of disruptive innovation theory. *International Journal of Management Reviews, 12*(4), 435–452.

Yunus, M. (1998). *Banker to the poor: The story of the Grameen bank*. London: Aurum Press.

Yunus, M. (2007). *Creating a world without poverty: Social business and the future of capitalism*. New York: Public Affairs.

Chapter 3
Clumsy Solutions, Messy Institutions and Cultural Change

The previous chapter looked at some of the reasons why people in large organisations want Design Thinking. Design thinking, as we have seen, promises businesses the type of innovation that secures organisational survival. The chapter also looked at reasons why large organisations may need Design Thinking. The reason, we hope to show in the following sections, is that Design Thinking encourages the type of cognitive and deliberative processes that result in what Roger Martin calls 'integrative thinking' (Martin 2009b). 'Opposable minds' (this is what Martin calls minds capable of integrative thinking), in turn, are more likely to mobilise the required diversity of perspectives on wicked problems to create what we have called 'clumsy solutions'. These types of solutions creatively integrate the wisdom of contending perspectives (while avoiding the inherent weaknesses) into innovative responses to wicked problems by using the tension between these frames.

Unfortunately, large organisations—whether they are businesses, ministries or executive agencies—experience great difficulties embracing integrative thinking. For organisations in the public sector this is all too apparent. On a daily basis, the media regales us with reports of policy failures at all levels—starting with climate change and ending with long-waiting times for life-saving medical procedures. Since large businesses are not accountable to the public in quite the same way as government and public administrations are, we rarely get the blow-by-blow account of management failures. But it is rather difficult not to notice the failure of a large, successful enterprise as they are swept away in Schumpeter's 'perennial gale of creative destruction'.

The reasons for this failure, thinkers from a wide range of disciplines seem to agree, are to be found in the way organisations work. The way we structure and run our institutions—particularly large organisations—seems to obstruct the mobilisation of opposing views we need to tackle the wicked problems that face us.

Why, then, is this the case? And what is to be done about it?

Wicked Problems, Innovation and Large Organisations

Christensen's 'Innovators Dilemma' or Schumpeter's original conception of business cycles driven by 'gales of creative destruction' suggest, somewhat counterintuitively, that successful organisations find it particularly difficult to seize or even recognise the opportunities created by innovation.

So, what is stopping large organisations from bringing about these path-breaking innovations?

Reasons for Organisational Failure

The simple answer (albeit with some very tricky implications) is that the things that make large organisations successful in their core business seem to get in the way of innovation. Peter Drucker argues that innovation needs to overcome what he calls the "gravity of existing success": the new, the contends, "…always looks so small, so puny, so unpromising next to the size and performance of maturity" (Drucker 2007, p. 103). Thus, the very set-up and constitution of large and successful organisations prevents people from identifying, let alone seizing path-breaking innovations. Failure, it would seem, is somehow in-built into large organisations.

The design researcher Kees Dorst points to five ailments or 'syndromes' that afflict organisations (Dorst 2015). First, Dorst observes that certain individuals and groups in organisations come to dominate problem-solving processes, often to the detriment of other voices and approaches. The ensuing controversy, typically acrimonious and bitter, between those who believe to 'own' the problem (and, of course, know what the best, appropriate or rational solution is to be) and those marginalised in the process paralyses problem solving. He calls this the 'lone warrior' syndrome. Second, large organisations attempt to solve problems by forcing essentially highly dynamic and changing problems into static and inflexible problem definitions. By 'freezing the world' in this way, Dorst argues that large organisations are highly adept at solving last year's problem. Third, organisations will always apply tried-and-tested solutions and conventional approaches to novel situations, even if these are patently inappropriate. When trapped in practices dictated by past success, organisations "…are blocking new thinking and reinforcing patterns of the 'self-made box'" (Dorst 2015, p. 16). Fourth, large organisations like to take "the rational high ground". Once organisations have found what they believe to be the most rational solution to a problem, they will defend that solution. For one, rationality imbues the organisation with moral authority: after all, a rational solution—legitimated through authoritative knowledge—is also the 'right' solution. Further, inflexibility and resistance to counter-arguments, Dorst argues, may also be driven by an "…acute fear of what might lie beyond the confines of this rationality, which is often referred to in terms of anarchy and chaos" (Dorst 2015, p. 17). In short, as the former prime minister and late Baroness Margaret Thatcher would have argued, "there is no alternative" (TINA).

Last, people in organisations, particularly successful organisations, may develop strong emotional ties to the organisation and begin to 'identify' with the practices that constitute this institution. Along with the other four organisational syndromes, Dorst tells us, this "pathological identification with current practices...is the absolute death knell to any innovation" (Dorst 2015, p. 17).

But why should that be? Why do institutions, particularly large organisations, suffer from these incapacitating diseases?

Roger Martin suggests that this may have something to do with the basic 'orientation' of firms and enterprises. He argues that large businesses have, more often than not, developed and honed capabilities that produce 'reliability'. For good reason. Reliability is rational; it emerges from decisions based on objective criteria, data (the more quantitative, the better) and logical algorithms. Large statistical models crunch numbers that accurately predict changes to existing systems—as long as the fundamental parameters remain stable. This data, seemingly freed of any bias by the workings of statistical models, can provide managers with the objective and, therefore, unassailable evidence to justify decisions for which managers will be called to account. And all this in a timely manner. Small wonder, then, that firms and enterprises have become taken in by what Martin calls the "reliability bias" (Martin 2009a).

But capabilities aimed at producing reliability, Martin argues, make it very difficult to respond to wicked problems. Essentially, organisational systems geared toward producing reliability are about being *demonstrably right*. Solutions that mobilise social and disciplinary plurality to deal with ambiguous knowledge, in turn, are about being what one could call *contestably right*. This, Martin tells us, requires a very different institutional logic, something he calls 'validity'. Unlike reliability, which aims to produce "...consistent, predictable outcomes" (Martin 2009b, p. 37), validity sets out to generate "...outcomes that meet a desired goal" (Martin 2009b, p. 37). For Martin, the latter requires judgement and interpretation. It requires a qualitative leap in understanding the American pragmatist philosopher Charles Sander Peirce called 'abduction' (c.f.Dorst 2015). It is this logic that enables people in organisations to not only recognise but also develop effective solutions to wicked problems.

However, Martin concludes, reliability unfortunately tends to trump validity in large organisations. After all, we live in a world in which we believe all effects to have an unambiguous cause: thus, failures result from poor decisions and poor decisions imply that someone must be to blame. It should come as no surprise that decision-makers prefer to rely on the rational, on the objective and on the evidence-based rather than on interpretation, the unprovable and conjecture. But precisely therein lies Clayton Christensen's 'Innovator's Dilemma': the very institutional set-up that reliably generates success with existing products and services creates real barriers to recognising the opportunities for breakthrough innovation, let alone seizing them.

If the set-ups in contemporary institutions are biased towards 'reliability', then, surely, the solution must be to transform these set-ups so that they are geared towards more 'validity'?

Transformation and Organisational Viability

Unfortunately, things are not as easy as all that.

While there is no shortage of schemes and frameworks for promoting entrepreneurship and innovation in both the private sector (e.g. Scrum, Agile, Lean, or Change Management) as well as in the public sector (e.g., New Public Management), the impact of these efforts is not always apparent (Huczynski 2012). In both the public and private sector, people in organisations complain of 'reform fatigue' after successive waves of organisational restructuring, realignments, trainings and reforms leave less time to deal with the what is perceived to be the core business. Reforms aimed to encourage entrepreneurship and innovation in the provision of public services often gets entangled in the debates about the justice and morality shifting public spending priorities (Pollitt 2003; Stoker 2006). Despite these programmes and reform efforts, nimble start-ups in the private sector and, increasingly, in the public sector continue to show up established players in terms of innovation.

It would seem that making organisations geared towards 'reliability' more 'entrepreneurial' or more 'innovative' is exceptionally difficult. Indeed, scholars, writers, journalists and practitioners acknowledge that transforming an organisation's set-up is, as Steven Denning of Forbes tells us, "one of the most difficult leadership challenges" (Denning 2011).

The reasons are fundamental to the way organisations work. Organisations are and need to be resistant to change. This is particularly true for established and successful organisations. Clayton Christensen and Michael Overdorf argue that all organisations, including businesses, are equipped with specific 'capabilities' (Christensen and Overdorf 2000). Much like the individuals that work in organisations, different sets of capabilities distinguish one organisation from another (Christensen and Overdorf 2000). These capabilities emerge from specific constellations of basic organisational characteristics. They determine what an organisation can do and, by the same token, they define what an organisation cannot do. We can refer to these distinguishing sets of capabilities as well as the ideas and values that support the capabilities as the *organisational culture*. While the specific terms in use will differ from discipline to discipline (and within disciplines from scholar to scholar), we can think of organisations as viable constellations of *structures and social relations, shared values and beliefs* as well as *processes and practices* (see Fig. 3.1).

The structures and social relations of an organisation are described by the patterns of transaction between the members of the organisation. Significantly, these patterns of transaction determine the distribution and deployment of resources in an enterprise, a ministry or a public service provider. Mapping the transactions of material and immaterial resources between reveals that some institutions feature stratified and vertical social relations. Examples here include classic line bureaucracies such as police departments in many European cities. Other forms of social relations exhibit more negotiated and horizontal relationships; examples here include groups of

Fig. 3.1 The institutional elements

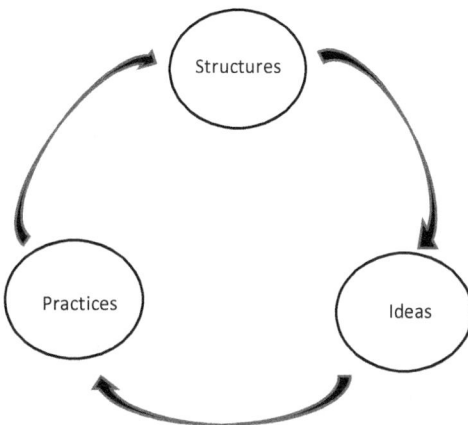

professionals, such as teachers, judges or hospital physicians. Some organisational cultures will encourage their members to distance themselves from other groups. For example, some religious orders, such as Benedictine monks (but unlike Franciscan monks), insist that its members reduce contact with the outside world to a well-regulated minimum. Other organisational set-ups work with a more fluid and disjointed membership.

Organisational cultures come replete with a set of shared values, norms and beliefs. These values and beliefs create a sense of togetherness or identity. By sharing values and norms, individuals can signify their membership in an institution or organisation. These shared values and beliefs provide both the normative and cognitive tools for making sense of the world. This is what we called 'frames' in Chap. 2. In business management, Christensen and Overdorf argue, these frames set the

> ... standards by which employees set priorities that enable them to judge whether an order is attractive or unattractive, whether a customer is more important or less important, whether an idea for a new product is attractive or marginal, and so on (Christensen and Overdorf 2000, p. 3).

In public management, Christopher Hood points out that these frames help individuals in organisations make sense of complex policy issues in order to formulate 'suitable' and 'appropriate' policy responses (Hood 1998). More importantly, these mental models structure lines of accountability. When things go wrong, as they invariably will, these mental models explain failure and, more importantly, apportion blame (Hood 1998; Douglas 1992).

Last, practices and processes determine the way organisations interact with and their environments. These are the procedures and processes that ensure the delivery of a service, the completion of a project, the ratification of decisions, or the setting of the management or policy agenda. Practices determine how conflicts are articulated and get resolved. Procedures and processes enable members to reward good and sanction bad behaviour. What is more, practices enable an organisation to engage with the outside world.

Organisations, then, consist of combinations of social relations, beliefs and practices that prove viable over time. Socio-institutional viability, in turn, depends on the extent to which these three elements mutually reinforce each other (Douglas 1981, 1987). This means that a particular configuration of social relations requires a set of values and mental models to justify this particular pattern of transactions. These norms and values, in turn, determine institutional practices and regulate their implementation. This then helps reproduce and enact the organisation in its wider institutional environment (Morgan 1986).

However, not all conceivable constellations of structures, ideas and practices are necessarily viable. Indeed, there are good reasons to believe that the range of viable ways of organising is rather limited (Douglas 1987; Weick and Sutcliffe 2015). While even a cursory survey of existing institutions is likely to present us with a mind-boggling variety of organisational forms, scholars of organisations seem to agree that only a few fundamental organisational forms or arche-types persist over time.

But what are these basic organisational forms?

Here, the work of British social anthropologist, the late Dame Mary Douglas, offers us a simple but powerful typology of archetypical ways of organising. This approach, sometimes called *Cultural Theory* (Douglas 1982, 1992; Thompson et al. 1990; Schwarz and Thompson 1990; Douglas and Ney 1998; Thompson 1996), is based on the simple insight that the manner in which we organise our social relations shapes the way we perceive the world and, consequently, the way we act on it. In this way, the approach sets out to identify the possible combinations of social relations, belief systems and practices—in other words, ways of organising—that are likely to be viable.

Cultural Theory locates four viable organisational archetypes along the grid and group dimension (see Box 3.1 for details). Each of these four ways of organising consists of mutually reinforcing social relations, beliefs and practices. *Hierarchies* feature highly stratified social structures supported by elaborate rules-systems as well as measures to sanction transgression and reward obedience. These organisational cultures help bring about 'reliability'. *Markets or individualism* provide individuals with the liberty to determine and negotiate transactions with others based on mutual self-interest. Individualist organisational cultures are geared toward bringing about 'validity'. *Sects or egalitarianism* offer individuals closed communities based on values of equality and justice. *Isolation or fatalism* is a way of organising in which trust in others is scarce; therefore, interaction is likely to be short-lived and strictly opportunistic. Box 3.1 provides a more detailed overview over Cultural Theory's contending ways of organising and disorganising.

> **Box 3.1 Four Ways of Organising and Disorganising**
> Cultural Theory maps viable ways of organising along two dimensions: grid and group. The vertical grid axis depicts the extent to which individual
>
> (continued)

Box 3.1 (continued)
behaviour is constrained by a system of social conventions. Moving up the grid dimension depicts social contexts in which a discriminating system of rules becomes increasingly dense and complex. The horizontal group axis, in turn, describes the constraints on an individual behaviour that result from membership in a group. Four stable organisational cultures emerge from these two dimensions. In their most generic form, these are usually referred as individualist (low grid, low group), egalitarian (low grid, high group), hierarchical (high grid, high group), and fatalist (high grid, low group).

Members of **individualist organisational cultures** prefer ego-centered networks that allow for maximum individual spatial and social mobility. Eschewing rules, traditions or customs, individuals regulate their relations with other free agents through negotiation and contract. For this reason, individualist organisational cultures are oriented towards outcomes. What counts here is the bottom-line. The niceties of process and status or the comfort of unanimity are, at best, a distraction if procedures cannot secure desired outputs and, more importantly, outcomes. What is more, the faster and more efficiently teams can generate these outputs the better for everyone involved. Speed and efficiency, in turn, emerges from healthy competition between smart and innovative individuals. However, the cost of speed and efficiency is often quality or accuracy. This is compounded by individualists' distrust of formal expertise and authority. This is why, individualist processes may produce 'awesome' and 'inspiring' innovations that, however, may simply be unworkable. Here, proponents equate dilettantism, erroneously, with economy. Similarly, the emphasis on the 'individual' designer or entrepreneur risks narrowing the scope of views and approaches required for effective integrative thinking. The voluntary and, ultimately, preference-based assignment of tasks potentially leads to issues and groups falling through the meshes of individual interests.

Egalitarian organisational cultures promote networks that do not differentiate between individual members. Egalitarian organisational cultures, then, are geared towards inclusion. Here, institutions are primarily supposed to provide a nurturing and protective environment for inherently good but highly fragile humans. On this view, a good organisation is one that provides a person with the autonomy from oppressive rules and the protection from ruinous competition. Inclusion means providing a place for the weak, the downtrodden and the marginalised within organisations and institutions. It also means giving a voice to those rarely asked and never heard. Egalitarian processes give would-be innovators the tools for securing the widest possible inclusion of views. However, including all conceivable stakeholders and ensuring their voices be heard makes for rather unwieldy design and decision-making processes. The egalitarian need for consensus decisions adds to the already

(continued)

Box 3.1 (continued)

considerable risk of sclerosis and paralysis. What is more, since egalitarians eschew formal authority and reject individual power, inclusion-oriented processes do not—and cannot—feature effective means of settling disputes and conflicts. With no way of settling disputes, conflicts very rapidly get reduced to issues of purity and virtue. The failure to reach consensus always implies an inability (or unwillingness) to understand truth and embrace virtue. Paradoxically, this can breed intolerance.

Hierarchical organisational cultures, by contrast, integrate knowledge and insights in terms of authority and expertise. These vertically structured organisations focus on the administration of rules and procedures. Assuring quality of outcomes means vetting and examining knowledge by appropriate procedures and suitably qualified personnel. On this view, not everything that may look like a good idea will necessarily provide the desired benefits in the long-run (the only run that counts). While diversity and plurality of knowledge are, in principle, a good thing, people working in hierarchies understand that not all participants in the process (and, by extension, their contributions) can ever be equal. This is the reason why contributions to solving wicked problems need to be vetted, summarised, and communicated by suitably qualified and appropriately authorised experts. In this way, hierarchical processes help us infuse expertise and quality into design. Hierarchies enable designers to appreciate the long-run view: what has gone before offers us some important clues about what to do now in order to secure results in the future. This trust in authority and the concomitant concentration of power in the hands of experts leaves hierarchical practices open to abuse and corruption. Since it is imperative that actions be appropriate and since hierarchies are focused on the long-run, process-oriented practices can become rather baroque and complicated.

Fatalist organisational cultures introduce the element of chance and unpredictability. For people in isolated social context, the world is a mysterious and inherently unknowable place. Fatalists witness many effects in the world but are deeply sceptical about claims to causality. It's not that an attempted solution is inevitably doomed to failure. Success—that is the development of an effective innovation—does happen: it's just that success, so the argument goes, has little relation to what people in organisations actually do. In short, we stumble over innovation by pure luck. The point here is that 'serendipity' always has a hand in whatever we do. Relying too much on our ability to control or even influence outcomes, fatalists argue, is giving hostages to fortune. Finally, fatalist puts a sceptical distance between putative causes and observed effects. It also allows design thinking teams to puncture illusions about teams and about potential solutions. Chance-oriented processes also enables teams to accept reality and roll with the punches. But fatalist

(continued)

> **Box 3.1** (continued)
> prescriptions are little more than a shrug of the collective shoulder in the face of wicked problems. Tackling messy challenges is a gamble: cooperation with others is a foolish undertaking. But, over time, fatalism corrodes the trust required to cooperate on anything. Fatalism can rob design teams of the vision - illusionary or not—they need to reframe wicked problems.
> The trick then, is to put together different types of practices that build on the respective strengths of each organisational culture and counteract the weaknesses.
> Source: Thompson et al. (1990)

In this sense, organisations are not merely patterns of transactions or resource networks but also ways of perceiving and acting upon the world (Thompson et al. 1990).

This goes some way in explaining why making large enterprises 'more entrepreneurial' or introducing an 'innovation culture' to public service providers may not only prove difficult but also rather risky. For one, effective organisational transformation requires sustained and, one might add, congruent changes of social relations, beliefs and practices. Change and reform processes aimed at only one or two of the three levels are unlikely to bring about the desired changes. Indeed, as Christensen and Overdorf point out, tinkering with individual elements may in fact do more harm than good (Christensen and Overdorf 2000). Injudicious change processes may, at best, simply not deliver desired organisational outcomes or, at worst, undermine existing organisational capabilities.

More In-Built Failure

There is, however, another fly in the ointment.

Even if efforts to transform organisational cultures were to be successful, reforms may move institutions from the frying pan into the fire. As we have seen, failure or the inability to innovate is built into the very fabric of an organisation geared towards reliability. A shift in the organisation from one viable type to another does not change the nature of wicked problems that the organisation faces: challenges are still complex and uncertain; knowledge is still ambiguous. This means that organisations aimed at innovation and entrepreneurship may feature their own in-built inabilities and weaknesses. In fact, each of the ways of organising features a specific mode of failure.

Hierarchies are good at creating and maintaining order. By enabling members to take the long-term view, hierarchical organisations draw on their expertise to create reliable and rational management processes. As long as everyone follows the rules laid down by competent authorities, nothing can go wrong. However, it is precisely these rules and processes that make hierarchies come unstuck. This is particularly true in turbulent and rapidly changing environments. Here, the trust in authority and expertise as well as the penchant for constructing baroque processes and rules becomes a liability. For one, authorities tend to discount knowledge, ideas or information from sources other than accredited experts. This deference to authority and authorised expertise in combination with complicated procedures make hierarchies rather cumbersome and inflexible.

Markets, in turn, operate in the here-and-now: opportunities are there for the taking for smart and hard-working individuals. Since all that really counts is the bottom-line (rather than the niceties of procedures), relations between individualists are only as useful as the tangible outputs they generate. In ego-focussed networks, members measure the desirability of outputs in terms of the utility and profit that accrues to the individuals involved. This enables members of ego-focussed networks to respond rapidly and flexibly to challenges and opportunities. That said, these types of organisations are far less proficient at recognising and understanding issues that may transcend individual interests. Here, things that are not in an individual's immediate interests simply do not appear in the individualist calculus of self-interest. Further, the pragmatic, sceptical and often irreverent view of authority and expertise ('if you're so smart, why ain't you rich?') also means that members of ego-focussed networks are not always as diligent in the collection and deployment knowledge as they may need to be: often ventures—whether business, policy or social—are built on rather shaky foundations in knowledge. In these cases, it is not entirely clear whether "failing often and early" actually means "failing unnecessarily".

Egalitarian organisations excel at inclusion and empathy. Trusting in the inherent good in people as well as in peoples' ability to do good, egalitarian networks aim to offer people an nurturing environment to fulfil their true human needs. Members of these types of organisations are highly sensitive to issues of justice and equity. This leaves them well equipped to empathise with and identify the interest of marginal and excluded groups. However, decision-making in egalitarian organisations can be cumbersome. Since no one can claim formal authority over others, everyone has to be heard and, more importantly, everyone has to agree, egalitarian networks have no way of resolving conflicts between members. Egalitarian conflict is not a clash of individual interests (to be resolved by competition) or a disturbance in the order (to be resolved by the application of rules) but a symptom of moral pollution. Since are all are equal, all have the requisite faculties for understanding and identifying (after adequate deliberation and discussion) the common good (or God's word, the true creed, real human needs, the Gaia's will, the planet's needs, etc.). Persistent conflict, then, can only be the result of succumbing to 'wrong ideas' or, worse still, malicious intent to exploit or undermine the group. Consequently, many egalitarian groups wish to protect themselves from pollution by constructing a 'wall of virtue' between themselves and the outside world (Douglas 1982, 1987; Douglas and Ney 1998). These types of organisations fail because their inability to resolve conflicts leads to festering infighting that paralyses the group (Hood 1998).

Isolation seems not to have all that much going for it. People in isolated social contexts trust nothing at all: not nature, not luck, not providence and certainly not other people. It's not that people are inherently bad or weak (and in need of guidance by strong institutions, as hierarchy argues); people are just capricious, unknowable and unreliable. But, oddly enough, this pragmatic cynicism helps inoculate people against the false promises of charlatans and delusions of prophets. When there is no common good and trade can only ever benefit those who initiate it, what some look to sell as a 'bold vision' is to isolates little more than the salesperson's cant. The downside of isolation and the sceptical pragmatism that it engenders, of course, is that it corrodes any basis collective action. When no one is trustworthy and chance dictates one's fate, the rational strategy is to 'default first' and get in your retribution before anyone else can.

Using this model, we can better understand why reform efforts are so difficult, particularly for successful organisations. Successful businesses, enterprises or social ventures have, almost by definition, forged viable configurations of social relations, values and practices. Effective organisational transformation needs not only to bring about enduring changes at all three levels (structures, ideas and practices), it also needs to make these changes compatible with one another so that the new organisational configuration is viable.

This is why many efforts at organisational transformation tend to be less effective than expected. For one, reform efforts that focus only on one of the organisational elements—say the values—are unlikely to have the desired effect. Instilling entrepreneurial values in organisations without changing management structures and processes may very well to lead to little more than an irritation as the old organisation co-opts, digests and adapts new values to old structures and practices. At worst, changes in only one or two organisational elements may cause severe turbulences that undermine the functionality of any institution or organisation.

But even if would-be reformers were to successfully transform organisations, they may do little more that replace one set of in-built organisational vulnerabilities for another. Installing an 'entrepreneurial culture' of risk-taking and opportunity-seeking into a business geared towards the risk-minimising and optimising habits of 'reliability' may indeed help overcome the "Innovator's Dilemma". However, this shift across the cultural map (from hierarchy to market) may very well come at the cost of exposing organisation to different types of vulnerabilities. The new risks are likely to be as perilous to organisational survival as the set of problems they replaced.

In sum, transforming large organisations—be they businesses, ministries or public service providers—so that they can more effectively embrace innovation, entrepreneurship and risk-taking is, at best, only part of the solution of adequately addressing wicked problems. For one, successful organisations—that is organisations that have found viable combinations of social relations, values and practices—are remarkably resistant to change. What is more, cultural change may simply replace one set of problems with another.

What is needed, then, is a way of setting-up organisations so that they can draw on a diverse set of institutional strengths without become susceptible to the specific forms of organisational failure.

From Ambidextrous to Multi-Dextrous Organisations

The veteran organisational theorist James March points to a way of—if not exactly resolving then at least—sidestepping Christensen's 'innovator's dilemma'. In one of his many seminal articles published in 1991, March identifies two opposed institutional modes of operation. One of the modes, which March calls 'exploitation', focuses on "...refinement, choice, production, efficiency, selection, implementation, execution" (March 1991, p. 71). The other mode, called 'exploration' is about "...search, variation, risk-taking, experimentation, play, flexibility, discovery, innovation" (March 1991, p. 71). Both modes are incommensurable. And yet, "...maintaining an appropriate balance between exploration and exploitation is a primary factor in system survival and prosperity" (March 1991, p. 71). Avoiding the 'innovator's dilemma', it would seem, calls for integrating contending institutional logics within a single organisation.

The business studies scholars Charles O'Reilly and Michael Tushmann call institutions that manage to bring both 'exploitation' and 'exploration' bear on wicked problems 'ambidextrous'. Being dextrous in contending institutional logics means having the "...ability to simultaneously pursue both incremental and discontinuous innovation...from hosting multiple contradictory structures, processes and cultures" (O'Reilly and Tushman 2013, p. 3). Ambidextrous organisations, they argue, do better on a wide range of indicators including sales, innovation and, of course, 'firm survival' (O'Reilly and Tushman 2013, p. 5). Roger Martin discusses ambidexterity in terms of the tension between 'reliability' and 'validity' (Martin 2009b). Indeed, for Martin Design Thinking itself is about finding and maintaining a 'balance' between the two contrasting modes of operation. Ambidexterity suggests that organisational survival may involve putting to work inherently incompatible modes of organising, of thinking and of acting within an institution.

But how can this work?

The idea of ambidextrous organisations has captured the imagination of researchers and practitioners alike (O'Reilly and Tushman 2013). This, however, does little to disguise the fact that the idea of bringing together fundamentally incompatible ways of organising, of thinking and of acting within a single institution is not trivial, not to mention a trifle counter-intuitive.

Indeed, organisational encounters of contending cultures are likely to set-off disputes and conflicts. While 'exploring' the uncertain and complex will entail some disagreement and argument, the confrontations between representatives of different institutional logics or cultures are unlikely to resemble a genteel scientific debate. The different institutional logics or cultures represent fundamentally different ways of operating and understanding the world. They are based on different structures of social relations and, significantly, different values. However, representatives and advocates of different institutional logics—'exploitation', 'exploration' and, we might add, 'inclusion' and 'isolation'—will have something to say about how best to solve wicked problems.

And what they have to say is unlikely to be compatible with one another. Frames associated with 'reliability' will tend to foreground risks and portray them as threats to the organisation in need of rational management. Advocates of entrepreneurial 'validity', in turn, will look at the same situation and see nothing but opportunities to be seized by individuals with the requisite courage, fortitude and intelligence. Perceptual lenses of egalitarian organisations will lead its members to focus on issues of justice, inclusion and inequity. Isolates will recognise none of this; nothing ever changes except perhaps the rhetorical guise of the same old story. Box 3.2 shows different cultural approaches to the issue of climate change. The problem is that this conflict, despite being couched in language that seems rational and objective, will be infused with and refer to fundamental beliefs about how best to respond to challenges (Douglas 1987; Thompson et al. 1990; Ney 2009).

Box 3.2 Four Stories About Climate Change

An analysis of the global climate change policy debate in the mid-1990s revealed three contending policy stories about global climate change (Thompson et al. 1998; Thompson and Ney 2000).

The first story—an **egalitarian tale of Profligacy**—singles out the consumption and production habits of the industrialised North as the fundamental cause of global climate change. The setting of this story is a world in which human wellbeing is intricately connected to the wellbeing of planet Earth, a highly fragile and vulnerable thing in need protection. The villains of the egalitarian tale are the inequitable structures of global capitalism that have driven human societies to the brink of ecological disaster. The profit motive and obsession with economic growth have instilled in us artificial wants (high calorie foods, fast cars, bottled water) fundamentally alien to our nature. What is more, the entire system is based on an inequitable global distribution of income and burdens: while the rich North wallows in excessive wants, the poor South is in dire want. Inequities, then, have generated unsustainable patterns of consumption and production. The general solution to the global climate change problem—that is, the heroes of the tale—is to put an immediate stop to these destructive tendencies. This means, among other things, adopting the strict precautionary principle for any activity and drastically reducing carbon dioxide emissions (mostly in the North). However, since global climate change is merely a symptom of the corruption of the global capital system, curbing global climate change will have to be part of a wider project of socio-cultural renewal.

(continued)

Box 3.2 (continued)

The second story, told by individualist advocacy coalitions, pins the degradation of the world's atmosphere on distorted resource price structures. The setting of the **individualist Prices story** is a world of markets and economic growth. In fact, economic growth is the basic motor that drives sustainable development: since climate change mitigation is likely to be costly, the global economic system must produce and release the required resources. This, in turn, means that markets must be allowed to function without governments impeding their self-regulatory mechanisms. However, these policy actors contend, this has not been the case. The villains of the Prices Story are misguided economic policies that have led to distortions in resource prices: the inevitable consequence is the relative overconsumption of natural resources that has led to the massive degradation of the environment. The heroes of this story, recounted by institutions such as the World Bank, are policies to break down the barriers inhibiting market mechanisms: these include global trade liberalisation as well as instruments such as carbon taxes or emissions permits.

The third policy story identifies uncontrolled population growth as the single most important cause of global warming. The setting of the hierarchical **Population Story**—a hierarchical tale—is a world in which humans are the custodians of the natural world. Our innate superiority over other species also gives us a moral obligation to manage our resources wisely. While economic growth is an inevitable part of any climate mitigation strategy, unbridled market forces are likely to wreak havoc on the social and natural order. Thus, policies for sustainable development that do not abandon civilisation (as the Profligacy Story proposes), call for the careful and judicious management of socio-economic activity. The villain of this story is uncontrolled population growth in the developing world. More mouths to feed and needs to satisfy translates directly into increased carbon dioxide emissions in particular and resource degradation in general. The heroes of this tale are policies and organisations that arrest rapid population growth through measures ranging from family planning campaigns to female education. Unlike the Profligacy Story, the onus for action is on the countries of the developing world.

Typically, fatalist or isolate stories are elusive. The conviction that there are but tenuous connections between policy (or any other kind of) action and discernible effects on climate change tends to be expressed in private but rarely articulated in public. A rare exception here is Robert J. Samuelson's 2014 opinion piece in the Washington post. Here, he argues that policy debates on climate change ought to come with the following disclaimer:

> Despite our belief that global warming poses catastrophic threats to many of the world's 7 billion inhabitants, we acknowledge that we now lack the technologies to

(continued)

> **Box 3.2** (continued)
>
> stop it. The purpose of our analysis and policy proposals is to create the political and economic conditions that foster the needed technologies. But there is no assurance that this will happen, and much time and money may be invested in futile and wasteful efforts (Samuelson 2014).
>
> He goes on to argue that the climate change debate is making very little headway because either side—the advocates of climate change policy and the climate change 'deniers'—have little or no common ground and insist on talking past each other. However, Samuelson argues that the "…central truth for public policy is: *We have no solution*" (original emphasis). What is more, while he contends that the technology may come to the rescue, "(a)s yet, no magical fix has emerged". The implication here is that we are at the mercy of serendipity (Samuelson 2014).

But surely this type of conflict distracts from the business of tackling wicked problems?

However, again somewhat counter-intuitively, scholars from a range of disciplines (Thompson et al. 1990; Schwarz and Thompson 1990; Weick and Sutcliffe 2015), suggest that this conflict—messy as it may be—helps tackle wicked problems and prevent characteristic organisational failures. As we saw in the previous chapter, frames-based accounts of wicked problems contain valuable insights as well as weaknesses. As Mary Douglas argues, each of the organisational cultures

> has its strengths, and in certain circumstances each culture has advantages over the others. And each has its weaknesses. But all four coexist in a state of mutual antagonism in any society at all times (Douglas 1996, p. 43).

This antagonism means that advocates of contending organisational cultures define themselves in contradistinction to alternative institutional logics. In terms of the Cultural Map (Fig. 3.2), this means that hierarchies defend against the threat of chaos from unregulated markets, social disorder and the dog-eat-dog world of isolation. Markets, in turn, allow competitive individuals to cast off the fetters of social status and regulation, the stuffy timidity of sectarian communities as well as the disheartening fatalism of isolation. Egalitarian communities provide a shelter for fragile humans from oppressive rules, the competitive dictates of the market as well as loneliness of isolation. Last, isolation provides respite from all the mugs that seem to actually believe the nonsense they spout. Thus, both cognitively and institutionally, the contending organisational cultures depend on one another. One the one hand, each organisational culture is well equipped to identify the weaknesses that emerge from blindspots in other frames. On the other hand, advocates of organisational cultures need the 'other' as a means to define and sharpen their own positions. It is a way of embracing ambiguous and contested knowledge by making use of the contention to avoid organisational vulnerabilities.

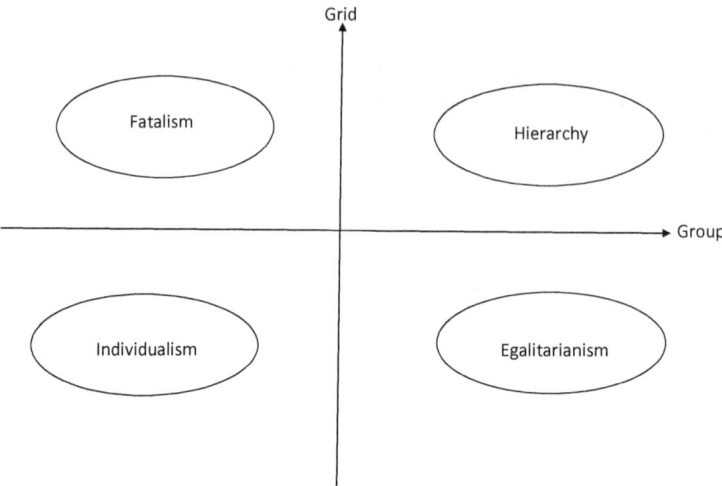

Fig. 3.2 The cultural map

In this way, then, the conflict between different ways of organising may contribute—indeed hold the key—to tackling wicked challenges in large organisations. Design-driven innovation, Roberto Verganti reminds us, is about uncovering 'new meanings' in artefacts and emerging technologies (Verganti 2009). For Roger Martin, as we have seen in the previous chapter, innovation is about 'integrative thinking'—the art and craft of forging innovative solutions from diametrically opposing ideas. In the context of organisational cultures in conflict, we can think of forging 'new meanings' through 'integrative thinking' as creatively and flexibly combining the insights and wisdom contained in contending solutions to wicked problems while at the same time avoiding the characteristic failures of each form of organising. In a very real sense, then, it is this tensions and conflicts between rival accounts of wicked problems that both enables and fuels 'integrative thinking'.

The outcomes of this process of integrative thinking in organisations are what we called 'clumsy solutions' in the previous chapter. Recall that these types of solutions creatively and flexibly combine, synthesise and, to use Martin's terminology, integrate contending partial solutions to wicked problems (Verweij 2006). In this way, clumsy solutions build on the inherent strengths of each organisational culture and avoids the pitfalls and weaknesses.

Boxes 3.3 and 3.4[1] outline some examples of clumsy solutions.

---

[1] The attentive reader will notice that these examples show how clumsy solutions feature only three of the four organisational cultures on the cultural map. This is because these so-called 'active' organisational cultures—hierarchy, individualism and egalitarianism—take part in policy debates about how best to respond to wicked problems. People in isolated social contexts, in turn, tend not to articulate their policy preferences (because they believe there is little point) or, if they do, will cynically use arguments from other organisational cultures to further rather narrow, situationally defined objectives. For this reason, fatalism is rather elusive.

Box 3.3 An Example of a Clumsy Solution
What are clumsy solutions? Briefly, they are responses to wicked design challenges that creatively and flexibly combine insights from contending and opposing organisational cultures. In his way, responses to wicked problems can leverage the strengths without succumbing to the interest weaknesses of contending organisational cultures.

What Does This Mean in Practice?

Water management in California is good example of a simple but effective clumsy solution (Lach et al. 2011). Traditionally, water management has been about providing and maintaining an elaborate engineering infrastructure. This complicated system of aqueducts, dams and basins transports water from the north and east of the state to the populous but rather arid southern parts of California. This physical infrastructure also came with an approach to water management that sought to "predict and provide" (Lach et al. 2011). However, as Lach et al. (2011) argue, mounting pressure from economic and population growth as well as new environmental concerns made it increasingly difficult to either predict or provide the water supply for California. Part of the problem, the researchers argue, was that water management necessitated the cooperation of different organisations and agencies with very different ways of perceiving and approaching the issue. In addition to the rational management approach of traditional water utilities, other institutional actors took a more individualist and market-oriented view of water management. For these actors, water is a commodity that, like any other commodity, responds price signals: water shortages point to distortions that prevent inherently efficient markets from clearing. Other actors still, those concerned with the well-being of eco-systems such as the Environmental Protection Agency (EPA), decry the commercialisation of what they see as a priceless ecological right: water. What is more, these agencies see heavy engineering of traditional water management as being an illegitimate infraction of nature in order to enable profligate and unsustainable water consumption habits. Yet all three organisational cultures were needed to find a solution to California's growing water problems. What was needed, then, was a solution that placated all three organisational cultures; in short, actors need a clumsy solution.

In Southern California, Lach et al. (2011) tell us, the clumsy response looked deceptively simple. Here, the three water utilities developed and deployed "an innovative rate structure" to charge consumers for water usage. In the past, utilities multiplied water use by same base rate. The new "conservation rate" retained a base rate but allocated a so-called 'conservation use target' for each water sector. Water use that exceeds the use target incurs a sharp rise in fees. This simple price structure, Lach et al. (2011) contend, incorporates three opposing principles: *parity, proportionality,* and *priority*. This rate structure allocates each household, as a human night, the same

(continued)

Box 3.3 (continued)
amount of water for drinking, cooking or washing; this creates the parity sought by egalitarian organisational cultures. The additional conservation use target allowance "...is determined by a formula that includes the area of each lot (determined from real-estate records), the evapo-transpiration rates at typical plantings and records of seasonal temperatures" (p. 232). This then, asserted the principle at proportionality at the heart of hierarchical approaches to rational water management. Last, the steep incline in price for water use exceeding the (hierarchically determined) conservation use target embodies the individualist norm of priority: households that feel they need water in excess of the conservation target can pay a premium to obtain a priority allocation. Pricing structures are also more likely to reflect real underlying scarcities, thereby strengthening markets and clarifying property rights. In this way, all three organisational cultures interact and integrate to create a workable solution to wicked water management problems in California.

This, then, is why managers of large organisations in the market, in the public sector as well as the citizen sectors may need to embrace organisational 'multi-dexterity'. Or, more precisely, this is why they ought to take seriously the underlying logic of organisational multi-dexterity: effective solutions to wicked problems emerge from the confrontation of the partial accounts (and solutions) that emerge from a diversity of contending organisational cultures. This, in turn implies that organisations need to create spaces in which actors can constructively engage with opposing ideas and practices—that emerge from contending organisational cultures—in order to forge clumsy solutions through team-based integrative thinking. In other words, rather than trying to shift organisations and their cultures across the Cultural Map of Fig. 3.2, it may make more sense to create spaces within these institutions that more closely resemble the Cultural Map itself.

Box 3.4 Clumsy Solutions and Design Thinking
Clumsy solutions have also emerged from Design Thinking processes.

At the Stanford d.school, a student team in the programme "Design for Extreme Affordability" set out to redesign incubators for developing countries. Believing that incubators for babies born prematurely are both too costly in the acquisition (they cost around about € 30,000,-) and too complicated in maintenance for health care system in developing countries, the team set out to Nepal to conduct user research. Upon finding fully functioning and well maintained incubators in the neo-natal facilities of Kathmandu's hospitals, the team was forced to reappraise their initial assumptions. It seemed that neither affordability nor maintenance were the real problem. The team was informed that these well equipped facilities were useful for premature babies

(continued)

Box 3.4 (continued)

born in the major cities. However, not all premature births take place in the urban areas of Nepal: the problem was one of accessibility to these facilities for babies born in rural and remote areas of this mountainous country. The team then shifted their research focus to these remote and rural areas. This research helped the team develop a portable incubator resembling a sleeping bag (Kelley and Kelley 2013).

This sleeping bag, called Embrace, is a clumsy solution. It appeals to egalitarian principles because it provides poor and marginalized parents with access to effective health care for their infants. What is more, the team was inspired by traditional and indigenous ways of carrying babies close to the body. Further, Embrace supports physicians and the medical system by bringing premature babies from rural areas into the purview of hierarchical health care provision (rather than, say, traditional medical practitioners). What is more, the sleeping bag is deceptively high-tech: it consists of an anti-microbal material that, once heated in an oven, maintains a constant temperature for about 5 h. This, then, requires bio-medical engineering expertise. Last, Embrace resonates with market-oriented actors: the technology is relatively cheap (at about $300 a piece) so that it is affordable for rural dispensaries and increases the general efficiency of the health care system in Nepal (Kelley and Kelley 2013).

Another example emerged from the HPI School of Design Thinking in Potsdam. When asked by a large multi-national parcel and post delivery company to help optimise delivery chains in cities of the future, the D-School jumped at the challenge. The problem was how best to organise the delivery of post and parcels in cities that feature little or no motor vehicle access. This is all the more pressing since both the volume and scope of goods delivered by post is set to increase steeply due to internet commerce (Barol 2010).

The D-School Team of students that worked on this problem in a 12-week project devised a solution that may revolutionise the business of delivering parcels in urban areas. The heartpiece of the solution is that the enterprise retreats from the actual business of delivering parcels and moves towards the coordination of a network of pro-sumers called "Bring Buddies". The "Bring Buddy" concept hinges on the insight that most city-dwellers make regular journeys through the city in which they live. This is particularly true for the areas that are unaccessible to motorised vehicles. Every day, people in cities need to make their way to work, bring the children to school, go shopping, or jogging, or take the dog for a walk. Many of these regular journeys are on foot, bicycle or public transport. Criss-crossing the cities at all hours, city-dwellers create an immense network of potential distribution pathways. And it is

(continued)

Box 3.4 (continued)

precisely these distribution channels that the "Bring Buddy" concept puts to use for large logistics providers.

The "Bring Buddy" would encourage city-dwellers to sign up to the scheme. The primary channel of communication between the "Bring Buddies" and the logistics provider is a mobile phone app. The logistics provider sets up parcel stations in the city along the regular pathways of the "Bring Buddies". Whenever something needs delivering, the mobile phone app would inform the relevant "Bring Buddies" via the app. Upon accepting the mission, the "Bring Buddy", on his or her daily journey, proceeds to the parcel station, picks up the package and delivers it to the address provided. In transit, the logistics firm can track, through GPS or similar technology, the progress and whereabouts of the parcel (Barol 2010). Each successful delivery is rewarded with points in an incentive system: both quantity and quality of delivery are rewarded. The Bring Buddy concept is currently being tested in Stockholm.

Simple as the idea seems, it engages all three so-called active solidarities. It appeals to egalitarian sentiments both is a formal and substantive sense. For one, the "Bring Buddy" involves people and their natural pathways through the city in the distribution of post and parcels. The "Bring Buddy" socialises of postal services, albeit not in any sense that Karl Marx would have foreseen. A positive externality, which the team explicitly points to, is that the "Bring Buddy" has the potential to increase social capital by increasing and intensifying the face-to-face interaction between city-dwellers. Another egalitarian aspect of the Bring Buddy is that it uses existing journeys more efficiently thereby cutting down the need for creating more carbondioxide emissions and making car-free urban areas viable.

The efficiency of the "Bring Buddy" also appeals to individualists. If citizens' urban pathways can be used as planned, then the logistics provider can service growing volumes while making huge savings in delivery infrastructure. What is more, the incentive system that rewards quality and quantity of delivery also resonates strongly with the individualist cultural bias.

But what's in it for hierarchy? Coordination, oversight and control are essential to the Bring Buddy concept. Starting from parcel station security and ending with GPS tracking of packages, the network of "Bring Buddies" needs effective control. And this is precisely what logistics providers are supposed to do. Indeed, the "Bring Buddy" concept suggests that logistics providers no longer deliver post and parcels. Instead, "Bring Buddy" turns the commercial aspects of postal delivery into tasks of management and coordination. Much like the NPM reforms transform ministries from service providers to coordinating facilitators, the Bring Buddy concept turns logistics providers into logistics coordinators. Or rather, it allows logistics providers to concentrate on coordination and oversight (Barol 2010).

Messy Institutions

How, then, can we set up spaces that allow us to constructively use the tensions between contending ideas to integrate the insights of these conflicting approaches? What type of processes will help people mobilise the contending institutional logics in 'multi-dextrous' organisations? How can we bring these (partial) insights to bear on wicked problems to generate 'clumsy' solutions?

Over the past decades, an astounding array of different methods and approaches that promise to solve wicked problems has emerged from fields as diverse as business studies, organisational studies, science and technology studies or public management (Ney and Verweij 2014a, b). These methods go by such promising names such as Action Science, Consensus Conferences, Deliberative Polling, Future Searches, or Foresight (just to mention a few).

But which of these many approaches is most likely to generate 'clumsy' innovations? Marco Verweij, a political scientist and leading Cultural Theorist, argues that, since mobilising and directing plurality of views in organisations is itself a complex and uncertain problem, the same logic that applies to clumsy solutions ought also to apply to the types of organisations that are most likely to generate clumsy solutions. These types of organisations are called *messy institutions*.

Four Roads to Clumsiness

For one, this means that would-be innovators in multi-dextrous organisations rely—indeed have little choice but to rely—on their 'perceptual lenses' when designing processes and methods for integrative thinking. We should, then, not be too surprised to find four ideal-typical models of solving wicked problems that correspond to four organisational provinces on the Cultural Map (Ney and Verweij 2014a, b). Each of these models lays out the 'best' way to put together Design Thinking teams, to create a conducive setting for generating clumsy solutions, to design an effective process and to moderate such a process. Table 3.1, adapted from Ney and Verweij (2014a, b), outlines the criteria and design principles set out by each organisational culture.

Egalitarian approaches insist that teams and groups consist of everyone affected by the issue in question. Such a group of equal stakeholders works best in a face-to-face setting when all other stakeholders are present. It is imperative that spatial arrangements and technology enable inclusion and encourage equal participation, particularly of socially marginalised groups. On this view, a good solution is one based on the broadest consensus possible. This means that everything from setting the agenda over the gathering and interpreting of information to the actual design of the solution be done collectively. Legitimate decisions—meaning consensual decisions—emerge from critical but also empathetic discussion in which individuals are encouraged to adopt a public interest perspective. Examples for these types of

Table 3.1 Design critieria for mobilising societal plurality

	Individualism	Egalitarianism	Hierarchy	Fatalism
Team				
Who should contribute	Those who want to be involved	Everyone affected by decisions	Authorities, experts and mediators—and those they designate/perceive as stakeholders	Those picked by random selection
How to attract/motivate people	Appeal to self-interest (personal absolute gain)	Appeal to outrage and solidarity	Appeal to sense of duty	No need, and (anyway) cannot
What behaviour to expect	Self-interested, rational, and open to exploring mutual benefits	Altruistic, concerned and caring (but some may covertly defend 'special interests')	Overly emotional, biased and short-sighted, when not properly guided	Haphazard, deceitful and amoral
Attitude towards economic, environmental and technological risks	Risk is opportunity	Risk needs to be minimized	Risk needs to be managed	Risk needs to be endured, unless it can be deflected to others
How to interact	Informally and competitively	Informally and empathetically	Formally and courteously	Randomly
Place				
When, where and with whom to contribute	At one's own time, in one's own space, and individually	When and where all the others meet	Depending on type of issue (with issue types and corresponding conditions set by experts)	Randomly
How to structure space in which deliberation and decision-making takes place	Fluidly (without clear, permanent boundaries or shapes)	As a round table: inclusive and equal	Depending on type of issue (with issue types and corresponding space determined by experts)	In an intimidating, impersonal manner, with space for 'back-room deals'
Design challenge	Reframed	Broader issues	Pre-structured with constraints	Random
Process				
How to divide tasks	Individual participants should define and choose their own tasks	All tasks should be undertaken collectively	Tasks should be allocated by experts on basis of expertise	Unsystematically

(continued)

Table 3.1 (continued)

	Individualism	Egalitarianism	Hierarchy	Fatalism
Which technology to use	Technology that is efficient and speeds up decision-making	Technology that can be used easily and collectively, strengthens social bonds, and gives a voice to the marginalized	Technology that can be used by experts to control information flow	Whatever
How to handle time	Time is precious and should not be wasted (as other opportunities beckon and the world won't stop)	Time should be suspended: everything hinges on the here and now	Time should be structured - with a formal agenda that distinguishes between beginning, middle and end	No need and not possible (time has stopped: nothing ever changes).
What information to use	Timely, sufficient and individually generated	Holistic and collectively produced (even if imperfect)	Complete, and produced (or screened) by experts and authorities	Secretive
How to determine the agenda	Every individual can add to the agenda	Through consensus/as a group (as one)	Pre-set by experts and authorities	Covertly ('hidden agenda')
How to take decisions	Outcome of an open competition between equals; or through bargaining and compromising ("splitting the difference")	Consensus revealed through empathetic talking and listening among group members	Expert-formulated synthesis of stakeholders' views	Unpredictably
How to learn from mistakes	By trial and error	Through critical group analysis	Through formal analysis undertaken by experts	Not possible
How to handle failure	Failure as a means of learning	Failure as a symptom of systemic inequities	Failure as a breakdown of functionality	Failure in inevitable, so best to accept failure

Source: Adapted from Ney and Verweij (2014a, b)

processes include Action Science (Schön 1996), the Learning Organisations (Senge 2006), Bohm Dialogues (Bohm 2013), or Open Space Technology (Owen 2008).

Processes that emerge from hierarchical organisational cultures trust authority and expertise. Here, groups charged with generating clumsy innovations need to be duly qualified experts, professional mediators and the responsible authorities. While these groups also feature the participation of users and stakeholders, it is the experts and authorities who appoint these stakeholders. Unlike egalitarian approaches, these process clearly distinguish between expert and lay participants. In hierarchical innovation processes, the setting will depend on the type of issue at hand: who contributes what, at what time and where will depend on how the experts for the issues set out the conditions and space for participation. To ensure an suitably high quality of deliberation and decisions, experts need to be in control of the deliberative process. Tasks need to be allocated to participants with the appropriate expertise. Similarly, the knowledge used to inform decision-making needs to be of the highest possible quality: this is why it needs to be authorised or, better still, produced by qualified experts. Hierarchical processes make use of technologies that enable the experts and authorities to control the flow of information. Decisions are based on the expert syntheses of stakeholder's views and perspectives. For example, Future Scenario Planning (Wack 1985) and Integrated Sustainability Assessment (Martens and Rotmans 1999) fall into this category (Ney and Verweij 2014a, b).

Individualist methods for tackling wicked problems emphasise competition and efficiency. Here, groups and teams consist of anyone who wants to get involved. Unlike hierarchical participants motivated by duty or the egalitarian innovators driven by outrage against injustice (hifalutin but probably disingenuous), participants in individualist processes are usually people that can make out some sort of gain or benefit for themselves. These approaches enable individuals to contribute to the process in their own time and on their own terms. Tasks are given to individual participants that ask for them: commitment and interest in the task are far more important than paper qualifications. For individualist processes, time is at a premium: any exercise that does not yield tangible outcomes is a unconscionable waste of time and opportunity. For this reason, technologies used in the process need to increase the speed and efficiency of deliberation, development and decision-making. This also means that innovation and problem-solving need a level and quality of information that is just enough to solve the problem at hand: here, 'satisficing' is a virtue (Simon 1945, 1978). Participants take decisions based on the relative performance of competing solutions or, if performance is not sufficiently discriminating, on bargaining. Examples for individualist processes are relatively scarce. The practices of tendering and evaluating competing solutions to development issues pioneered by the Bill and Melinda Gates Foundation serve as a possible example (Ney and Verweij 2014a, b).

Fatalist processes introduce the chance and unpredictability into problem-solving. Since there is no way to motivate people (except through deceit), deliberating groups emerge through random selection and compulsion. The most conducive setting for deliberation and problem-solving, so the argument goes for fatalists, is an impersonal and intimidating setting that discourages collusion and cooperation. Moderating deliberation and problem-solving under these conditions means accepting that people are inherently unknowable, unpredictable and, therefore, untrustworthy.

Four Sets of Strengths and Weaknesses

As we would expect, each of these family of processes for generating clumsy solutions has specific strengths and weaknesses. Egalitarian processes tend to be well suited for ensuring inclusion and equality. But since they place less value on efficiency, they tend to take up an inordinate amount of time and resources. Much like socialism in Oscar Wilde's quip, the key weaknesses of egalitarian processes are that they "take up too many evenings". And even after lengthy discussion, results may not be forthcoming.

In turn, individualist ways of solving wicked problems are all about ensuring effective and efficient performance. Indeed, proponents of individualist approaches take a very dim view of anything that is perceived to waste valuable time and resources. As a result, participants of individualist processes to solving wicked problems will tend to look for the quick win, which could mean cutting corners in terms of the quality of knowledge and the scope of inclusion.

Hierarchical processes are good at deploying authority and expertise. This enables deliberative processes such as Consensus Conferences to draw on reliable, tested and authoritative knowledge. However, it also discounts and thereby marginalises the voice of non-experts from problem-solving and innovation. Deliberation can then appear as little more than a show orchestrated by the authorities in order to rubber-stamp decisions made elsewhere (Ney and Verweij 2014a, b). Observing due process in the collection of data and evidence can also mean that hierarchical methods for addressing wicked problems can become rather involved and complicated.

Finally, fatalist approaches introduce the random into problem-solving. This can have two (beneficial) effects. First, contrived randomness—as Christopher Hood calls it—injects a dose of scepticism and distrust into problem-solving and innovation processes (Hood 1998). While this does not sound terribly constructive, distrust and scepticism can help prevent the type of strategic collusion that hi-jacks deliberative processes for private interests: since people are inherently unknowable and unpredictable, collusion is unlikely to yield any benefits (except perhaps for the instigator of such collusion). Second, contrived randomness can create an awareness among participants that innovation is often results from serendipity or, more prosaically, sheer luck. However, a little distrust and scepticism goes a long way. Stronger doses of contrived risk corroding the very basis of deliberation and problem-solving: if there is little anyone can do to solve wicked problems, why bother?

Relying on any particular process for problem-solving and innovation is therefore likely to leave organisations vulnerable to in-built weaknesses and blind-spots. However, the relative strengths of each process can help balance the weaknesses of contending approaches. The individualist emphasis on efficiency and output as well as the hierarchical insistence on managing deliberation can help overcome egalitarian proclivities to get lost in their search for consensus. In turn, the egalitarian insistence on maximum inclusiveness and the public interest perspective can counter the risk of (re)producing social disparities that inheres in individualist processes. Hierarchical notions of expertise and due process can help avoid mistakes caused by enthusiastic and rash dilettantism. The critical and inclusive spirit that infuses egalitarian processes as well as the individualist empowerment of stakeholders helps counter the hierarchical deference to expertise and authority that can alienates stakeholders.

Thus, clumsy solutions are more likely to emerge from processes that engage and make use of all four ways of innovating and problem-solving. These organisations are likely to be more pluralist—in terms of structures, ideas and practices—than the types of organisations built to generate 'reliable results'. These organisations are also more likely to be turbulent. Here, debate and discussion in these organisations is likely to be lively and full of conflict. Actors will thematise values and beliefs as well as facts and figures. But even the debate about facts and figures will be suffused with values and beliefs.

This, then, is what we may call a 'messy institution'.

Messy Institutions and Design Thinking

As strange as it may sound, it would seem that more mess—harnessing contending organisational structures, ideas and practices—may help organisations avoid the 'Innovator's Dilemma'. These organisations may be better placed than organisations predominantly geared towards 'reliability' (such as large bureaucracies), 'validity' (such as start-ups) or 'inclusion' (such as social enterprises) alone. Messy institutions allow actors in organisational contexts to integrate opposing models of tackling wicked problems that profit from the insights but avoid the pitfalls of any individual (partial) solution.

Messy institutions empower people in organisations in three ways. First, messy institutions provide the 'organisational space' for creative synthesis to take place. In this way, messy institutions delineate a public sphere (or partial public sphere) in which deliberation and *team-based integrative thinking* can occur. This space—both physical and socio-institutional—needs to encourage and empower the type of activities that bring about integrative thinking within and across teams. This includes critical inquiry, open debate and deliberation as well as to explore the unthinkable.

Second, messy institutions populate this space with a wide range of contending frames, paradigms and perceptions. This collection forms a reservoir of ideas, accounts and solutions (albeit partial) that are the raw material for creative synthesis and team-based integrative thinking. This is also the source of contending problem formulation.

Last, messy institutions make available the practices that help actors to forge effective responses to wicked problems. Drawn from contending organisational cultures, this plurality of practices and processes enables innovators to select and guide teams, collect data, generate insights, make decisions and construct solutions in ways that capitalises on the inherent strengths of organisational cultures. Messy institutions tailor their processes in order to enable a lively and often conflictual debate. At the same time, these practices are designed to ensure that conflict does not deteriorate into the intractable controversies amenable to resolution on by authority and force but by reason and good design.

Conclusion

The 'Innovator's Dilemma' is, at its core, an organisational problem. The inability to recognise or, even more frustrating, act upon opportunities offered by so-called disruptive innovations is something that seems to be built into the fundamental make-up of some organisations. As we have seen, this seems particularly true for successful organisations. Businesses, public service providers or social ventures that have, to use Peter Drucker's phrase, "created a customer", have set up a viable (meaning mutually supportive and reinforcing) relationship between organisational structures, governing norms and values as well as processes and practices.

Viability means that organisations reproduce themselves at all three levels. This also means that viable organisations have developed effective defences to 'deflect' attacks at all three levels. As we have seen, viability and success suggest that confronting the 'Innovator's Dilemma' by implementing programmes designed to introduce a more 'entrepreneurial' culture may be considerably more difficult (as well as prone to failure) as they at first may appear. Cultural change - if it is to be effective - needs to bring about sustained transformation at all three organisational levels. Lessons from politics and policy-making suggest that these types of reforms generate immense resistance to change (Ney 2009). More often than not, would-be reformers do not have the stomach for this type of reform. This is true for both the public as well as the private sectors.

Further, even if it were to be successful, cultural transformation may not make a business or social venture more innovative or less vulnerable to the 'perennial gale of creative destruction'. Using Mary Douglas' typology of organisational cultures, this chapter has shown how different (but limited) options for socio-institutional viability make up a map of organisational cultures. Each of the ways of organising comes with a specific set of 'perceptual lenses' that helps make sense of the world in an inherently selective way. These perceptual lenses provide a coherent albeit partial account of what is, and more importantly, what should be going on with any particular wicked problem. Each way of organising also comes replete with a specific frames and a repertoire of practices. Consequently, each way of organising is good at recognising and dealing with certain aspects of complex and uncertain problems. Conversely, each way of organising also has in-built blind-spots and weaknesses. There are things about wicked problems that remain hidden to organisations: luckily, the things that remain hidden are different for different types of organisations.

This is why simply shifting the organisational culture from one province of the cultural map to the other may merely replace one set of vulnerabilities with another. So while reforms may change an organisation geared towards reliability (or hierarchy on the Cultural Map) towards validity (or individualism) may help overcome the "Innovator's Dilemma", it may very well leave the business incapable of effectively scaling and reliably delivering their solutions. Indeed, the Cultural Map (Fig. 3.2) suggests that people working in any of the other organisational provinces face specific 'dilemmas' of their own.

The ways of organising do not merely coexist. As we have seen, these ways of organising are mutually antagonistic and constant competition with one another. Each of these ways of organising features a viable combination of structures, ideas and practices. Yet, at the same time, each defines itself in contradistinction to rival organisational cultures and, perhaps somewhat paradoxically, depends on the other cultures for its own institutional reproduction. This is why contending ways of organising keenly perceive the respective weaknesses and vulnerabilities of contending organisational cultures. Thus, each way of organising offers useful insights about and partial solutions for wicked problems. As we saw in Chap. 2, solutions that creatively integrate these contending approaches are called 'clumsy solutions'.

Dealing with wicked problems, then, involves mobilising contending ways of organising and bringing their insights to bear on complex and uncertain challenges. Rather than shepherding organisations across the Cultural Map, change processes need to transform business and public institutions so that they more closely resemble the map itself. We can call these types of organisations 'messy institutions'. Since these types of organisations incorporate a wide plurality of organisational cultures, they feature a rich and variegated reservoir of ideas, perceptions and solutions. Messy institutions are 'multi-dextrous' in that they encompass organisational cultures that encourage both reliable exploitation and exploration for validity (following March and Martin). Yet, messy institutions extend the concept of ambidexterity to include two further basic institutional capabilities: inclusion and isolation.

But how can we transform large organisations into 'messy institutions'? What is needed is an approach or method that that can do two things. First, this approach needs to operate at all three organisational levels: that is the level of structures, the level of ideas as well as the level of practices. Second, the approach needs to not only create a broad plurality of ways of organising, it also needs to enable actors within organisations to mobilise this plurality for constructing innovations that address wicked problems.

Recent research suggests that Design Thinking is one of a range of approaches that enables organisations (or, more precisely, people that work in organisations) to do just this. The remainder of this book will take a critical look at how people in large organisations have used Design Thinking to transform their institutional settings at all three levels. First, Design Thinking helps would-be innovators create appropriate socio-institutional spaces for teams to engage in team-based integrative thinking. The next chapter—Chap. 4—looks at the way Design Thinking has affected socio-institutional spaces. Further, the methods and mindsets of Design Thinking allow this space to be 'populated' with contending views, perspectives and practices. Chapter 5 discusses how Design Thinking creates a rich reservoir of (contending) ideas and practices that for the 'raw material' for team-based integrative thinking. Chapter 5 also outlines how Design Thinking can help people encourage and institute a contentious pluralism of ideas and beliefs. Last, Design Thinking also provides the methods and processes that empower design teams in large organisations to constructively build on insights that emerge from contending frames without succumbing to in-built vulnerabilities and weaknesses. Chapter 6, then, shows how the introduction of Design Thinking practices shapes large organisations.

References

Barol, B. (2010, November 26). bring.BUDDY: DHL crowdsources your grandma. *Forbes*.
Bohm, D. (2013). *On dialogue*. London: Routledge.
Christensen, C. M., & Overdorf, M. (2000). Meeting the challenge of disruptive change. *Harvard Business Review, 78*(2), 66–77.
Denning, S. (2011, July 23). How do you change an organizational culture. *Forbes*.
Dorst, K. (2015). *Frame innovation*. Boston, MA: MIT Press.
Douglas, M. (1981). *Edward Evans-Pritchard*. New York: Penguin Books.
Douglas, M. (Ed.). (1982). *Essays in the sociology of perception*. London: Routledge and Kegan Paul.
Douglas, M. (1987). *How institutions think*. London: Routledge and Kegan Paul.
Douglas, M. (1992). *Risk and blame: Essays on cultural theory*. London: Routledge.
Douglas, M. (1996). *Thought styles: Critical essays on good taste*. London: Sage.
Douglas, M., & Ney, S. (1998). *Missing persons: A critique of personhood in the social sciences*. Berkeley, CA: University of California Press.
Drucker, P. F. (2007). *The essential Drucker* (Classic Drucker Collection Edition) London: Butterworth-Heinemann.
Hood, C. (1998). *The art of the state: Culture, rhetoric, and public management*. Oxford: Oxford University Press.
Huczynski, A. (2012). *Management gurus*. London: Routledge.
Kelley, T., & Kelley, D. (2013). A solution for poor mothers, when expensive hospital incubators won't do. *The Eye: Slate Design Blog*. Retrieved March 4, 2014, from http://www.slate.com/blogs/the_eye/2013/11/04/embrace_infant_warmer_creative_confidence_by_tom_and_david_kelley.html
Lach, D., Ingram, H., & Rayner, S. (2011). You never miss the water till the well runs dry: Crisis and creativity in California. In M. Verweij & M. Thompson (Eds.), *Clumsy solutions for a complex world: Governance, politics and plural perceptions* (pp. 226–240). Basingstoke: Palgrave Macmillan.
March, J. G. (1991). Exploration and exploitation in organizational learning. *Organization Science, 2*(1), 71–87.
Martens, P., & Rotmans, J. (1999). *Climate change: An integrated perspective*. London: Springer.
Martin, R. L. (2009a). *The design of business: Why design thinking is the next competitive advantage*. Boston, MA: Harvard Business Press.
Martin, R. L. (2009b). *The opposable mind: Winning through integrative thinking*. Boston, MA: Harvard Business Press.
Morgan, G. (1986). *Images of organisation*. London: Sage.
Ney, S. (2009). *Resolving messy policy issues*. London: Earthscan.
Ney, S., & Verweij, M. (2014a). Exploring the contributions of cultural theory for improving public deliberation about complex policy problems. *Policy Studies Journal, 42*(4), 620–643.
Ney, S., & Verweij, M. (2014b). Messy institutions for wicked problems: How to generate clumsy solutions. Available at SSRN 2382191.
O'Reilly, C., & Tushman, M. (2013). Organizational ambidexterity: Past, present and future. *The Academy of Management Perspectives, 27*(4), 324–338. https://doi.org/10.5465/amp.2013.0025.
Owen, H. (2008). *Open space technology: A user's guide*. San Francisco, CA: Berrett-Koehler.

Pollitt, C. (2003). The essential public manager. In P. Christopher (Ed.), *The essential public manager* (pp. 26–51). Maidenhead: Open University Press.

Samuelson, J. (2014, May 11). On climate change, we have no solution. *The Washington Post*.

Schön, D. A. (1996). *Organizational learning II: Theory, method and practice*. New York: Addison-Wesley.

Schwarz, M., & Thompson, M. (1990). *Divided we stand: Redefining politics, technology and social choice*. Hemel Hempstead: Harvester Wheatsheaf.

Senge, P. M. (2006). *The fifth discipline: The art and practice of the learning organization*. New York: Broadway Business.

Simon, H. (1945). *Administrative behaviour*. New York: Free Press.

Simon, H. (1978). Rationality as process and product of thought. *American Economic Review Papers and Proceedings, 68*, 1–16.

Stoker, G. (2006). Public value management: A new narrative for networked governance? *The American Review of Public Administration, 36*, 41–57.

Thompson, M. (1996). *Inherent relationality: An anti-dualist approach to institutions*. Bergen: LOS Center.

Thompson, M., & Ney, S. (2000). Cultural discourses in the global climate change debate. In E. Jochem, J. Sathaye, & D. Bouille (Eds.), *Society, behaviour and climate change mitigation* (pp. 65–92). Dordrecht: Kluwer.

Thompson, M., Ellis, R., & Wildavsky, A. (1990). *Cultural theory*. Boulder, CO: Westview Press.

Thompson, M., Rayner, S., & Ney, S. (1998). Risk and governance Part II. *Government and Opposition, 33*(3), 330–354.

Verganti, R. (2009). *Design-driven innovation: Changing the rules of competition by radically innovating what things mean*. Boston, MA: Harvard Business Press.

Verweij, M. (2006). Is the Kyoto protocol merely irrelevant, or positively harmful, for the efforts to curb climate change. In M. Thompson (Ed.), *Clumsy solutions for a complex world* (pp. 31–60). Basingstoke: Palgrave.

Wack, P. (1985). Scenarios: Shooting the rapids: How medium-term analysis illuminated the power of scenarios for shell management. *Harvard Business Review, 63*(6), 139–150.

Weick, K. E. A., & Sutcliffe, K. M. (2015). *Managing the unexpected: Sustained performance in a complex world* (3rd ed.). Hoboken, NJ: Wiley.

Chapter 4
Creating Social Spaces for Exploration

If organisations are to tackle wicked problems, the last chapters have argued, they need to become 'multi-dexterous' or 'messy' institutions. It is these types of organisations that enable people to generate 'clumsy solutions'. They create the conditions for multidisciplinary teams to work with opposing and even contradictory ideas that originate in different institutional logics. By engaging in what we have called—drawing on Roger Martin's work (2009b)—'team-based integrative thinking', multidisciplinary teams in messy institutions can forge these contending ideas into effective responses to messy challenges. The previous chapters also argued that Design Thinking could move large organisations geared to reliability towards multi-dextrous messiness. The introduction of Design Thinking potentially affects large organisations at the level of structures, at the level ideas as well as the level of practices.

So, how can Design Thinking help large organisations become 'multi-dextrous' and 'messy'? How can Design Thinking help organisations embrace ambiguous and contested knowledge? And how have efforts to implement Design Thinking affected large organisations at the level of structures, ideas and practices?

The following three chapters will address this question by looking closely at some of the available empirical evidence. This chapter will direct our attention to the way Design Thinking initiatives[1] shaped (or failed to shape) organisational structures. The subsequent chapter (Chap. 5) takes a close look at how the implementation of Design Thinking has affected the reservoir of ideas in the institutions studied. Chapter 6, then, reviews the way Design Thinking provides messy practices to enable Design Thinking teams to forge clumsy solutions.

---

[1]We can define the term 'design thinking initiative' as a formal programme of organisational change and reform. Programmes of this sort explicitly budget and deploy financial, human and capital resources to implement the methods and mindsets of design thinking in parts or the whole of the organisation. 'Design thinking initiatives' are formally endorsed and sanctioned by the management of the organisation in question. This definition, then, excludes informal endeavours by individual employees or managers to introduce design thinking to organisations.

Our argument relies on several existing studies of the implementation of Design Thinking in large private and public sectors organisations. Although the implementation of Design Thinking is still a rather young field of research, we can draw on several excellent studies. The work of Lisa Carlgren, Ingo Rauth and Maria Elmquist (Carlgren et al. 2014a, b; Rauth et al. 2014) compares Design Thinking initiatives in six large multi-national organisations in the private sector. These organisations include enterprises from sectors as diverse as IT, health care, consumer goods and consumer electronics (Carlgren et al. 2014a, b; Rauth et al. 2014). Holger Rhinow's work (2018) takes an in-depth look at the implementation of Design Thinking in a large German enterprise. Here, Rhinow concentrates on the role of project managers in the Design Thinking process. Similarly, Eva Köppen (2016) critically examines the same Design Thinking initiative by focusing on the way empathy shapes the norms and practices in the enterprise. Katrin Dribbisch (2016) compares the introduction of Design Thinking to several different departments of a central ministry in Singapore. Her work sets out to ascertain how large organisations adopt, adapt and translate the practices of Design Thinking to local institutional conditions.

In what follows, then, we take a close look at the way the introduction of Design Thinking affected the structures of the different organisations. After a brief conceptual introduction, the subsequent section looks at how different Design Thinking initiatives affected the organisational structures of large organisations. One section focuses on the structural changes while another section looks at the costs and potential problems associated with these reforms. The final section briefly reviews some of the lessons to be drawn from the different experiences of implementing Design Thinking in large organisations.

Space, Deliberation and Mini-Publics

Everyone who has ever taken part in a Design Thinking workshop will know that space plays a key role. At the D-Schools, all the furniture is on wheels, students and faculty do most of their work standing up and all vertical spaces are a plane onto which to project thoughts and ideas. The room set-ups change as the day wears on. The underlying idea is that the spatial set-up of where we work will shape what we can or cannot achieve.

Social spaces are no less important to Design Thinking. In order for Design Thinking teams to innovate, they require a suitable social space that corresponds to their physical innovation space. Just like the physical space needs to support team creativity and autonomy, the social space needs to enable 'team-based integrative thinking'.

What, then, brings about 'team-based integrative thinking'?

Effective 'team-based integrative thinking' emerges from critical deliberation. The term 'deliberation' and the accompanying notion of 'deliberative democracy' have emerged from democracy theory in the past decades (Fishkin 1991, 2009, Bohman 1998; Fischer 2003). They describe a way of taking decisions—usually but not necessarily of public relevance—based on a prior debate between participants of the process. Here, debate describes the exchange and competition of arguments about the issue at hand. Unlike, say, negotiation or bargaining, the aim here is not so much to find a compromise or to strike a deal between competing interests. Instead, deliberation is supposed to allow participating citizens to explore the issue at hand in order to find the 'common good' or 'public interest'. Similarly, unlike voting, deliberation is not about aggregating individual preferences. Rather than assuming individual preferences remain fixed or are not amenable to change, deliberation offers individual participants the opportunity to *transform* their preferences in the light of proffered arguments. Of course, transforming individual preferences through deceit, dissembling or even by force is not permissible: not only does this undermine the normative claim of being a fundamentally democratic process, it is also unlikely to produce effective (meaning clumsy) solutions to wicked problems. On this view, finding solutions that best serve the 'public interest' requires a particular type of debate in which, as much as is possible, the 'force of the better argument' (Habermas 1987; Dryzek 1990, 1993) is the strongest currency.

So how do social spaces support critical deliberation in a diverse team of T-Shaped people?[2]

First, social spaces need to support and protect open-ended and exploratory inquiry of the design challenge. Social spaces need to provide teams with both the *freedom from* external interferences as well as the *freedom to* investigate the design challenge as the team sees fit. By neutralising (or, at least, relativizing) external constraints—be they performance indicators, targets, or mission statements—these negative and positive freedoms help safeguard that teams look for, find and listen to the 'force of the better argument'. Ensuring an open and exploratory inquiry means to allow that "decisions", as Weick and Sutcliffe (2015) put it, "migrate to experts". In our context, migration of decisions to experts means that teams find and listen to the person (or persons) most qualified to provide insights about the design challenge regardless of the status and organisational location of these actors. Weick and Sutcliffe (2015) point out that "...if you want decisions to migrate to experts, then you need to loosen the rigid hierarchy, know where the experts are, and have mechanisms to get to them" (Weick and Sutcliffe 2015). In an open-ended, user-centric inquiry, the experts of user and stakeholder experiences may very well be the users and stakeholders themselves. Social spaces must therefore not only enable Design Thinking teams to hear these experts *qua users*, they also need to support the teams in forming and acting upon their own judgement about what they hear from these experts. Design Thinking teams need the sovereignty to reframe the design challenge in terms of how they interpret the contending perspectives they hear from 'expert' users and stakeholders. While external voices—say of the organisation's management—may enter the Design Thinking team's social space at any time, they should (ideally) carry no more weight or significance than any other voice. In short, social spaces need to furnish Design Thinking teams with the *autonomy* to explore and reframe the design challenges.

---

[2]Recall from Chap. 1 that T-Shaped people bring to the team specialist expertise that sets them apart from other team members (the stem of the T) as well as interests and preferences that connects them to other team members (the bar of the T).

Second, effective social spaces are an arena for hosting a lively or even turbulent debate about the design challenge among diverse T-Shaped people. This means supporting critical debate of contending views within the team; a debate that may very well feature conflict as the team members work juxtapose contending accounts of design challenges. This debate—if it is to tackle the complexity and uncertainty of wicked problems—must allow 'all voices to be heard and responded to' (Thompson 1996, 2003). However, the stronger the internal differentiation of individual team members, the less likely is critical debate. Conversely, deliberation that supports team-based integrated thinking requires that all team members are primarily accountable to each other as equal T-Shaped individuals. Thus, social spaces need to provide modes of *accountability* that empower equal T-Shaped people.

In sum, social spaces for team-based integrative thinking need to be what Archon Fung (2003) calls 'mini-publics': autonomous spaces that support pluralist, critical and open-ended deliberation about wicked design challenges among equal T-Shaped people.

Carving New Organisational Spaces Out of Institutional Silos

Design thinking, as we have seen, helps teams tackle wicked problems by harnessing the creative potential of diversity in teams. The organisers of academic Design Thinking programmes, such as the ones at HPI School of Design Thinking in Stanford, Potsdam or Cape Town, can choose from a pool of applicants and then assign teams according to reflect disciplinary, gender, ethnic and cultural diversity. However, unlike universities, actors in large organisations are forced to contend with vertical organisational structures or, in more popular parlance, *organisational silos*. As a rule, organisational silos tend to feature vertical forms of decision-making (Colebatch 2009) and hierarchical patterns of transactions (Thompson and Ney 1999; Hood 1998). Assembling Design Thinking teams in large, vertically structured organisations is predicated on carving new social spaces out of a hierarchical institutional landscape. Before any team-based integrative thinking can take place in large organisations, then, Design Thinking initiatives must reconfigure patterns of transactions and organisational structures.

How has this played out in large organisations?

The available evidence indicates that Design Thinking initiatives mapped new social spaces onto existing organisational landscapes that resembled mini-publics.

Both Holger Rhinow (2018) and Eva Köppen (2016) studied the introduction of Design Thinking in a large German software enterprise. Katrin Dribbisch (2016), in turn, looked at the implementation of Design Thinking in several departments of a central ministry in Singapore.[3] In all cases, the ostensible aim of the initiatives was to improve and exploit the innovative potential of the respective organisations.

How, then, did the Design Thinking initiative affect organisational structures at these organisations? Design Thinking teams in both organisations carved out deliberative spaces in two interrelated ways.

First, the Design Thinking initiatives in the organisations equipped Design Thinking teams with considerable *autonomy*. Rhinow (2018) describes how the Design Thinking initiative empowered teams to manage themselves and reframe design challenges. For one, Rhinow argues, briefings for Design Thinking projects were far more open than for other types of projects within the corporation. These open project briefs did not explicitly match tasks to the expertise of individual team members– such as, say, software developers. In effect, then, Design Thinking teams themselves needed to distribute assignments among team members: Rhinow tells us that team members, rather than project managers, defined who did what. Employees at the software enterprise, Rhinow recounts, perceived this to be a "big difference" to other design and production processes (Rhinow 2018, p. 125). Moreover, distributing tasks implied that teams needed to engage more intensively with the substantive aspects of the design challenge than in the conventional projects. One of Rhinow's respondents remarks that teams discussed the purpose and ends of their work rather than merely looking for means to answer a pre-determined question. Specifically, Design Thinking teams were encouraged to reframe the design challenge. These reframed challenges, members of the Design Thinking teams reported, would often noticeably depart from the original project brief (Köppen 2016). In this way, teams also wielded autonomy also vis-à-vis external constraints. Autonomy over defining themes meant that teams dealt with the entire Design Thinking process themselves thereby obviating, or at least weakened, the need for coordination from the outside (Köppen 2016). This threw into stark relief other working practices, even ostensibly agile and flexible practices such as Scrum, at the corporation (Rhinow 2018).

Evidence suggests that this autonomy enabled teams to not only listen to stakeholder voices but also base their own judgement on what they heard from users. Rhinow (2018) points out that team members articulated their own opinions and perspectives on contested issues. What is more, by interacting with users and stakeholders, Design Thinking team members were in a much better position to form and, more importantly, defend these opinions within the team and to outsiders (Rhinow 2018). Rhinow also tells us that Design Thinking team members expressed appreciation for the playful engagement with the data from user research (Rhinow 2018). Team members particularly seemed to enjoy the fact that engagement with users need not necessarily and inexorably lead to the development of new products and services: here, exploratory user research implied getting to know users and their environments. Similarly, Rhinow shows how the nature of debate and conversation within teams changed: expertise, seniority or function—whether internal or

---

[3]Köppen, Rhinow and Dribbisch anonymised their data and result; the names of the organisations and of individual respondents have not been published.

external—no longer automatically bestowed authority to arguments. Rather, team members seemed to argue as participants of their "mini-publics" appealing to the authority of user research findings. For Singapore, Dribbisch recounts how civil servants point to the deliberative, collaborative and team-based elements in Design Thinking. Teams, these civil servants told Dribbisch, were effective because they avoided "...the usual structural hierarchy or authority by basing decisions on user research" (Dribbisch 2016). In this way, the new-found autonomy enabled teams to pursue an open-ended and exploratory inquiry. Not only did it encourage thematic exploration and, significantly, redefinition of the design challenge, it also rendered user and stakeholder voices at least as authoritative as expert or management opinion.

Second, the Design Thinking initiatives introduced new forms of *accountability* both between teams and the wider organisation as well as within Design Thinking teams themselves. Köppen finds that the introduction of Design Thinking teams caused a marked shift away from a predominantly *vertical form of decision-making*—based on authority, control and ownership—and to more *horizontal forms of accountability*—geared towards autonomy, cooperation and consent (Colebatch 2009). Similarly Rhinow (2018) reports that his respondents pointed to a shift of responsibility away from the 'Product Owners' towards the collective responsibility within pluralist Design Thinking teams. Although the formal title of 'Product Owner' persisted in Design Thinking teams, the coordination function had moved sideward to the team coaches (usually external Design Thinking specialists) while their decision-making power had diffused downward to the team itself (Rhinow 2018). Within teams, the Design Thinking initiative replaced vertical and hierarchical for more horizontal and egalitarian forms of accountability. Köppen (2016) notes that individuals were now being held to account by their peers rather than their line managers. Moreover, within teams at this corporation, specialist knowledge and expertise no longer necessarily or immediately conferred status among Design Thinking team members (Rhinow 2018). This seemed to 'shelter' individuals from the pressures of hierarchical line management: therefore, Köppen likens them to 'protective spheres' (Köppen 2016, p. 180).[4] This, Rhinow points out, encouraged team members not only to form their own opinions about design challenges but also to debate the these perceptions within the team. Team members resolved or at least managed these disputes with democratic means of conflict resolution—e.g. majority voting (Rhinow 2018, p. 117). Likewise, Dribbisch argues that civil servants in Singapore believed Design Thinking "...builds stronger teams and engenders confidence in people because it empowers everyone to contribute" (Dribbisch 2016).

In sum, by establishing multi-disciplinary and diverse Design Thinking teams, Design Thinking initiatives carved autonomous social spaces out of the institutional

---

[4]Designating the mini-publics as 'protective spheres' is, however, somewhat misleading. Deliberative spaces may offer 'shelter' from hierarchical oversight. Yet, they cannot protect individuals from other, more egalitarian forms of social accountability and the critical scrutiny that goes along with it.

geography of large organisations. These spaces provided Design Thinking teams with autonomy from the wider organisational constraints. This meant that the teams could implement structures and practices of self-governance. Further, this autonomy enabled teams to explore and, more importantly, reframe the wicked design challenges.[5] The literature points out that thematic autonomy also implies a shift of accountability away from vertical line management towards shared responsibility within the team. In these teams, evidence suggests, distinctions based on formal status, function or expertise are less significant than they are in the rest of the organisation. In these spaces, team members feel encouraged as well as enabled to form their own opinions about challenges. What is more, Design Thinking initiatives seem transform the quality of debate among team members. In sum, the available evidence suggests that Design Thinking teams in large organisations function, at least for some of the time, like 'mini-public' that enable free and critical deliberation (Fung 2003).

Expanding and Narrowing Strategic Options for Organisations

What were the impacts on the organisations studied? There is evidence to suggest that the introduction of Design Thinking teams expanded the sets of institutional strategies available to organisations. Carlgren et al. identify how Design Thinking initiatives changed ideas and practices that map onto Cultural Theory's typology of organisational forms. In their sample of large organisations, the researchers contend that Design Thinking initiatives led to an appreciable increase in "openness, empathy and optimism" (Carlgren et al. 2014a, p. 414)—a shift down-grid towards egalitarianism. Further, they point to the emergence of more rugged and combative deliberative practices. By shifting away from consensus-seeking towards a more action-oriented pragmatism, the introduction of the methods and mindsets of Design Thinking seems to have shifted the organisations in Carlgren et al.'s sample towards a more individualist set of practices (Carlgren et al. 2014a, p. 414). Finally, and remarkably, Carlgren et al.'s findings also seem to suggest that the Design Thinking implementation schemes in the sample of six large organisations they studied enabled organisations to (re)embrace hierarchical values. The researchers found that Design Thinking practices have helped top-management to take the long-term view rather than obsessively focussing on short-term stop-gap solutions.

Similarly, both Köppen and Rhinow as well as Dribbisch argue that many employees embraced the new forms of autonomy and accountability of the new social spaces for Design Thinking. For some at the large German software

---

[5]When Design Thinking teams deal with wicked problems, we can think of these problems as 'wicked design challenges'.

corporation, Köppen argues, empathetic work practices made possible in the new social spaces extended their repertoire of action and, therefore, were at the very least enabling and, in some cases, empowering (Köppen 2016, p. 138). In Singapore, Dribbisch tells us, deployed the new forms of autonomy and accountability to remodel both relations within the teams as well as the interaction with citizens.

However, the studies also show that these Design Thinking Teams or mini-publics sat rather awkwardly in the wider organisational landscapes. In particular, the Design Thinking initiatives created a whole new set of social distinctions at individual and organisational level. More importantly, when Design Thinking initiatives left project managers torn between two countervailing institutional logics, they found ways to wrest back control over autonomous and self-accountable teams. This, then, narrowed the scope of organisational strategies.

Individual Discomforts, Professional Grievances

Creating mini-publics within the large organisations studied seems to have caused considerable turbulence. In the German software enterprise, the Design Thinking's empathetic practices had decidedly mixed impacts (Köppen 2016). While undoubtedly beneficial for some employees, the empathetic practices of Design Thinking seemed far less benign for others (Köppen 2016).

At the individual level, Köppen argues that the Design Thinking's emphatic work regime dissolved old social distinctions. At the same time, however, these social spaces created new ways of distinguishing individuals. Design Thinking teams introduced a wide range of changes to the interaction between colleagues: these included the informal address within teams (e.g. using first names or the informal '*Du*' rather than the formal '*Sie*'), the sharing of personal information (e.g. 'so how was your weekend?', 'how are the kids?'), the revealing of one's emotions through the frequent teams check-ins, check-outs and warm-ups. Some employees perceived these changes to be liberating and even empowering (Köppen 2016, p. 155). Others, however, reported that the 'team gaze' was not only intrusive but also constraining and limiting (Köppen 2016, p. 180). Rather than formal and hierarchical distinctions, Köppen suggests that the new regime differentiated those who can readily adapt to new emphatic tools and mindsets from those who move clumsily through this more informal, subjective world; those whose expertise is devalued by the credo of the 'beginner's mindset' from those whose social skills are in high currency; those classed as 'difficult team-members' compared to those who can rely on their charisma for authority. Köppen suggests that in many instances, Design Thinking teams did not create mini-publics but rather simply replaced vertical patterns of accountability with horizontal forms of coercion.

At organisational level, Design Thinking's emphasis on T-Shaped people seemed to erode the value of specialist technical skills. For example, one of Köppen's informants felt that the new empathetic practices and techniques devalued his specialist skills as a coder. Further, the professionally trained UX designers at the software company perceived Design Thinking as a deskilling and, therefore, degradation of their work. As a result, the professional designers Köppen interviewed felt vulnerable and beleaguered (Köppen 2016, p. 239). Similarly, Carlgren et al. (2014a, b) also uncovered profound scepticism of professional designers towards the popularisation and, in their eyes, desecration of design skills: as one of their informants argues, "'...a lot of designers want to hold that close to their chest, like 'this is a skill set that is unique to me, why would I give that away'..." (quoted in Rauth et al. 2014, p. 29).

Significantly, middle-management[6] at the large software organisation saw the mini-publics as a threat. Team autonomy, self-governance and a high degree of thematic responsibility questioned the role of project managers. Indeed, Köppen argues that much of the rhetoric and practices that accompanied the introduction of Design Thinking implicitly cast middle-management as the obstacle to the free exchange of ideas and opinions. The fact that external Design Thinking coaches would exclude project managers from Design Thinking team meetings did little to disperse the suspicions of middle-managers at this enterprise (Köppen 2016, p. 241).

This is why some project managers, viewed with alarm the many changes brought about by the Design Thinking initiative. Project managers interviewed by Rhinow observed, with considerable misgivings, how open project briefings—designed to encourage open-ended exploration—led to what they viewed as wasteful and unnecessary discussions in the teams about what users to approach during fieldwork (Rhinow 2018). A project manager complains to Rhinow that "...one needs to know at least, what it is one wants to achieve. And that was formulated very vaguely [in the project briefing]..." (Rhinow 2018). Another manager, echoing this desire for clear guidance, goes on to bemoan the fact that his team needed to conduct research to identify a target industry; an arduous and seemingly pointless exercise to him. Indeed, this respondent describes the exploration phase in Design Thinking as little more than 'drifting' ("*orientierungslos*").

The changes, Rhinow argues, left project managers feeling that they had lost of control over 'their projects'. And for good reason: project managers were still held to account by their superiors for the progress (or lack of progress) of these projects. Managers report of not knowing how Design Thinking projects at the corporation developed and, more importantly, what to report back to their superiors (Rhinow 2018). Consequently, project managers in Rhinow's study were openly critical of the pluralist modes of decision-making in Design Thinking teams. They argue that the 'Product Owners'—meaning themselves—ought to provide teams with a clear objectives and a framework for achieving these objectives (Rhinow 2018).

---

[6]Middle-management here refers to former project managers.

Three Patterns of Resistance: Disruption, Agenda-Setting and Manipulation

Rhinow's findings suggest that, at least for this enterprise, the norms of 'reliability' are rather deeply entrenched. Project managers looked upon practices of exploration as an inefficient distraction. As a result, Rhinow contends, managers developed three strategies to reassert control over autonomous Design Thinking teams: disruption, agenda-setting and manipulation. Significantly, these strategies also describe the implementation of Design Thinking in other large organisations.

Disruption: Controlling Self-Governance and Accountability

One strategy involved undermining team autonomy by imputing a lack of capability as a reason to re-impose external coordination. Here, actors directly undermine and weaken practices of self-governance within teams.

At the large German software corporation, managers disrupted team autonomy by dividing the Design Thinking team and parcelling out different tasks of the Design Thinking process to subteams. In the spirit of efficiency, one project manager created a core team of 3–4 persons to which other team members were to occasionally contribute. She tasked one of these subteams to conduct interviews before the project had properly kicked-off (Rhinow 2018). Moreover, the project manager felt that the Design Thinking team, consisting of software developers, was ill-equipped to conduct a meaningful synthesis of the empirical material. Following the Design Thinking coach's (what seems now like ill-considered) advice, the product manager prepared a synthesis and creates a persona on her own. She presented the outcomes to the team that, unsurprisingly, reacted with considerable irritation. They protested against being left out of the creative reframing and team-based integrative thinking. The product manager, in turn, interpreted the team's complaints as yet another instance of developers' inability to properly apply empathy tools or understand team-based integrative thinking: she aborted the project.

In Singapore, this disruption took place at the level of the Design Thinking process as a whole. Dribbisch shows how the Singaporean ministry adapts Design Thinking by emphasising some elements to the detriment of others. In particular, she outlines how the Singaporean civil service downplays the role prototyping and testing. Ostensibly due to a perceived lack of skills in these areas, Design Thinking projects at the ministry concentrate on user research, synthesis and ideation (the Problem Space i.e. the part that deals with the complexity of wicked problems). However, most Design Thinking projects in the ministry engage in very little prototyping, testing and iteration (the Solution Space i.e. the part that deals with the uncertainty of wicked problems). Indeed, Dribbisch contends that many Design

Thinking projects at the ministry have "...hitherto stopped at the interviewing stage and not proceeded to the prototyping phase" (Dribbisch 2016).

Whatever this case says about the empathetic capabilities of software developers or civil servants, it certainly points to a fundamental misunderstanding of the role of teams in the Design Thinking process. The team-based integrative thinking that goes on in the synthesis phase is the key to generating 'clumsy' innovations. It is during the observation and synthesis phase that Design Thinking practitioners *qua* teams confront their own assumptions. Through critical reframing during the synthesis process, teams open up innovation spaces. Teams define and delimit these spaces through integrative thinking. What drives creative synthesis, in turn, is open and conflictual deliberation. And high-quality deliberation presupposes a holistic appreciation of the design challenge. In this context, splitting the team and parcelling out individual tasks to be reassembled at a higher level is a false economy: denying the team the experience of synthesis undermined the efficacy of the process. Indeed, deliberation itself is as important—arguably even more so—than the concrete outputs of this process (i.e. personas, point-of-view statements, etc.). These artefacts help express or articulate the process of deliberation in which the team fuses contending ideas and accounts of wicked problems into a space or platform for innovative and clumsy solutions.

Similarly, curtailing the Design Thinking process after the Observe and Synthesis phase, as Dribbisch (2016) reports, also disrupts team autonomy. Here disruption is a sin of *omission* rather than, as in Rhinow's study, one of *commission*. Nonetheless, it weakens the autonomy of the team within the social space, by forfeiting a crucial opportunity for learning. If the Design Thinking process is to be an exploration into the unknown, then teams need the freedom to investigate solutions as well as user perceptions. In a very real sense, solutions and prototypes are artefacts that help teams to learn more about users and stakeholders. Recall from Chap. 1 that Design Thinking is an iterative process. Teams learn by constantly confronting their assumptions with user and stakeholder perceptions. Testing prototypes with users, then, is pivotal to the learning journey. Rapid prototyping and testing allows Design Thinking teams to deal with the inherent uncertainty of wicked problems. All interpretations, regardless of whether teams mobilise contending perceptions, are little more than propositions or gambles (see Chap. 1). They are, in short, risky. Yet, effective exploration requires that teams do not shy away from these risks. The higher the perceived costs of interpretation and 'getting it wrong', the less likely it will be that Design Thinking teams truly explore. In turn, early prototyping and testing of ideas keeps the costs of 'getting it wrong' low: failing early supports rapid learning. This, in turn, encourages exploration. Disrupting the ebb and flow of the Design Thinking process, then, undermines team autonomy by depriving teams of the space, methods and practices to manage the inherent uncertainty (and therefore risk) that makes problems wicked.

Agenda-Setting: Controlling Autonomy

A second set of strategies for restricting team autonomy involved setting team agendas externally. Here, managers created artefacts and outputs before projects ad begun. In one case, some team members had conducted user research and built a prototype before the project had properly started. The research and the prototype, Rhinow observes, effectively fixed the goals for the team before it could explore the design challenge. Setting the team's agenda in this way, Rhinow concludes, constrained the innovation space the team could stake out for itself. All that was left for the team was to flesh out and concretise a general idea fed into the team by middle management.[7] Rhinow reports that team members resented relinquishing control over their own agenda, unwilling to merely rubber stamp or, worse still, beautify an idea that had been imposed on them (Rhinow 2018).

Another, somewhat related strategy involved narrowing the scope of conflict by focusing deliberation on one particular class of outcomes. Rhinow shows how project managers insisted that teams generate new applications of the technology that makes up the mainstream business of the organisation. Referring to the putative demands of 'sponsors' within the organisation, the manager argued, if an outcome were not to feature this technology "...then somehow the target has been missed. Then we may have served the wishes of the customer but our sponsors would, of course, complain" (Rhinow 2018). Rhinow reports how Design Thinking teams members felt this insistence on and reference to technological constraints to be a severe limitation to their creativity and innovation. A respondent pointed out that prescribing technology undercuts the team's ability to "wow" the user.

A final means of controlling team agendas was to tie teams to a very narrow project briefing. The team in question, one of Rhinow's informants argues, never really managed to liberate itself from the strictures imposed by the design challenge. The team offered some resistance by re-interpreting interview data to question and contest the constraints of the brief. While this is arguably precisely what Design Thinking teams ought to be doing with interview data (that is, using the data and insights to reframe the initial design challenge from the point of view of users), project managers elevated (or relegated) these findings to such a level of abstraction so as to be uncontroversial. One of Rhinow's respondents speaks of managers "levelling" or "normalising" uncomfortable findings (Rhinow 2018).

Political scientists know agenda-setting to be a particularly insidious but highly effective strategy for controlling decision-making (Bachrach and Baratz 1962). Unlike disruptions, it limits autonomy indirectly. Rather than hindering the team's exploration by affecting mechanisms and practices of self-governance, agenda-setting draws tight limits around the area in which teams are allowed to explore. What is more, agenda-setting tends to constrain exploration to areas and issues that are relatively 'innocuous' to the actors setting the agenda. While this ensures

---

[7] In a very real sense, the role for the team in this case harkens back to traditional (mis)conceptions of design—as merely decorative but not generative (Buchanan 1992).

stability and continuity within an organisation, agenda-setting can very effectively stifle any substantive change. In terms of innovation, 'agenda-setting' is a recipe for what Christensen (2000) calls "sustaining" or "incremental innovation" that provides users with the equivalent of Henry Ford's 'faster horses'.

Manipulation: Controlling Debate

The last set of strategies involved controlling the debate within Design Thinking teams by manipulating the methods and mindsets of Design Thinking. Deliberation and the necessary conflict that fuels it are vulnerable to non-deliberative or strategic uses. When actors deploy deliberation and argument to pursue exclusively strategic goals[8] the quality to debate and deliberation in mini-publics degrades. This may lead, among other things, to the polarisation of positions within a team in which debate becomes an "intractable policy controversy" (Ney 2014). Here, contending team members are no longer willing to listen to opposing arguments. Instead, team members deploy facts and arguments strategically to defend polarised positions. This compromises team-based integrative thinking.

Both Köppen's and Rhinow's studies revealed instances in the Design Thinking initiative of the large German software enterprise in which team members and managers very consciously manipulated Design Thinking methods for strategic purposes. Köppen shows how some team members quickly became adept at wielding the new empathy tools to their advantage. In Köppen's study, a team member recounts her strategic use of empathy in the team. An interviewee reports that she feels comfortable with the new empathetic regime because she can deftly deploy the new tactics—particularly empathetic mirroring—to drive her ideas in team work and deliberation (Köppen 2016, p. 150). In contrast, another respondent has few skills in deploying empathetic methods and tools strategically. Further, and more worrying, both Köppen and Rhinow point to instances in which product managers strategically deployed Design Thinking methods to reassert the power relations of the *ancien regime*. Rhinow's research found an instance in which a product manager had a team repeat the ideation phase until they come up with the 'right solutions', i.e. ideas that better resonated with the manager's expectations.

Lessons Learnt

We can draw four general lessons from the implementation of Design Thinking spaces in large organisations.

---

[8]Or, as Habermas (1987) puts it, "non-generalisable interests".

Design Thinking Causes Alienation Too

Part of the motivation for introducing Design Thinking was to counter the alienation felt by many in large and vertically structured organisations. The studies, however, indicate that alienation and marginalisation is not the sole province of hierarchical line bureaucracies. The findings from Köppen, Rhinow and Dribbisch show that shifting from one mode of accountability to another alone does not necessarily create open spaces for deliberation. Köppen's deft analysis describes how the introduction of empathetic working practices, at least in some cases, created social spaces that shifted parts of the organisation—in terms of Cultural Theory outlined in Chap. 3— from the hierarchical to the egalitarian quadrant. Instead of creating an open space for deliberation, empathetic practices and norms gave rise to new social divisions and forms of social control.

The key lesson here is to avoid throwing out the 'clumsy' baby with the hierarchical bathwater. Design Thinking reformers need to resist the temptation of merely replacing one set of social constraints with another. *If the aim of the introduction of Design Thinking is to create 'messy institutions' or 'multi-dextrous organisations' then the changes ought to extend—not limit—the available repertoire of organisational responses to wicked problems. Shifts of accountability and legitimacy must complement and extend existing institutional logics.* Would-be reformers, then, need to forge viable settlements between different contending institutional logics (6 2003).

Senior Management Support May Not Be Enough

The evidence also suggests that the injunction to secure 'senior management buy-in' for Design Thinking reform initiatives may be a truism. Of course, top-management consent and even enthusiasm for Design Thinking initiatives is imperative. Unlike organisations in which individual employees have a high degree of autonomy (such as, say, universities), using 'guerrilla tactics'[9] to introduce Design Thinking is probably not advisable.

However, as we have seen, top-management support merely is the necessary condition. Rhinow's account of how project managers wrested back control from Design Thinking spaces suggests that 'mini-publics' in large organisations are vulnerable at operational level. The cases show that despite endorsement from senior management, project managers successfully undermined the mini-publics. *While senior management can extend symbolic protection to Design Thinking teams, it is middle-managers that have to ensure the integrity of these mini-publics from one day to the next.* Alienating and even antagonising middle-management by

---

[9]Such as those used at the Stanford d.school.

insinuating that they are the problem Design Thinking is supposed to solve, may not be conducive to the implementation of Design Thinking.

Design Thinking Spaces Need Protection at Operational Level

Design Thinking spaces, then, need looking after in their day-to-day work. Someone must guard and defend the autonomy and self-governance of the Design Thinking space. This 'Design Thinking Guardian' would ensure that access to the Design Thinking remains free for contending views and perspectives. The 'Design Thinking Guardian' would also protect the space from external pressures to keep team-based integrative thinking exploratory. Significantly, this would include managing the flow of communication between Design Thinking teams and the rest of the organisation. *In essence the 'Design Thinking Guardian' would help translate the outputs of Design Thinking teams (personas, points-of-views, low resolution prototypes, role-plays, etc.) into a language more readily understood by actors in other parts of the organisations.*

The idea of the 'Design Thinking guardian' requires rethinking of the role of the project managers. Instead of being held to account for project outputs and outcomes, 'Design Thinking Guardians' would be something more akin to an agent or advocate for the Design Thinking team. Like any good agent, the 'Design Thinking Guardian' would look for suitable and interesting wicked problems for the team. Like any advocate, the 'Design Thinking Guardian' would have to be able to make a convincing case for the Design Thinking teams and their spaces. What is more, the 'Design Thinking Guardian' would strive to create and sustain the conditions in which Design Thinking teams can engage in integrative thinking. Thus, 'Design Thinking Guardians' not only understand the methods and mindsets of Design Thinking but would also be highly knowledgeable about the workings of the organisation.

New Management of Interfaces

The experience of implementing Design Thinking in large organisations throws into stark relief the significance of managing interfaces between the Design Thinking spaces and the rest of the organisation. In a very real sense, the success of a Design Thinking initiative in a large institution will not merely depend on how adept Design Thinking practitioners are at team-based integrative thinking. *More importantly, success or failure of any Design Thinking initiative will also hinge on how well Design Thinking spaces can integrate as well as irritate other organisational provinces in the institutional landscape. Thus, managing the interaction and exchange of Design Thinking spaces with will increasingly define leadership in messy institutions.*

The cases suggest that there may be (at least) three different types of interfaces that require management. The first, and perhaps most obvious, type of interface is structural. If Design Thinking teams carve out social spaces within organisations that sit awkwardly in and across vertical structures, the junctures between the 'mini-publics' and the rest of the organisation are likely to chafe. The second interface concerns less formalised but nonetheless significant boundaries between different groups and (political) constituencies within the organisation. For example, as we have seen, professions within organisation—such as UX designers or software developers—are wary of approaches like Design Thinking that set out to blur the boundaries between different professional groups. Researchers who study Design Thinking initiatives in large organisations invariably point to political wrangling over the definition and ownership of 'design' (Liedtka and Bennett 2013; Carlgren et al. 2014b; Köppen 2016). Last, research suggests that Design Thinking teams create new emotional interfaces between individuals (*qua* T-shaped people). As we have seen, recoding patterns of transactions within social spaces, and thereby by recoding individual status within teams, Design Thinking initiatives can give rise to considerable uncertainty among organisational actors. And if social spaces set up 'mini-publics'—meaning spaces in which teams need to negotiate and renegotiate the patterns of transaction and accountability—then successful implementation of Design Thinking practices is predicated on managing the individual emotional interfaces.

Conclusion

As we have seen, implementing the methods, mindsets and practices of Design Thinking can shape the institutional structures in large organisations. Studies suggest that setting up and managing teams of heterogeneous T-shaped people carves new social spaces out of established, mostly hierarchical, organisational landscapes. At the level of institutional structures, studies suggest that Design Thinking initiatives provide teams of T-Shaped people with autonomy as well as horizontal forms of governance and accountability. In this way, initiatives redraw boundaries within organisations and reconfigure patterns of transactions between organisational actors. We have also seen that the new social spaces encourage new forms of exploration and interaction. For one, thematic autonomy allowed teams to determine and develop project objectives rather delivering goals defined elsewhere in the organisation. Further, the studies point out that autonomy and vertical accountability encourage individual team members to form, deliberate and, significantly, change their opinion on relevant project parameters. In short, evidence seems to suggest that Design Thinking initiatives set up 'mini-publics' across the vertical boundaries of large organisations.

And yet, scholars also argue that the impacts of mapping new social spaces onto established institutional landscapes have been a mixed blessing. On the one hand, studies, particular the comparative work of Carlgren et al. (2012, 2014a, b), show

Conclusion

that setting up Design Thinking teams in large organisations can expand the repertoire of institutional strategies: this includes, it would seem, not only egalitarian and entrepreneurial (or individualist) strategies but also an expanded menu for hierarchical institutional action. Additionally, new social spaces and the empathetic set of practices they introduce seem to have enabled individuals to discover, activate and mobilise different skill sets; skill sets, no less, that have promoted creativity and innovation within these teams.

On the other hand, studies also suggest that the new social spaces seem to come with their own set of thorny challenges. First, while mini-publics and their new practices of exploration and horizontal accountability seem to have empowered some organisational actors, this seems to have taken place at the cost of devaluing other specialist skills. Left unchecked, the evidence suggests, this can lead to perceived marginalisation and exclusion of individuals as well as specific professions. In particular, studies argue that the perceived de-skilling or downgrading of technical skills—such as user design or coding—can introduce an explicitly political dimension to Design Thinking initiatives. Here the debate within the organisations about Design Thinking can derail into an unedifying political conflict about the ownership or relative position of a particular skill set (Liedtka and Bennett 2013). What is more, several cases also highlight the risk of injudiciously alienating middle management. Finding themselves stuck between Design Thinking teams encouraged to explore and higher management who demand exploitable project results, middle managers looked for (and found) ways of reasserting control over Design Thinking teams. Rhinow portrays the way product managers limit the scope of conflict by disrupting teams and the process, setting agendas, as well as manipulating methods in order to determine outputs.

The evidence from the studies points to the following lessons:

- First, people championing Design Thinking in large organisations need to be aware that autonomous and horizontally structured Design Thinking spaces still need to instigate cooperation among team members. These new forms of ensuring cooperation may feel refreshing to employees used to a predominantly hierarchical organisation. At the same time, these new forms of bringing about social solidarity (check-ins, check-outs, warm-ups, informal address, etc.) may not suit everyone.
- Second, the prescription to enlist the support and endorsement of senior management may be merely the necessary condition for a successful Design Thinking initiative. Findings from Köppen (2016) and Rhinow (2018) contend that the alienation of middle-management led to effective patterns of resistance that undermined both the autonomy and the horizontal patterns of accountability within Design Thinking spaces.
- Third, the new social relations generated in Design Thinking spaces are highly vulnerable to manipulation at operational level. These spaces (and the teams within them) require protection at the level of project management. Thus, project managers need to become 'Design Thinking Guardians' that can defend the integrity of Design Thinking spaces, ensure the conditions for open-ended

exploration and, most importantly, advocate the outputs of Design Thinking teams in the wider institutional environment.
- Last, if large organisations are to transform into messy institutions, then the management of the interfaces between Design Thinking spaces and the rest of the organisation are more likely to determine the way institutions effectively respond to wicked problems.

The methods and mindsets of Design Thinking, then, are capable of bringing about the type of change at the level of institutional structures needed to transform large organisations into 'multi-dextrous' or messy institutions.

Yet, how have Design Thinking initiatives fared at the level ideas?

References

6, P. (2003). Institutional viability: A neo-Durkheimian approach. *Innovation: The European Journal of Social Science, 16*(4), 395–415.
Bachrach, P., & Baratz, M. (1962). Two faces of power. *American Political Science Review, 56*, 1947–1952.
Bohman, J. (1998). Survey article: The coming of age of deliberative democracy. *Journal of Political Philosophy, 6*(4), 400–425.
Buchanan, R. (1992). Wicked problems in design thinking. *Design Issues, 8*(2), 5–21.
Carlgren, L., Elmquist, M., & Rauth, I. (2012). *Implementing design thinking in large organizations*. Proceedings of the IPDM Conference 2012, Manchester.
Carlgren, L., Elmquist, M., & Rauth, I. (2014a). Design thinking: Exploring values and effects from an innovation capability perspective. *The Design Journal, 17*(3), 403–423.
Carlgren, L., Elmquist, M., & Rauth, I. (2014b). Exploring the use of design thinking in large organizations: Towards a research agenda. *Swedish Design Research Journal, 1*(14), 47–56.
Christensen, C. M. (2000). *The innovator's dilemma: When new technologies cause great firms to fail*. New York: HarperBusiness.
Colebatch, H. K. (2009). *Policy*. Maidenhead: Open University Press.
Dribbisch, K. (2016). Translating innovation: The adoption of design thinking in a Singaporean Ministry.
Dryzek, J. S. (1990). *Discursive democracy: Politics, policy and political science*. Cambridge: Cambridge University Press.
Dryzek, J. S. (1993). Policy analysis and planning: From science to arguments. In F. Fischer & J. Foreste (Eds.), *The argumentative turn in policy analysis and planning*. Durham, NC: Duke University Press.
Fischer, F. (2003). *Reframing public policy: Discursive politics and deliberative practices*. Oxford: Oxford University Press.
Fishkin, S. (1991). *Democracy and deliberation: New directions for democractic reform*. Cambridge: Cambridge University Press.
Fishkin, S. (2009). *When the people speak*. Oxford: Oxford University Press.
Fung, A. (2003). Survey article: Recipes for public spheres: Eight institutional design choices and their consequences. *Journal of Political Philosophy, 11*(3), 338–367.
Habermas, J. (1987). *Theorie des Kommunikativen Handelns Bd.2* (*vierte Auflage*). Frankfurt am Main: Suhrkamp.
Hood, C. (1998). *The art of the state: Culture, rhetoric, and public management*. Oxford: Oxford University Press.

References

Köppen, E. (2016). *Empathy by design: Untersuchung einer Empathie-geleiteten Reorganisation der Arbeitsweise*. Konstanz und München: UVK Verlagsgesellschaft mbH.

Liedtka, J., & Bennett, K. B. (2013). *Solving problems with design thinking: 10 stories of what works*. New York: Columbia University Press.

Martin, R. L. (2009). *The opposable mind: Winning through integrative thinking*. Boston, MA: Harvard Business Press.

Ney, S. (2014). The governance of social innovation: Connecting Meso and Macro levels of analysis. In M. D. Jones, E. A. Shanahan, & M. K. McBeth (Eds.), *The science of stories*. New York: Palgrave Macmillan.

Rauth, I., Carlgren, L., & Elmquist, M. (2014). Making it happen: Legitimizing design thinking in large organizations. *Design Management Journal, 9*(1), 47–60.

Rhinow, H. (2018). Design thinking Als Lernprozess in Organisationen: Neue Chancen Und Dilemmata Für Die Projektarbeit. Doctoral thesis, University of Potsdam, Potsdam.

Thompson, M. (1996). *Inherent relationality: An anti-dualist approach to institutions*. Bergen: LOS Center.

Thompson, M. (2003). Cultural theory, climate change and clumsiness. *Economic and Political Weekly, 48*, 5107–5112.

Thompson, M., & Ney, S. (1999). Consulting the frogs: The normative implications of cultural theory. In M. Thompson, G. Grendstad, & P. Selle (Eds.), *Cultural theory as political science* (pp. 206–223). London: Routledge.

Weick, K. E. A., & Sutcliffe, K. M. (2015). *Managing the unexpected: Sustained performance in a complex world* (3rd ed.). Hoboken, NJ: Wiley.

Chapter 5
Hunting, Gathering and Taking It Home: Bringing New Perspectives and Perceptions into Organisations

Popular images of Design Thinking usually depict groups of (predominantly) young people jumping around and plastering multi-coloured sticky notes all over walls, windows and whiteboards. While these images accurately portray the lively atmosphere of Design Thinking, they are a little misleading. They suggest, not entirely unreasonably, that the generation of ideas using brainstorming techniques—something we like to call 'Ideation'—is how the Design Thinking process helps teams bring about innovation. And it is of course true that teams come up with innovative solutions (or, to be precise, concepts of solutions) during these brainstorming sessions. However, ideation responds to questions that open up new vistas and perspectives. It is creative synthesis—or integrative thinking—that generates these questions. During synthesis, Design Thinking teams define and delimit new problem spaces by using stakeholder needs and perceptions to shift their own perspective on the design challenge. By better understanding the worlds of users as well as the problems these worlds generate for users, Design Thinking teams reframe design challenges in way that allows for new and counterintuitive solutions. It is here, then, that innovation takes place or, more precisely, is made possible.

How, then, does synthesis enable or create innovation? Recall that the methods and mindsets of Design Thinking allow small, pluralist teams of T-Shaped people to engage in 'integrative thinking' (Martin 2009). Working in Design Thinking spaces—both social and physical—Design Thinking teams bring contending and conflicting perspectives to bear on wicked design challenges. This encounter of contrending approaches gives rise to effective responses to wicked problems if teams can creatively incorporate the wisdom inherent in each of the contending perspectives without succumbing to the in-built normative and cognitive blindspots.

Yet, apart from the social space (discussed in the previous chapter) and practices to help teams reframe design challenges (discussed in the following chapter), forging clumsy solutions requires a variety of contending perspectives, beliefs and views. This chapter will look at how Design Thinking creates this pluralist and heterogeneous reservoir of ideas and perspectives. In particular, then, this chapter reviews existing evidence on the way Design Thinking teams in large organisations have used qualitative research methods to fuel team-based integrative thinking. In addition to driving creative synthesis and, thereby, innovation, setting up a pluralist reservoir of contending ideas and beliefs also shapes organisational cultures.

The following sections, then, review how Design Thinking initiatives have introduced user research and how this has affected structures and working practices. The last two sections look closely at some of the problems Design Thinking reformers experienced in large organisations. The final section reviews the lessons we can draw from the introduction of user research in large organisations.

Hunting, Gathering and Taking It Home: Strengthening Diversity in Teams and Giving Users a Voice in the Design Process

In the previous chapter, we saw how Design Thinking teams in can rearrange the nodes and boundaries of vertical institutional landscapes of large organisations. Design Thinking teams create social spaces—supported by physical creation spaces—in which individuals can (more or less) freely and critically deliberate about wicked design challenges. These social spaces, resembling what students of deliberative democracy call 'mini-publics' (Fung 2003), create the conditions for team-based integrative thinking.

However, team-based integrative thinking needs fuel or raw material to drive and inspire creative reframing. This material comes in the form of contending perspectives and accounts of a particular wicked problem. Thus, team-based integrative thinking needs a pool of contending ideas as its source of sustenance. The wider and deeper this pool of contending ideas, the richer integrative thinking is likely to be.

Where can find such a variety of ideas and concepts?

First, setting up and running Design Thinking teams helps mobilise the inherent plurality within large and vertically differentiated organisations. Large organisations, almost by definition, host a wide diversity of individuals; this is particularly true for organisations with a global reach. And yet, these organisations find it immensely difficult to encourage individualism and diversity. Large institutions value employees for their command of particular skills or the proficiency in specific working practices that align with and further the perceived mission of the organisation. Vertically structured institutions tend to group members in terms of these skill sets or working practices. Departments in organisations define themselves in terms of these specialised skills and procedures. Membership in these departments is determined by what individuals have in common, say a qualification and proficiency in computer programming or human resource management, rather than what sets them apart. As we have seen, this makes up the stem of the T-Shaped profile. Emphasising this stem creates pressures on individuals to conform by playing down all the other things that make up their personality. All these elements—the bar of the T-Shaped profile—tend to get relegated from the workplace as irrelevant distractions. Unlike vertically structured organisations, as we have seen, Design Thinking teams as 'mini-public' encourage their members to form, deliberate and transform their own views about design challenges. Significantly, however, the Design Thinking teams studied explicitly encouraged individual members to draw upon the skills and knowledge usually associated with the bar of the T-Shape; in this sense, Design Thinking teams are predicated on a more holistic involvement of individual members (Köppen 2016; Rauth et al. 2014). By the same token, then, by emphasising both the stem and the bar of the T-shape, Design Thinking teams tease out the inherent variety and diversity in large organisations.

Second, another way to enrich and feed the reservoir of contending ideas is to go out looking for them. A pivotal element of Design Thinking is user and stakeholder research. Relying on the methods of the qualitative social sciences,[1] Design Thinking teams empathise with users and their lifeworlds in order to ascertain their needs. Doing this means deploying three general research approaches (see also the Chap. 1). First, Design Thinking teams *observe* users and stakeholders. Here, Design Thinking teams use ethnographical methods developed to understand and compare different cultures and socio-institutional contexts. The idea is to make sense of the way users structure, interact with and move through their social and physical spaces. In particular, Design Thinking teams aim to get a sense of how wicked problems manifest and unfold in the world of the user and how users deal with them. Second, Design Thinking teams may *engage* with users. As a rule, this involves a range of qualitative interview methods designed to elicit the views and perceptions of stakeholders. More importantly, qualitative interviews aim to generate insights about how users attach meaning to and make sense of their social and physical environments. Last, Design Thinking teams may *immerse* themselves in the lifeworld of the users. Here, Design Thinking teams set out to experience problems and challenges as users might. How might a disabled person experience alighting an underground train during rush hour? How might an injured person experience the A&E department of the local hospital? How might tourists experience public transport if they cannot read the local script?

Unlike social scientists, design thinkers do not use qualitative research methods to create knowledge about user groups, cultural contexts or institutions that could stand up to the rigours of scientific scrutiny. Instead, Design Thinking teams look to empathise with users in order to inspire the design of new and sustainable responses to wicked problems. We can think of these research methods less as tools for informing research than as vehicle for making users and stakeholders heard in problem-solving processes.

---

[1] As well as the more commercialised variations from market and consumer research.

This is what Plattner et al. (2014) call 'hunting and gathering'. User and stakeholder research creates conduits for a plurality of views into the organisation. By moving across organisational boundaries into the wider institutional environment, members of Design Thinking teams enrich the pool of contentious ideas with concepts from the 'outside'. Moreover, hunting for and gathering user insights also yields different ways of expressing notions already floating around in the 'ether' of the organisation. Significantly, engaging users and stakeholders can also give these actors a voice in organisational problem-solving processes. Methods of how to capture and articulate user perceptions, emotions and experiences differ considerably. Some approaches, such as observation and interviews, give users with a rather mediated and proximate voice in the Design Thinking process. Here, Design Thinking teams empathise with users predominantly through vicarious experiences of their lifeworlds. Other methods, most prominently action research or co-creation, include stakeholder voices more directly. In this case, Design Thinking teams profit from first-hand experience.

What impacts have these methods and approaches had on real organisations?

Mobilising Diversity

Researchers have been keenly interested in both the impacts of new forms of accountability as well as of 'hunting and gathering' on the diversity of ideas in large organisations. All studies point out that user-research prominently in all of the Design Thinking initiatives (Rauth et al. 2014; Carlgren et al. 2014a, b; Köppen 2016; Dribbisch 2016). The available evidence suggests that the organisations embraced user engagement and that this implied a significant departure from established ways of working. Further, the studies show that user research and stakeholder engagement actually managed to include user and stakeholder perceptions in the Design Thinking process. That is, engagement with users enriched the pool of ideas and concepts in the organisations. What is more, studies point out that user research contributed to a transformation in the quality of deliberation within teams. Last, there is some evidence to suggest that user insights led to the design of better products and services.

Teasing Out Diversity Within Teams

As we saw in the previous chapter, Design Thinking initiatives stake out social spaces in large organisations for teams of T-Shaped people to deliberate. Recall how horizontal forms of accountability Design Thinking initiatives encouraged deliberation within the teams. In addition, however, the studies suggest that the new forms of accountability and the attendant team-building practices also aimed at promoting a more holistic engagement of individuals with their teams and the design challenges. This is true both at the level of team composition as well as, more significantly, at the level of each individual team member. Köppen (2016) reports how Design Thinking team interactions featured the use of empathy tools designed to activate and mobilise the bar of team members' T-Shaped profile. Here, these empathy tools encouraged team members to go beyond their professional expertise when engaging with the team as well as when grappling with design challenges.

Similarly, research into the implementation of Design Thinking in six large organisations conducted by Lisa Carlgren and her colleagues (2014a) seems to echo these findings. Within the Design Thinking teams set up in these initiatives, it was easier to make

> …room for different personalities, and hiring individuals with different backgrounds and of different ages, and creating networks of the like-minded. Interviewees described hearing co-workers say they had found a place in the organisation where they felt at home, a place where it was 'OK to think differently' (Carlgren et al. 2014a, p. 412).

Hunting and Gathering: Incorporating User Voices in Design Processes

By the same token, the introduction of user and stakeholder research also significantly departed from conventional working practices of the large organisations studied. While the Design Thinking initiatives introduced a range of user-research methods, the Design Thinking teams—be they in the Singaporean ministry or the German enterprise—concentrated on *engaging* with users through qualitative interviews and user tests (Köppen 2016; Dribbisch 2016; Rhinow 2018).[2]

The Design Thinking initiative at the German software enterprise encouraged Design Thinking teams to work with users and, more importantly, also enabled access to users (Köppen 2016; Rhinow 2018). For most employees this was a new experience: in the past, interaction with customers had been reserved solely for marketing and sales staff. Both Köppen (2016) and Rhinow (2018) report that the Design Thinking teams studied enjoyed this new experience. By the same token, a product manager reported that users seemed to appreciate participation in or at least contributing to product development (Rhinow 2018). Much of this, Köppen surmises, was because employees saw user research as a welcome change from the routine (Köppen 2016, p. 151). Indeed, for Köppen, this represents a 'radical change' in user orientation for the organisation.

In Singapore, civil servants also regarded hunting and gathering as a significant departure from previous working practices. A civil servant interviewed by Dribbisch (2016) tells her that the ministry

---

[2]That said, Rhinow reports of a "fly-on-the-wall" approach where Design Thinking teams sat next to a colleague and observed how this colleague interacted with a computer.

...used to do things without asking our customers and without asking people and we just did things, design things that we think people want, instead of going down and asking people what exactly it is they want and they need... (Dribbisch 2016).

In the past, Dribbisch reports, the Ministry would design services based on expert assessments with very little contribution from citizens. If at all, Dribbisch tells us, civil servants would elicit feedback from users once the particular service had been implemented. Consequently, user-induced change to services was, if at all, incremental; more often than not, change was little more than symbolic. More importantly, Dribbisch contends that the Design Thinking initiatives at the policy-making department in the Singaporean ministry brought about a fundamental shift in the way civil servants looked at interaction with citizens *qua* users. Before, the ministry launched new services using a 'pilot': these were essentially marketing exercises to promote a finished service or product. After the exposure to Design Thinking, Dribbisch notes that civil servants rely on user research and, to a lesser extent, user tests to inspire and shape service innovations (Dribbisch 2016).

The studies show that 'hunting and gathering' created a richer pool of ideas and perspectives by providing users with a voice in the Design Thinking process. The Singaporean civil servants Dribbisch (2016) interviewed valued user and stakeholder research because it provided them with fresh perspectives on public service provision. At a time of increasing distrust of the civil service and government, Dribbisch found that qualitative interviews had become a meaningful way to reach out to and connect with citizens. Against the backdrop of strictures on critical debate in the Singaporean public sphere, civil servants saw user engagement as an effective way to gauge citizen and user needs. Here, Design Thinking practices created an opportunity for civil servants to understand the needs of citizens as users: indeed, Design Thinking allowed them '...to see through the eyes of people, hear them and just improving lives [...] from their point of view' (quoted in Dribbisch 2016).

At a more fundamental level, Dribbisch finds that the Singaporean civil servants at the different departments of the ministry adopt the underlying logic of user-centred design: effective solutions, they tell her, emerge from a deep appreciation and understanding of user needs (Dribbisch 2016). This meant that user research practices also helped the Singaporean civil service to approach and include citizens in problem-solving processes (Dribbisch 2016). Civil servants interviewed expressed the hope that user-centred practices of Design Thinking would help restore trust in the government and the civil service (Dribbisch 2016). Dribbisch (2016) argues that Design Thinking

> ...seems to have sparked a more serious effort to understand 'the ground', i.e. customers and stakeholders [...] This is also encouraged by the management [...] and represents a shift from the past, in which the government did not focus on understanding and involving citizens and other stakeholders (Dribbisch 2016).

Indeed, Dribbisch points out that in the Design Thinking initiative at different departments of the ministry led to plans for introducing co-creation project such hackathons (Dribbisch 2016).

The Benefits of a Rich Pool of Ideas

Whenever teams meet and engage with users, learning occurs—at least potentially. How, then, have new working practices that encourage a diversity of ideas and perceptions shaped learning processes in Design Thinking teams? And how has a richer pool of ideas affected the outputs of Design Thinking teams?

Confronting Assumptions

The studies indicate that user and stakeholder research affected the way Design Thinking teams confronted and dealt with their assumptions. Providing users with a voice in the problem-solving process, Rhinow (2018) suggests, enabled Design Thinking teams to question and change their own perspectives (Rhinow 2018).[3] For example, a design team in Rhinow's study had assumed that fellow-employees at the large software enterprise were unhappy with the ticketing system. This was not an unreasonable assumption since the results of an earlier survey of employees had suggested considerable dissatisfaction with this ticketing system. User research into an alternative system—based on a concept of a user community—however showed that employees liked the ticketing system *per se* but thought that it had been poorly implemented (Rhinow 2018). By the same token, Dribbisch finds evidence of how the confrontation with user needs helped Singaporean civil servants probe their assumptions. For the civil servants, user research "...revealed surprising insights about the target group and proved previous assumptions about them wrong" (Dribbisch 2016).

In addition to qualitative, in-depth interview, Rhinow points out that the testing of prototypes also served as a way for teams to ascertain user needs. A team leader, Rhinow reports, cites an instance in which a prototype based on voice recognition software (figuratively) fell on deaf ears with users during tests. While the team initially experienced considerable frustration, Rhinow reports how further iteration and testing led the team to develop an idea that users appreciated (Rhinow 2018). Engaging with contending user perceptions, then, not merely supports teams but actually creates the argumentative conditions in which teams can critically examine and discover the blind-spots and inaccuracies of their assumptions.

---

[3]In the jargon of deliberative democracy, engagement with user voices brought about the 'transformation of preferences' and assumptions.

Designing Better Outputs

Giving users a voice in the Design Thinking process, it would seem, also enabled teams to design better responses to wicked problems. At the large German software enterprise, engagement with users helped teams to find a common purpose. Rhinow argues that many of the employees in the organisation expected the methods of Design Thinking—in particular user-research—to create a common understanding within development teams about goals and potential outcomes. Understanding users and their needs, many of Rhinow's respondents argue, adds purpose and meaning to efficient but otherwise value-neutral processes such as Lean.[4] Whereas processes such as Scrum allow teams to efficiently develop software, the argument went, there is nothing in these methods to prevent teams from producing "...the biggest pile of rubbish" (interviewee quoted in Rhinow 2018). For employees in this large software enterprise, engaging with users added quality or, more precisely, meaning to software development by helping teams to find a real problem for products to address.

In their study of Design Thinking initiatives in six large enterprises Carlgren et al. (2014a) found that, on the whole, working with users helped teams generate more variegated ideas which led to the development of better products (or, at least, created this impression among their respondents). Notably, researchers found that empathy work with users and stakeholders increased the acceptance of solutions (Rauth et al. 2014).[5] They conclude that user research enabled the Design Thinking teams in these organisations to embark on learning journeys in which they successfully articulated, confronted and transformed their assumptions about users, products and solutions.

Similarly, Dribbisch reports that user and stakeholder research resulted in the design of more user-friendly public services. Not only did the ministry redesign their IT user interfaces, Dribbisch tells us that Design Thinking

> ...was also used to enhance the customer experience [...]. For example, the re-design of the first service centre was intended to go beyond the regulatory function and create a more welcoming service experience [...]. Design Thinking was therefore applied to improve service flows and the customer experience [...] (Dribbisch 2016).

In sum, giving users and stakeholders a voice in design processes created a richer reservoir of ideas in the large organisations analysed by the scholars. What is more, the research also suggests that these voices enabled teams to critically confront their unquestioned assumptions and, in the jargon of deliberative democratic theory, transform their preferences. In this way, then, the practices of hunting and gathering

---

[4]Arguably, efficiency is a very strong and jealous value.

[5]This, of course, echoes the standard argument in favour of citizen participation and deliberation. Not only do citizen participation processes yield normative benefits (i.e. it is morally good for democracies to involve citizens in the decisions that affect their lives) but also functional or instrumental benefits (i.e. the quality of outputs and outcomes is better and these decisions are more readily accepted by citizens) (Bohman 1998).

that these Design Thinking initiatives introduced to large organisations, helped fill the new social spaces with a rich plurality of ideas.

The Difficulties of Setting Up a Richer Pool of Ideas (And an Open Question)

Yet for all the perceived benefits and advantages of user engagement, empathy and deliberation, the available evidence suggests these changes were fraught with difficulty (Köppen 2016; Dribbisch 2016; Rhinow 2018). For one, user-oriented working practices do not suit everyone; as with empathetic work practices (see previous chapter), the introduction of user research and stakeholder engagement posed real challenges for some employees. Further, the studies point to a lack within the organisations of the skills needed for effective team-based integrative thinking. What is more, the studies also uncovered the strategic use and misuse of user research methods. Last, existing research is silent about the scope of diversity created by the introduction of Design Thinking practices.

Marginalisation and Exclusion

Just like the use of empathy tools for managing teams, Köppen argues that the new user-oriented working practices did not necessarily suit everyone. Her research suggests that, although generally appreciated as a new and interesting experience, user engagement can feel threatening and intimidating for some employees. For example, approaching users proved stressful for more introverted Design Thinking team members. These employees report feeling threatened by situations in which they need to build a rapport and gain empathy with what were de facto strangers. Likewise, Dribbisch reports that Singaporean civil servants saw Design Thinking as "personality-driven". Design thinking, so the argument goes, is "...team-based and requires its practitioners to be open-minded and outgoing during interviews..." (Dribbisch 2016); she found that some civil servants will fit the bill but others will not.

Rhinow's research shows how empathy-based Design Thinking skills and mindsets became a means of marginalising both individuals and entire professions (Rhinow 2018). Some respondents intimated that they believed developers to be ill-equipped for engaging with users and clients. Unsurprisingly, this scepticism about the empathetic capabilities led to unproductive tensions in the Design Thinking teams under observation (Rhinow 2018).

Moreover, needs and insights gleaned from user research, Köppen observes, not only inspire teams but also became a new measure of relevance. Köppen observed how team members would refer to user needs and insights to hold other team members to account (Köppen 2016). While this need not be a problem per se, research on the large German software enterprise suggests that not all participants were prepared for or suited to these changes. In particular, some individuals (rightly) perceived this shift in argumentative authority as further evidence of how Design Thinking undercuts and devalues professional skills and managerial status.

Lacking Skills

Accusations of empathetic incompetence can, of course, only bite if there are justified doubts concerning capability and skill. The available evidence suggests that the lack of skills in research and data analysis affected the quality of the Design Thinking process.

Köppen reports of incidents in which team members misrepresented, misunderstood or simply misheard what users were telling them in interviews. Worryingly, this apparently also included 'selective listening' during interviews. These distortions were exacerbated both by the ubiquitous time-pressure that accompanies Design Thinking exercises as well as the fact that interviews are rarely recorded and analysed. The upshot was that Design Thinking team members heard what they want to hear. One of the coaches interviewed complained that interviewers often would hear only what confirmed their initial assumption (Köppen 2016, p. 197). A project manager tells Köppen that "...I think we had a relatively good picture from the outset. The [...] interviews then just confirmed that picture" (Köppen 2016, p. 196). Köppen argues that during many Design Thinking exercises she analysed, empathy techniques did not always provide an insight into users' lifeworlds. Rather, project managers and team members deployed user data to confirm their unquestioned assumptions and preconceived bias. This is why a project manager expressed his discomfort about a perceived lack of qualitative research skills in his Design Thinking team. Instead of the team engaging users and conducting interviews on their own, this project manager would have wished for the support of an experienced researcher or professional ethnographer during the fieldwork (Rhinow 2018).

Likewise in Singapore, Dribbisch reveals that civil servants harboured considerable doubts about their own Design Thinking skills. In particular, working closely with an agency specialising in Design Thinking seems to have made civil servants more acutely aware of the levels of skill involved in activities such as synthesis or prototyping (Dribbisch 2016).[6] Feeling that they "...as a government agency were not as advanced as the design consultancy...", Dribbisch continues, the ministerial department focused on service delivery backgrounded prototyping and testing. The problem, Dribbisch quotes a consultant from the design agency, is that the Ministry seeks to reduce Design Thinking to a process and a set of tools. What tends to get lost

---

[6]Which is somewhat ironic, given that Design Thinking is supposed to foster 'creative confidence'.

in this approach is that the activities that make up the process require considerable skill in the application of these tools. As the design consultant tells Dribbisch:

> They [the ministry] think that Design Thinking is just a process, a four-step process. [...] But as much about Design Thinking is about tools, it's about culture actually as well, but that's where it flourishes, cooperation, diversity, starting with a great question, not starting with an answer so they're taking it very figuratively Design Thinking here is what are we saying (interviewee quoted in Dribbisch 2016).

Misuse and Misunderstanding

In addition to issues of power, competence and skill, research findings point to a more fundamental misuse and misunderstanding of the methods of user research. Köppen tells us of instances in which members of Design Thinking teams emotionally manipulated users during interviews. By 'playing a part', Design Thinking team members hoped to find an angle or need that the enterprise could exploit (Köppen 2016, p. 204). Köppen argues that the misrepresentation of user voices is not the result of conscious foul play. Instead, she points out that the simplification of qualitative research methods and reduction of emphatic tools to serve strategic ends—namely discovering commercially exploitable user needs.

Further, Rhinow reveals considerable confusion among team members about how different tools and methods contribute to innovation through team-based integrative thinking. For example, Rhinow observed one team that had collected far too much data and was consequently overwhelmed with the data analysis. Part of the problem, Rhinow suggests, seems to be a deep-seated reluctance to discard data. Trained as engineers or natural scientists, Design Thinking team members found it very difficult to "let data go to waste". At some level, then, teams look to the data to provide generalizable explanations or 'validated' insights rather than inspiration for innovation (Rhinow 2018).

Norms of good scientific practice also contributed to the methodological confusion. In particular, the question of the amount of data that enables teams to 'validate' user needs and insights attracted considerable controversy. Project managers in the Design Thinking initiative of the large software enterprise would reject Design Thinking team outputs—mostly personas and point-of-view-statements—if they were based on what managers perceived to be too few interviews (Rhinow 2018). At the same time, team members complained to Rhinow in interviews that data from sample sizes of 20 qualitative interviews proved far to unwieldy.[7] The temptation here, Rhinow argues, is to introduce 'sciency'-sounding measures of validity or, worse still, demand that results be representative. Another project manager, who

---

[7]Twenty qualitative interviews generate an immense amount of data that would keep a team of experienced social scientists busy for many weeks.

seems to have understood the idea of using user research as a source of inspiration, complained to Rhinow that teams wasted their time conducting 30 odd interviews instead of concentrating on a few interviews with extreme users:

> Yes, but 30 from what? And ... if you interview 30 people at the supermarket, you can still completely off target [...] they may not know enough about my problem to generate insights. And then it makes far more sense to sit down for a day and think what the extremes are and go into them. That was a very nice insight for me (Rhinow 2018).

How Diverse Is Diversity?

Last, the studies tell us very little about the scope of diversity generated by Design Thinking initiatives. This should come as no great surprise. None of the studies explicitly focussed on cultural change and none were informed by a comparative framework of organisational culture (such as Cultural Theory, see Chap. 3). However, the question of how diverse a reservoir of ideas needs to be is anything but trivial. According to the conceptual framework outlined in Chaps. 2 and 3, forging effective responses to wicked problems in design challenges requires a *requisite variety* of ideas, concepts and perceptions. If each organisational logic grasps some important aspect of a complex and uncertain issue, then effective responses need to include each organisational logic. Following the typology of organisational cultures outlined in Chap. 3, this would mean that a *requisite variety* in the reservoir of ideas would feature views from each quadrant of the Cultural Map (see Fig. 3.2). Omitting or, worse still, excluding these concepts and perceptions risks leaving the responses vulnerable to the in-built weaknesses and blindspots inherent in each institutional logic. As a result, responses to wicked problems created by Design Thinking teams are likely to fall foul to so-called 'unexpected consequences'; unexpected only from the perspective of an individual organisational culture.

Lessons Learnt

What lessons we can take away from the benefits and costs of enriching the pool of ideas? What issues do would-be reformers in large organisations need to be aware of? And how can an implementation project for Design Thinking avoid potential pitfalls?

Acknowledge Shifts of Accountability and Legitimacy

Bringing in user-perspectives through 'hunting and gathering' is likely to shift existing standards of validity and modes of argumentation in large, vertically structured-organisations. Understanding user needs and insights as new measures of relevance is part of this shift. It is likely to affect the way members within a team argue about design challenges as well as the way the team discusses issues with actors from other parts of the organisation. It signifies a transition from a formal, hierarchical legitimation of power based on authorised expertise to an altogether more murky, subjective form of legitimacy based on what we may call 'epistemic sovereignty'. Here, power and legitimacy accrue to actors who can generate meaningful interpretations of what user needs and insights mean for the organisation. These interpretations become more significant the more these actors can make them stick. While these shifts are congruous with horizontal and egalitarian patterns of transactions within the Design Thinking teams (see previous section), they do not necessarily empower all members of Design Thinking teams or users in the design process. Indeed, organisational actors who rely on a more formalised and expert-oriented argumentative strategies now need to contend with new and fundamentally incommensurate modes of argumentation.

The First Lesson Is to Anticipate These Shifts in the Patterns of Accountability and Legitimacy When Introducing Design Thinking into Large Organisations The shift in legitimacy and power should come as no surprise (see Chap. 3 or the previous chapter). For one, making user voices heard in the design process is likely to empower deliberation over expert assessment. This is inimical to Design Thinking and is unavoidable if any team-based integrative thinking is to occur. And yet, evidence suggests that members of Design Thinking teams and managers appeared somewhat unprepared for the impacts of 'hunting and gathering' on both relations in the Design Thinking team and relations between Design Thinking teams and the wider organisational landscape (Köppen 2016).

The Second Lesson Is Not to Deny or Ignore the Effects These Shifts, Whether Beneficial or Not Each shift across the cultural map produces different—but not necessarily less stringent or less oppressive—strategies for coercion and pressures towards conformity (Douglas 1987, 1996). Mini-public or not, members of Design Thinking teams need to cooperate if they are to create innovative responses to design challenges. So, just like any other form of social organisation, Design Thinking teams need to ensure the cooperation of its members. This calls for what the social anthropologist Dame Mary Douglas refers to "heavy tactics of persuasion" (Douglas 1996, p. 32). Champions of Design Thinking in organisations—be they Design Thinking intrapreneurs or external coaches—need to acknowledge that Design Thinking practices can be every bit as oppressive and coercive as management in a traditional line bureaucracy. It is as naïve to believe that Design Thinking can do without coercion as it is disingenuous to deny the potentially deleterious effects of less hierarchical forms of social accountability for individual employees.

Enable Continuous Learning

The available research points out that poorly develop research skills potentially undermine the value of user and stakeholder research for Design Thinking teams. As we have seen, organisations are caught in a vicious cycle. On the one hand, underdeveloped research skills produce poor user data that, in turn, increases the likelihood of mediocre insights and innovations. On the other hand, actors in these organisations themselves often have so little confidence in their (emerging) skills that they prefer to curtail or omit crucial parts of the Design Thinking process.

The Lesson Here Is That Mastering Design Thinking Implies Continuous Learning Initially, the learning curve for Design Thinking is rather shallow. It does not take much in terms of instruction to acquire the basics needed to *practice* Design Thinking. The tools are simple; there is little in the way of theory; the playful approach to teaching makes everything seem easy. In fact, given a skilled and experienced Design Thinking coach, teams with very little or, indeed, no previous exposure to Design Thinking can successfully tackle wicked problems. What is more, teaching Design Thinking through simple but effective experiences of the method does little to dispel the impression that Design Thinking is easy to learn.

But this is deceptive. All phases of the process call for specialist skills. This applies to the observation phase as well. Collecting, compiling and analysing qualitative data is a skill. Like any other skill, exercising it competently requires good instruction, some talent and a lot of practice. While Design Thinking celebrates dilettantism by encouraging 'the beginner's mindset', this can be a problem when attempting to give users a voice in the Design Thinking process. If teams do not use stakeholder voices to challenge their assumptions in the team, then these voices lose their significance for the process of team-based integrative learning. Indeed, team-based integrative thinking is unlikely to take place.

This means that, despite a shallow learning curve, organisations will need to invest in building—and continuing to build—Design Thinking capabilities at several levels. At one level, any sustainable implementation of Design Thinking requires investment in Design Thinking coaching and facilitation capabilities. In a very real sense, it is the well-trained, highly skilled and experienced Design Thinking coaches that make hard work seem easy (c.f. Rhinow 2018). In order to ensure that Design Thinking teams can engage in team-based integrative thinking, it may make sense to invest in a coaching team that can access the required skills with appropriate proficiency. At another level, Design Thinking requires so-called 'T-Shaped People'; that is, people with an in-depth specialisation (the stem of the 'T') as well as a set of more general skills (the bar of the 'T'). Any sustainable implementation of Design Thinking in a large organisation will need to enable design thinkers to develop both the stem and the bar of their 'T'. Most design thinkers in large organisations will not have trained to be qualitative social researchers. For them, developing the bar of the 'T' implies acquiring and improving skills such as qualitative interviewing or ethnographic observation.

Balance Exploration and Exploitation in Methods

The misappropriation of user research reflects the difficulties of separating the logic of exploration from the prevalent logic of exploitation. User and stakeholder research is most effective when it is open-ended and exploratory. Yet, the studies suggest that Design Thinking teams felt constrained by business imperatives (whether imposed by managers or self-imposed by effective socialisation). Much of the misappropriation of empathy tools and qualitative methods emerge from the inherent tensions between new, more egalitarian working practices and the pressures of daily business (Köppen 2016). Both Köppen (2016) and Dribbisch (2016) find that the pressures of the mundane—be it software development or public service provision—crowd out empathetic and exploratory user research. Both researchers find that actors in large organisations perceive qualitative and ethnographic research to be unduly time-consuming. What is more, qualitative research—even in its curtailed form—produces immense amounts of data that quickly overwhelm inexperienced Design Thinking teams. As a result, actors are quick to sacrifice research and team-based integrative thinking to perceived (and rather conventional) conceptions of organisational efficiency (Dribbisch 2016; Köppen 2016).

The risks, however, to the Design Thinking teams are real. Strategic communication with users—or, more prosaically, 'faking it'—undermines the trust upon which meaningful exchange with users about their lifeworld can take place. This jeopardises the new relationships with users and stakeholders. Without these insights into the lifeworld of users, teams will not be able to open innovation spaces in which teams can develop clumsy solutions to wicked problems.

The Lesson Here Is That 'Defending' Design Thinking Spaces *Qua* Mini-Publics (See Previous Chapter) Also Extends to 'Hunting and Gathering' Just like the access to the Design Thinking space as well as deliberative practices need protection, so too does user and stakeholder research. In practice, this leaves would-be Design Thinking reformers in a double bind. On the one hand, Design Thinking teams need to ensure that the logic of reliability does not contaminate 'hunting and gathering' user insights. On the other hand, Design Thinking teams will—sooner or later—also have to show that their work is relevant to wider organisational objectives. Transferring the findings of open-ended user research (as well as the outputs of subsequent explorative but user-oriented ideation and prototyping processes) into viable products, services and processes is a conscious as well as a deliberative process. Significantly, transfer is unlikely to occur by itself; indeed, effective integrative thinking that leads to reframing is more likely to sit uncomfortably in existing organisational structures. Thus, transfer of the outputs of an exploratory Design Thinking process into organisational realities not easy; if it was easy, the ideas to be transferred are probably not all that innovative. In short, the conscious transfer of Design Thinking outputs into wider organisational realities needs to be an integral part of any Design Thinking initiative in large organisations. Short-circuiting that discussion by splicing organisational imperatives into user-research is a false economy: it constrains the type of inquiry and undermines trust needed to empathise with users.

Ensure a Requisite Variety of Voices

Finally, how can we know whether the reservoir or pool of ideas is sufficiently rich to spark inspiration? As we have seen, applying quantitative standards of representativeness to the process of 'hunting and gathering' user voices makes little sense for two reasons. First, user research is meant to inspire rather than inform. Second, even if Design Thinking teams were to set out to conduct an ethnographic study, quantitative conceptions of representativeness say very little about the reliability of qualitative data. And yet, a richer and more variegated reservoir of ideas is more likely to inspire teams to create robust and workable responses to wicked design challenges. The answer, then, is not to increase the number of interviews, observations or immersion exercises to fulfil an arbitrary quantitative standard. Rather, Design Thinking teams need to ensure that they can capture as wide a variety of ideas as possible.

The Lesson Here Is That Design Thinking Teams Need to Develop Fieldwork Strategies Capable Hunting and Gathering as Wide a Variety of Ideas as Possible This will entail finding and recording contentious and potentially irritating views by, for example, looking at the margins and extremes of a user or stakeholder group. Further, by applying the fundamental Design Thinking principle of iteration to user research, teams can make sure to 'hunt down' a crucial stakeholder voice. Comparative frameworks, such as the typology of organisational cultures introduced in Chap. 3, can help teams both set out their fieldwork strategy as well as help gauge the diversity and variation of the reservoir of ideas.

Conclusion

Team-based integrative thinking needs contending ideas. By confronting their own assumptions and perceptions with opposing ideas, Design Thinking teams can forge 'clumsy solutions' to wicked design challenges. We can think of all of the ideas and concepts available for in an organisation as a pool or a reservoir. The more variegated and pluralist this pool of ideas, the more effective integrative thinking is likely to be.

But where do these opposing ideas and concepts come from? One source is the inherent pluralism of large organisations: we saw in the previous chapter, Design Thinking initiatives carve open social spaces out of the wider institutional landscape. Here, studies suggest, Design Thinking teams have created social spaces that encourage employees to emphasise the skills and interests that define them as individuals (rather than as employees). In these spaces, individuals deliberate as members of mini-publics. But in teams of 5–8, this is a rather small pool of ideas.

This is why Design Thinking teams go out 'hunting and gathering' for insights from users to enrich the pool of contending ideas and concepts. Here, Design Thinking teams rely on the methods of qualitative social sciences. By observing users in their environment, by engaging stakeholders in interviews or by immersing into the world of customers or citizens, Design Thinking teams can build the empathy that can inspire 'clumsy solutions' to wicked design challenges.

User and stakeholder research has been a central aspect of the Design Thinking initiatives in large organisations. The available evidence suggests that 'hunting and gathering' user insights has brought about real changes in large organisations. For one, user and stakeholder research has allowed Design Thinking teams to work with a wider variety of perceptions and concepts than would otherwise have been available. In this sense, then, 'hunting and gathering' has enriched 'the ether' within these organisations. What is more, research helped Design Thinking teams focus on users and their needs thereby bringing these stakeholders into the Design Thinking process, albeit indirectly. Significantly, studies indicate that the 'hunting and gathering' change the modes of discussion, debate and argumentation in Design Thinking teams. In all the organisations analysed, data from users helped teams critically confront their own assumptions and perceptions. Ultimately, it would seem as if the user insights—or rather the integrative thinking these insights made possible—led Design Thinking teams to generate better and more user-centred products and services.

However, studies also indicate that providing users with a voice in design processes of large organisations is fraught with difficulty. First, Design Thinking's injunction to approach users—clients and citizens—led to significant discomfort with employees in some of the organisations analysed. More importantly, the perceived ability to approach users and stakeholders became a means of marginalising both individuals as well as entire groups (e.g. software developers). Second, researchers found significant gaps in the skills and capabilities required to conduct qualitative user research. The misunderstandings and misrepresentations, they agree, undermined integrative thinking and synthesis. Last, the studies indicate that Design Thinking teams also deployed the methods of user research strategically. In addition, patchy appreciation of qualitative research on the one hand as well the use of these methods in Design Thinking on the other led to the misappropriation of these approaches. Instead of hunting and gathering user insights for inspiration, Design Thinking teams were looking to satisfy specious standards of validity.

The findings of the studies point to the following lessons:

- Providing users and stakeholders with a voice in the design process, however vicariously, is likely to affect patterns of accountability and legitimacy. It is important for would-be Design Thinking reformers to anticipate these changes. In particular, Design Thinking champions need to acknowledge both the beneficial and potentially deleterious impacts of these shifts in validity and argumentation. If Design Thinking initiatives are to promote the development of a 'messy organisation', people implementing Design Thinking had best avoid simply replacing one set of social constraints with another. Instead, the focus needs to be on finding viable settlements between different institutional logics of an organisation.

- Establishing Design Thinking in a large organisation implies continuous learning. Although Design Thinking has a relatively shallow learning curve, practicing Design Thinking does require a certain level of proficiency and competence at activities such as user and stakeholder research. Any sustainable implementation of Design Thinking in a large organisations will not only need to establish sufficiently variegated coaching capabilities, it will also need to invest in continually improving the core skill Design Thinking skill set, including user and stakeholder research.
- Striking a balance between exploitation and exploration also seems to apply to the practice of user and stakeholder research. Available research shows how actors misappropriate and even strategically misuse research methods. The reason seems to be that the logic of exploitation or reliability seeps into user and stakeholder practices. 'Hunting and gathering', it would seem, requires a similar level of operational protection as Design Thinking spaces themselves.
- Design thinking teams need to devise fieldwork strategies that can ensure as wide a variety of ideas as possible. Crucially, this implies using qualitative rather than quantitative measure of variance and diversity. In practice, this will mean looking for users and stakeholders at the margins or extremes of user groups. Furthermore, Design Thinking teams need to apply the principle of iteration to the process of 'hunting and gathering' user voices. Comparative frameworks of organisational cultures, such as Cultural Theory, may help teams put together fieldwork strategies as well as gauge the degree of variety the reservoir of ideas.

How, then, do Design Thinking teams take these ideas and forge them into effective (meaning 'clumsy', see Chap. 3) responses to wicked design challenges?

References

Bohman, J. (1998). Survey article: The coming of age of deliberative democracy. *Journal of Political Philosophy, 6*(4), 400–425.
Carlgren, L., Elmquist, M., & Rauth, I. (2014a). Design thinking: Exploring values and effects from an innovation capability perspective. *The Design Journal, 17*(3), 403–423.
Carlgren, L., Elmquist, M., & Rauth, I. (2014b). Exploring the use of design thinking in large organizations: Towards a research agenda. *Swedish Design Research Journal, 1*(14), 47–56.
Douglas, M. (1987). *How institutions think.* London: Routledge and Kegan Paul.
Douglas, M. (1996). *Thought styles: Critical essays on good taste.* London: Sage.
Dribbisch, K. (2016). *Translating innovation: The adoption of design thinking in a Singaporean Ministry, doctoral thesis.* Potsdam: University of Potsdam.
Fung, A. (2003). Survey article: Recipes for public spheres: Eight institutional design choices and their consequences. *Journal of Political Philosophy, 11*(3), 338–367.
Kingdon, J. W. (1984). *Agendas, alternatives and public policies.* Boston, MA: Little Brown.

References

Köppen, E. (2016). *Empathy by design: Untersuchung einer Empathie-geleiteten Reorganisation der Arbeitsweise*. Konstanz und München: UVK Verlagsgesellschaft mbH.

Martin, R. L. (2009). *The opposable mind: Winning through integrative thinking*. Boston, MA: Harvard Business Press.

Plattner, H., Meinel, C., & Leifer, L. J. (2014). *Design thinking research: Building innovators*. Berlin: Springer.

Rauth, I., Carlgren, L., & Elmquist, M. (2014). Making it happen: Legitimizing design thinking in large organizations. *Design Management Journal, 9*(1), 47–60.

Rhinow, H. (2018). Design thinking Als Lernprozess in Organisationen: Neue Chancen Und Dilemmata Für Die Projektarbeit. Doctoral thesis, University of Potsdam, Potsdam.

Chapter 6
Design Thinking and Messy Practices

The previous chapters looked at how Design Thinking can help organisations create the institutional preconditions for addressing wicked problems. Chapter 4 reviewed the way Design Thinking creates the social spaces needed for effective team-based integrative thinking. Chapter 5, in turn, showed how empathy work in teams and with users provides a gateway for contending perspectives into these spaces. As we have seen, exploring the life-worlds of users and stakeholders helps people in organisations find inspiration for innovation beyond the boundaries of their organisations. It also helps would-be innovators to identify and mobilise contending perspectives within large organisations.

The social space and the reservoir of ideas are the necessary condition—the workshop and the raw material respectively—for constructing responses to wicked design challenges. However, just like a cake does not bake itself by merely bringing the ingredients into close vicinity of one another, innovative solutions to wicked problems do not just miraculously emerge from pluralist institutional spaces. On the contrary, clumsy solutions need to be brought about; they need to be consciously wrought by team-based integrative thinking from contending ideas and frames. As we saw in Chap. 3, so-called messy institutions—that is organisations that feature both a plurality of frames as well as a corresponding variety of organisational practices—are particularly well equipped for generating innovative solutions to wicked problems. These pluralist practices also provide the blueprint for bringing about a multi-dextrous organisation capable of tackling wicked design challenges.

To what extent, then, have Design Thinking initiatives in large organisations managed to introduce the practices required for effective team-based integrative thinking? And how have these practices impinged on wider organisational cultures?

This chapter contends that while Design Thinking potentially features a 'messy' plurality of practices (as stipulated in Chap. 3), Design Thinking initiatives have not always been successful in implementing this plurality in large organisations. While these Design Thinking initiatives managed to diffuse new practices into the organisation, they seemed less effective in forging innovations. Part of the reason, we contend, is that teams lacking the requisite variety of practices experienced considerable difficulties with effective team-based integrative thinking. Conversely, Design Thinking initiatives that furnished teams with sufficiently variegated practices tended to create outputs that sit awkwardly in wider institutional environments.

This argument will take a little longer to develop. Based on concept of 'messy institutions' introduced in Chap. 3, we first outline four distinct types of practices that characterise Design Thinking. Here, we look to the practices that have developed in the schools of Design Thinking in Stanford, Potsdam and Cape Town (and, by extension, IDEO) as a baseline. The subsequent section then explores the relative strengths and weaknesses of each set of practices. Further, this section also explores the way Design Thinking teams put this plurality of practices into action to bring about effective team-based integrative thinking. The chapter then goes on to outline practices implemented in large organisations against the backdrop of what goes on in the schools of Design Thinking. The chapter concludes with the lessons that emerge from the comparison of practices in different institutional settings.

Messy Design Thinking

If we want to solve the pressing challenges of our time, we can no longer rely on a single way of organising or single form of knowledge. Recall that each way of organising outlined by Cultural Theory allows us to understand something important about any wicked design challenge. At the same time, each way of organising comes with its own blind-spots and vulnerabilities. Table 6.1 outlines the characteristic strengths and vulnerabilities associated with the practices of each organisational culture. Tackling complex and uncertain problems, as we saw in previous chapters, requires bringing the valuable insights that emerge from different types of organisational cultures to bear on these wicked challenges. At the same time, innovators need to avoid the in-built blind-spots and vulnerabilities of frame-based accounts of wicked problems. This is, as we have seen, what Roger Martin calls 'integrative thinking' (Martin 2009b).

Table 6.1 Characteristic strengths and vulnerabilities of each organisational culture

	Individualism	Egalitarian	Hierarchy	Fatalism
Trusts	Market mechanisms, individual leadership and competition	Malleability of social norms; inherent good of people	Substantive and moral authority of experts	No one; the inherent unpredictability of nature
Downplays	Inherent market distortions and dilettantism	Self-interest of actors	Expert complacency and dangers of concentrating power	The ability to effect change
Vulnerable to	Increasing inequality	Free-riding; Irrelevance and festering conflict	Bureaucratic inertia and corruption	Passivity and manipulation

Source: Adapted from Ney (2012)

But how do these generic strengths and vulnerabilities emerge from the practices that we associate with Design Thinking? As a base-line for our exploration, we will look to both the schools of Design Thinking in Stanford, Potsdam and Cape Town as well as to the methods and mindsets developed by IDEO. The reasons are both historical and organisational. First, the origins of this particular flavour of Design Thinking are David Kelley's work at Stanford University and IDEO. Second, and more importantly, all three schools of Design Thinking funded by the Hasso-Plattner Foundation as well as IDEO are relatively independent—both organisationally and financially—from their wider institutional contexts. In this sense, they are ideal-types[1] that help us analyse, gauge and understand the implementation of Design Thinking in other organisations. We can identity four families of practices at the different schools of Design Thinking and at IDEO: output-oriented practices, inclusion-oriented practices, process-oriented practices and chance-oriented practices. Table 6.2 systematically outlines these families of practices.

We will discuss each in turn.

Output-Oriented Practices

Design Thinking is fundamentally geared towards producing tangible outputs in a relatively short period of time. Arguably, this output-orientation explains the attractiveness of Design Thinking for many organisations, particularly businesses. The output-orientation results from a set of methods and processes that promote efficiency, flexibility and performance.

Design Thinking, as we have seen in Chap. 4, thrives when work-spaces are flexible and can adapt readily to the needs of the team. As Scott Doorley and Scott Willhot argue, Design Thinking workspaces take into account that we are intelligent apes (Doorley and Witthoft 2011). For this reason, custom-made design spaces consist of furniture that acts as basic building blocs for individually configured work spaces. Tables, white-boards and, most importantly, the red sofas are moveable. Foam cubes—quite apart from furnishing the ammunition for pitted battles among boisterous students—allows teams to model landscapes or create new spaces.

This flexibility not only support the creativity of Design Thinking teams, it also creates the work conditions for teams to produce innovations. As the photographs in Fig. 6.1 show, Design Thinking workspaces, unlike most other types of working environments, do not impose any particular spatial order upon individuals and groups. On the contrary, the flexibility of the spaces aims at releasing and strengthening the individuality of each design team. This enables teams to build

---

[1] Arguably, the fourfold typology of organisational cultures is the fundamental ideal-typical model in this exposition. Just as we use this model to calibrate and analyse practices in the schools of design thinking, we will use the articulation of the four sets of cultural practices in d.schools to make sense of design thinking initiatives in large organisations.

Table 6.2 Messy practices in design thinking

	Individualism	Egalitarianism	Hierarchy	Fatalism
Team				
Who should contribute	Anyone who is motivated and wants to contribute; T-shaped people: Team members are encouraged to explore new fields of opportunity	Design thinkers should be intrinsically motivated to solve wicked problems; cocreation	Experts for specialized inputs and contributions	
How to attract/motivate people	Let design thinkers choose the design challenges and projects they want to work on	Intrinsic motivation to solve wicked problems for and with users and stakeholders		
What behaviour to expect	Competitive	Cooperative and sharing		Overconfidence; needs management
Attitude towards economic, environmental and technological risks	Rapid and low-resolution prototyping allows teams to take risks at a relatively low cost			
How to interact		Cooperatively	Coaches enforce rules	
Place				
When, where and with whom to contribute	Flexible workspaces; trans-disciplinary teams	Team works together in the workspace; individual work discouraged; splitting implies sharing	Clear times, set in advance; teams determined beforehand by coaches	
How to structure space in which deliberation and decision-making takes place	Flexible to suit the needs of each individual team member at each point	Over time, workspace becomes the home of the team	Coach use space for didactic reasons	
Design challenge	Reframed	Broader issues	Pre-structured with constraints	
Process				
How to divide tasks	According to individual interests and motivation; expertise not necessarily needed	Based on a discussion and consensus in the team	Coach decides to break deadlock	

(continued)

Table 6.2 (continued)

	Individualism	Egalitarianism	Hierarchy	Fatalism
Which technology to use	Technology to impress and inspire; effective and simple	Technology that enables all team members to express their creativity	Appropriate for the stage of the project	
How to handle time	Time is a scarce and precious resource; time-boxing		Coaches reinforce time-boxing and agendas	
What information to use	Pragmatic and easy to gather	All sources of information and knowledge are equally probable sources of inspiration; look for the voices usually marginalised		
How to determine the agenda			Coaches determine and enforce agenda and the design challenge	
How to take decisions	Aggregation of preferences in matters concerning substance	Team related issues are based on consensus	Coaches break up deadlock and force decision	
How to learn from mistakes	Trial and error learning	Feedback and discussion from all team members to all team member and coaches	Expert coaches provide feedback on ideas and prototypes	Let teams fail to appreciate the inherent impossibility of ever solving wicked challenges
How to handle failure	Failure as a means of learning			Failure is inevitable, so best to accept failure

Source: Adapted from Ney and Verweij (2014b)

environments to suit their preferences. Some teams prefer open and expansive spaces that feature different 'sites'. Other teams, in turn, prefer to huddle around the table, using the whiteboards as a projective space for their outputs. Others still prefer to hide away.

Design teams are what Tom Kelley calls "hot teams". Design teams are hot if and only if they perform (Kelley 2001). Whoever can bring about that performance leads the team. This is why it is the team member who can contribute most to moving the team along in responding to the design challenge that takes the lead. Typically, this is independent of age, formal qualifications, rank or seniority.

Fig. 6.1 Design thinking workspaces. Credit: Kay Herschelmann

The lynchpin of any Design Thinking exercise is the practice design thinkers refer to as 'time-boxing'. Borrowing from methods such as Scrum or Lean Start-Up, all tasks and phases in Design Thinking are completed in so-called *design sprints*. Time is a valuable resource, so Design Thinking exercises ration it stringently (some would argue, brutally). New recruits to Design Thinking acutely feel the time pressure and an ubiquitous complaint we hear from them is the "I wish we had more time to complete the tasks". Experienced design thinkers typically point to the admittedly rough and ready prototypes: sprints may be stressful, but they enable teams to get the job done.

Design thinkers also adopt a rather pragmatic approach to the type of knowledge and information that feeds team-based integrative thinking. Here, valuable knowledge consists of insights, experiences, information and impressions that inspire innovation. In this sense, then, knowledge need not be authoritative or representative or, in a very fundamental sense, real, accurate or correct. Indeed, teams might find inspiration in stereotypes, misconstruals, mistakes or mystical accounts. While, as we saw in Chap. 5, design teams rely on qualitative and ethnographic research methods, they are not conducting a scientific investigation.

Pragmatism and efficiency similarly determine decision-making. Here, teams of design thinkers—essentially egalitarian groups (see next section)—rely on aggregating their preferences by voting rather than expending time and energy seeking an invariably elusive consensus. Teams choose between options—usually but not exclusively concerning the idea the team will take forward in the process—by relying on dot voting or, at times, secret voting techniques. The iterative nature of the Design Thinking process mitigates the cost of losing a vote: 'outvoted' ideas do not disappear but may become relevant in a later cycle or iteration of the Design Thinking process.

For voting to be meaningful, the team needs more than one option to choose from. The generation of ideas (or the ideation process), is all about creating choices for teams. Here, Design Thinking teams set out to create as many responses to the design challenge—which has been reframed in the light of user needs—as possible. The underlying logic is that quality follows quantity. Or, rather, after having relieved themselves of the "same-old-stuff", team members' can then concentrate on novel ideas.

Design Thinking teams learn through trial-and-error. Rapid prototyping and testing provides the teams with knowledge about what might and what might not satisfy the needs of users and stakeholders. These tests with users help teams determine what is worth developing and what to discard. In some cases, tests may indicate that the idea and the prototype are moving in the right direction. In other cases, user tests may show—very rapidly—that an idea is not nearly as good as it seemed during ideation and prototyping. This type of feedback can lead a team to completely abandon the idea and cycle as far back as the Observe phase (something Lean Start-Up pundits call a 'pivot').

In sum, Design Thinking features a considerable number of output-oriented practices. This, as Ney and Verweij point out, is somewhat anomalous for processes that aim to generate clumsy solutions (most processes seem to concentrate on inclusion- and process-oriented practices). The practices promote flexibility, efficiency and trial-and-error learning (Ney and Verweij 2014a). As Table 6.2 shows, output-oriented practices concentrate on the dimensions of process and space.

Inclusion-Oriented Practices

Design Thinking, at least our flavour of it, emerged from California's Silicon Valley. Thus, we might come to expect a strong individualist and entrepreneurial accent in the way we practice Design Thinking. But, just like California itself, we also find in Design Thinking practices that foster inclusion and unconditional equality.

As we have seen, many of the individualist practices focus on the Design Thinking process to empower Design Thinking teams to get things done. Inclusion-oriented practices, in turn, tend to revolve around team interaction. Design Thinking teams work best when participation in them is voluntary. This also means that there are no formal barriers—or at least no barriers that derive from the method itself—for anyone to join a Design Thinking team. Some Design Thinking exercises encourage the active involvement and participation of users and stakeholders in so-called co-creation processes (Bason 2010; Stickdorn 2012).

But why should people participate in co-creation processes? Ultimately, Design Thinking is about tackling (wicked) problems (as discussed in Chap. 2). There may, then, also be an element of intrinsic motivation to be a part of a team dedicated to facing up to messy challenges. Since weak intrinsic motivation makes for poor and ultimately ineffective Design Thinking teams, effective team management finds ways to generate intrinsic motivation. A very effective way of fostering intrinsic motivation in Design Thinking teams is to allow them to define (and redefine) how to approach design challenges according to the interests and capabilities in the team.

Whatever else it may be, Design Thinking is essentially a team activity (Kelley 2001; Plattner et al. 2014). Design Thinking happens when people work on solving a wicked problem in a team. Whether it is in the workspace or in the field, teams operate as a unit. Of course, Design Thinking teams, like any other type of team, will split up and distribute tasks. For example, Design Thinking teams will typically go into the field in smaller sub-teams or they will split-up to build different prototypes. However, team members go to great lengths to share insights or information with others. This is what the Design Thinking jargon refers to as 'syncing' or 'on-boarding'. Yet, flippant jargon aside, this process is fundamental to the functioning of Design Thinking teams: members of Design Thinking teams feel keenly the corroding force of asymmetries of information, interaction, resources, attention, or, indeed, anything. All members of Design Thinking teams are equal and any temporary asymmetry or inequality needs to be rectified before it becomes dysfunctional.

Similarly, team spaces are always accessible for each member at any time. Or the team space is equally inaccessible for any member. While team spaces are flexible and adaptable, the wheels on tables, whiteboards and seats are peculiarly unsuited to ordering space in terms of rank, seniority or distinction. However, the spatial arrangements enable teams to exclude the outside world constructing, quite literally, a wall of virtue. What is more, coaches encourage teams to develop their spaces over time: team spaces evolve to become both the home and collective memory of the team.

Since the effectiveness of Design Thinking teams depends on maintaining egalitarian structures and practices, integrating new members into an existing team will always be a challenge. From the very first day of a Design Thinking project, teams are encouraged to develop their own ways of cooperating, interacting and decision-making. As the project progresses, these practices (particularly if the team members believe them to work) become habitual and institutionalised. New members to the team need to undergo a process of socialisation and acculturation; they need to learn, understand and, most importantly, accept these somewhat idiosyncratic ways of going about things. This includes the culture of discussion and conflict resolution, the taboos ('Andrew is vegan, so no dishes containing meat for the team pot-luck') as well as the team rituals (such as the check-out handshake). But the integration of a new member—apart from being disruptive and time-consuming—also introduces status to the group (at the very least the status of a new-comer) which can undermine the basic premise of egalitarianism among team members. This is why design thinkers try to avoid adding new members to existing teams.

Design Thinking and design thinkers, as we saw in the previous section, take a rather pragmatic approach to knowledge and information. If knowledge inspires creative reframing, integrative thinking and innovation, it is good enough. However, pragmatism in application relies on egalitarianism in procurement. Design thinkers assume that all sources of information and all types of knowledge can inspire innovation. This implies that no form of knowledge—such as, say, science—is any more likely to spark creative synthesis as any other. Due diligence in the innovation process (which, remember, grapples with wicked problems) means that design thinkers actively seek out and give a voice to stakeholders usually overlooked, ignored and marginalised.

User-research for Design Thinking teams always looks for and embraces the views and experiences of extreme-users. These may be people who find new and innovative ways of deploying products and services (Suri 2005). Significantly, this includes people who use products and services illicitly or people whose situation or special needs call for innovative adaptation. The logic here is that understanding these needs—special and marginalised as they may seem—may be the doorway to making better products and services for everyone. In this way, then, Design Thinking gives a marginalised and overlooked voices a place in the problem-solving process.

Similarly, Design Thinking generates knowledge for innovation by immersing in the world of users. In the past, anthropologists would live in what were then believed to be remote areas of the world to participate in the everyday life of their chosen subjects of study. Design thinkers adopt a similar approach with users and stakeholders who, at first sight, seem far more familiar to us than, say, the Trobriand Islanders must have seemed to Bronislaw Malinowski. For design thinkers, immersion could imply using a product or service that is the subject of the design challenge.

By generating empathy at this experiential level, Design Thinking teams can become advocates for the users and stakeholders for which they create innovations. In a very real sense, the innovations and artefacts Design Thinking teams create, make the user's case and give them a voice in large organisations.

The testing phase illustrates just how powerful a voice this can be. The injunction for Design Thinking teams is to produce prototypes that enable users to experience the idea. This, then, is another way of empowering users and stakeholders in the innovation process. Since members of design teams attempt to 'defer judgement' while generating and working on ideas, users and stakeholders are the only actors in the process with anything resembling a veto.

Not everything is put to the vote in Design Thinking. Teams typically base decisions that affect the way a team cooperates and interacts on a consensus among team members. In order for the process of consensus-building to run as smoothly as it possibly can, teams and coaches rely on a battery of methods and tools. These can range from simple discussion to formal mediation. Whatever methods the team brings to bear, it is crucial that everyone is 'on board' or, at the very least, does not feel left out. Box 6.1 describes inclusion-oriented governance practices at the design studio Dark Horses.

Box 6.1 Sociocracy at Dark Horse

Dark Horse is an innovation agency that applies the methods and mindsets of design thinking to find effective responses to wicked design challenges. The agency was founded by the first class to graduate from the HPI School of Design Thinking in Potsdam. Seeking to reproduce the experience of the d-school, they set up the internal organisation, particularly the team work, of the agency along egalitarian lines based on inclusion-oriented practices. All 30 of the graduating class are equal owners of the Dark Horse agency. After experimenting with and, following the good tradition of design thinking, failing at several different models of work distribution, the 30 Dark Horse owners developed a messy, and therefore workable, approach. Project work is strictly voluntary; each owner-consultant works on projects according to their interests, rather than skills or specialisation. At the same time, each owner informs the others about how much of their time they plan to devote to Dark Horse projects over a specific period. However, the owners take turn for taking charge of core organisational functions—such as management, back-office, communication or development of new organisational tools and structures: this model understands that some formal hierarchy is inevitable, but avoids the concentration of power in the hands of a few owners. Dark Horse also features fixed decision opportunities (Cohen et al. 1972), such as weekly meeting. Here, participation is voluntary and is determined by the relevance of the issues to be discussed and decided upon to the individual owner. Other meetings, such as periodic strategy meetings, are mandatory. Decision-making

(continued)

> **Box 6.1** (continued)
> at Dark Horse's meetings rely on inclusion-oriented practices. In particular, the agency has implemented principles of 'sociocracy' (Buck and Villines 2007). Apart from rotating electing and rotating functions, decision-making is based not on majority voting but on building a consensus. At Dark Horse, everyone has a veto; however, exercising this veto also entails providing the group with an alternative proposal.
> Source: Löffler (2015).

As a rule, competitive behaviour within and between teams is uncommon (and unwelcome). Interaction between team members is informal and always aims to support collaboration. Executive education in Design Thinking simulates the informal and emphatic atmosphere typical for the student teams. This means that often the formal address in many European languages is replaced by the informal mode of communication. This signals that distinctions based on status or seniority are to play no role during the Design Thinking exercise.

The same is true for interaction between teams. While teams working on the same challenge compete at one level, coaches ensure that the teams also regularly share their insights with the competing team. What is more, teams are encouraged to share resources (such as, for example, contact in the field or tips for observation). Often teams will coordinate the way they approach the challenge: one team will explore one aspect of the design challenge while another will look at an entirely different angle. For example, if two teams working on redesigning the experience of learning a foreign language, one might explore the recent experience for recent immigrants or refugees while another will might concentrate on the learning experience for foreign students. The aim, however, is not for one team to create a competitive advantage over the other: the teams will share their insights in the hope of broadening their own solution space with the insights of the other team.

Process-Oriented Practices

Seasoning and spices are essential to the overall taste of a good dish. But seasoning, if it is to bring out rather than overpower the taste of the main ingredients, is best used sparingly. Messiness, like clumsiness, does not necessarily require that each in organisational culture be represented 'equally'. Indeed, Perri 6 argues that advocates of specific organisational cultures will favour and champion for different types of 'settlements' between contending organisational cultures (6 2003). As Table 6.2 shows, the main ingredients for Design Thinking, at least the Stanford or HPI flavour, are output- and inclusion-oriented practices. But in order to allow the full effects—the taste—of these practices to unfold, they requires some deft seasoning with hierarchical and fatalist ways of solving wicked problems.

Fig. 6.2 T-shaped persons.
Credit: Kay Herschelmann

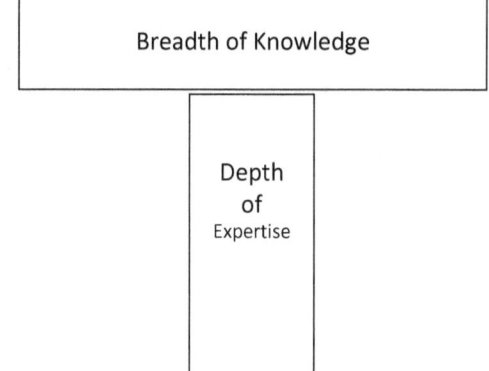

As we have seen, expertise and specialised knowledge confers neither status nor authority onto individual design thinkers. However, that does not mean that expertise and specialist knowledge play no role in Design Thinking. On the contrary, Design Thinking is about harnessing, blending and directing different types of expertise. This is why Design Thinking teams consist of so-called 'T-Shaped' people (see Fig. 6.2). Design Thinking need people that have the ability to reach out to others in the team (the horizontal bar of the T): these are not only the empathy and team-work skills but also the basic curiosity that drives individuals to try new things and push the limits of their particular horizons. But, in order to make a unique contribution to the team, individual members need depth in specialist knowledge (the stem of the T). This specialist expertise constitutes part of the reservoir of frames and ideas from which creative synthesis needs to draw. This is the reason why the D-School in Potsdam prefers post-graduate to undergraduate students for the D-School programme: post-graduates are more likely to have developed a T-shaped knowledge profile.

Rules play an important role in Design Thinking at several levels. Design Thinking may be something that happens in 'hot teams' and flexible workspaces but it takes place at clearly defined times set well in advance. As we have seen, teams are encouraged to formulate rules to guide their interaction. Coaches then ensure that teams observe these rules. Time-boxing implies that Design Thinking sessions are planned in detail (the technical term for this is 'micro-timing') and that these plans are rigorously implemented.

Coaches (or the functional equivalent) are responsible for ensuring that teams respect the rules in Design Thinking. They help teams structure the day and then enforce this structure. Keeping time is a coach's key responsibility: coaches make sure that tasks do not bleed into one another. Coaches set agendas or, where they do not, they enforce agendas that teams set themselves.

Apart from transdisciplinary teams and variable spaces, the success of Design Thinking depends on the integrity of the Design Thinking process. Just like Edward de Bono's 'six thinking hats' separate different modes of reflecting on an issue, the Design Thinking process forces teams to concentrate on specific modes of reasoning in a specific order (De Bono 1989). The Design Thinking process allows teams to step through the somewhat opaque logic of creative synthesis (see Chap. 2, Cross 2011) without getting sidetracked by discussion or lost in irrelevant details. However, this is predicated, on the one hand, on maintaining the integrity of the process and, on the other, the fidelity with which this process mirrors or reproduces the underlying logic of creative synthesis.

This, in turn, requires careful process management by coaches or moderators. Coaches ensure that team focus on the specific tasks for each phase. This also implies that teams need to follow the sequence of phases laid out by the Design Thinking process. This is the case even if a short-cut seems more profitable or if the activities in the present phase seem confusing or even pointless (see next section). Coaches encourage team members to 'trust the process' even if neither logic nor progress are immediately apparent to the team.

Significantly, 'trusting the process' is about following the rules—both implicit and explicit—dictated by the generative logic of each phase. Looking at the entire Design Thinking process, the first three phases—Understand, Observe and Synthesis—concentrate on grasping, defining and, significantly, redefining the problem (formulated as a design challenge). This is where teachers and coaches the HPI D-School in Potsdam admonish students to "switch off their solution engines": these phases are about exploring the problem in terms of user needs and opening up new spaces for innovation through reframing. The latter three phases—Ideation, Prototyping and Testing—concentrate teams on finding solutions. Here, there is little value for teams to discuss and criticise earlier (re)framings of the challenge. Coaches remind teams that trusting the process means that there be a chance to re-visit the reframed problem at a later stage, quite possibly with more and better—meaning user-generated—data. Thus the integrity of the process—the sequence of phases, the tasks within each phase as well as the transitions between each phases—is crucial if the logic (or magic) of creative synthesis is to unfold.

Chance-Oriented Practices

If hierarchical practices are a rich spice to be used sparingly, then fatalist practices are the equivalent of red chillies. Fatalist practices corrode trust and undermine interaction. Overdoing fatalism risks making the Design Thinking experience, quite literally, unpalatable. And yet, fatalist practices are an important way of grounding Design Thinking teams. Failure is a key aspect of Design Thinking. Admittedly, failure in Design Thinking is all about output-oriented trail-and-error learning; teams are encouraged to 'fail forward' and fail early to succeed later.

However, creating an awareness of failure and learning to accept failure requires creating isolation and fatalism. This is particularly important for people learning the methods and mindsets of Design Thinking. Here, coaches will set tasks that are impossible to complete. This include providing too little time or too little (or not the right) information. Another strategy is to let student teams work on the type of wicked problems that have no ultimate or comprehensive solutions. Issues such as homelessness (a didactic design challenge in the so-called 2nd project of the HPI D-School's Basic Track) allow students to experience that some problems or issues cannot be solved. Any response to the design challenge that student teams devise can never more than ameliorate the situation. No matter how 'inspiring' or 'awesome' their innovations, they can do little more than "make life a little more bearable" for the homeless (as one student team put it).

Strengths and Weaknesses of Contending Practices

How do these conflicting types of processes interact to produce workable and innovative responses to wicked problems?

As we have seen, processes associated with contending organisational cultures feature characteristic blindspots and vulnerabilities. Left unchecked, cognitive and normative blindspots in the frames make us miss potential opportunities. These weaknesses are likely to undermine the effectiveness and benefits of the particular type of process. Since organisational cultures define themselves in antagonistic contradistinction to one another, individual frames enable their advocates to pinpoint the vulnerabilities in other frames (Douglas 1987; Douglas and Ney 1998; Thompson et al. 1990). This is why processes of each organisational culture contain the 'antidote' to the vulnerabilities of the other cultures.

Avoiding Dilettantism

Individualist organisational cultures emphasise competition. Their output-oriented processes and procedures promote and institutionalise competitive behaviour. While this orientation towards output enables teams to get things done, competition can also be unhelpfully divisive. Competition within and between Design Thinking teams motivates individual members to produce, it can also lead to a rather narrow definition of what is and what is not to count as productive. This, in turn, may lead to the marginalisation of team members that are perceived to be 'unproductive'. What is more, competitive pressures make the 'quick win' irresistible. Indeed, not going for the quick win and "getting it out there" before the competition is, in the eyes of the individualist, almost a sign of negligence. However, output-orientation of this type does little for the quality of the innovation. Or, indeed, its originality. Disregard for expert knowledge and authority (which often goes hand-in-hand with overconfidence in the team's abilities and knowledge) risks dilettantism.

Working with "hot teams" (Kelley 2001) means that the status and authority individual members bring into the team does not determine who does what. And this most emphatically includes leadership and the organisation of tasks. Apart from the danger of dilettantism, relying too heavily on the "hot" aspect of the team—meaning getting things done through individual motivation—also leaves teams vulnerable to internal divisions as the fastest and most motivated individuals pull ahead without the others. Here, the inclusion-oriented team processes offer potential antidotes and therapies: frequent team meetings that not only discuss the substantive progress but also take a reading on the emotional state of individual team members (so-called checking-in) go some way to ensuring that all team members are included in the process. Similarly, when several design teams work on the same design challenge simultaneously—as is the case at the D-School in Potsdam—coaches encourage the sharing of insights and ideas across teams (see above). Frequent presentations—designed to elicit critical (albeit constructive) feedback rather than to sell a particular idea—as well as techniques explicitly aimed at idea-sharing ensure that good ideas diffuse through the school as a whole. For example, after teams have completed an ideation session, coaches will urge teams to go "idea shopping". Here, team members visit workspaces of other teams to look for ideas and innovations in other workspaces to take back and apply to one's own challenge. So while teams are encouraged to compete, the Design Thinking community treats outcomes as open knowledge that is supposed to benefit everyone.

Last, output-oriented processes and individualist mindsets leave teams vulnerable to overconfidence and, in the extreme, arrogance. Not only do teams celebrate the "beginner's mindset", teams also begin to see themselves as genius benefactors bringing light in form of brilliant innovations into the benighted existence of their chosen user group. This is particularly germane for projects aimed at social innovation, roughly half of the projects at the D-School in Potsdam and about 80% of the projects at the Stanford d.school. The real danger here is that design teams confuse sympathy for empathy; innovations may fail to address the very real problems with which these user-groups, often people at the margins of society such as the homeless (2nd Project D-School Potsdam), refugees (2nd Project D-School Potsdam, 3rd Project D-School Potsdam 2015) or poor mothers in rural Nepal (d.school Stanford), have to grapple. Here, then, is where the use of fatalist, chance-based methods can help counter overconfidence: by forcing teams to experience and confront the inevitability of their own ultimate failure (Embrace, while brilliant, makes women in rural Nepal no less poor; D-School innovations for helping refugees learn German have not stopped the civil war in Syria nor the discrimination they encounter in Germany), fatalist practices and mind-sets help ground and direct ambition in humility.

Preventing Paralysis

Egalitarian organisational cultures assume that people are inherently good. Thus, communities and teams that do away with corrosive competition or oppressive regulation are well suited to bringing out the very best in people—given time and patience, that is. And this is precisely where inclusion-oriented processes fall down: they take a lot of time. Since egalitarian procedures aim for consensus, decisions and choices may be a long time coming, if, indeed, they ever arrive. What is more, processes geared to inclusion provide protagonists with few effective means of settling disputes or conflict. If consensus is the only legitimate outcome of debate, conflict will be blamed on 'special interest', on 'weakness of the faith' or 'doctrine' or on the inability to recognise the true needs of the team. This, perhaps somewhat paradoxically, can lead to intolerance of other views and divergent patterns of behaviour.

In order to avoid the paralysis and in-fighting of typical in sectarian groups, design thinkers (and Design Thinking coaches) draw on processes from contending organisational cultures. Output-oriented processes—most prominently time-boxing and rapid prototyping—set very clear objectives and limits to debate. Coaches—authoritative experts on the Design Thinking process—enforce these limits by curtailing unproductive discussion—that is, any discussion that prevents Design Thinking teams from 'doing' the tasks needed to move the process on. At the same time, however, these grievances expressed in discussion—such as they are—are not allowed to ferment: instead, coaches and teams postpone these discussions to the designated slot—usually the team check-out—or a set aside time to discuss these issues later.

The same goes for decision-making during the Design Thinking process. Given the diversity of Design Thinking teams, consensus on substantive issues (rather than team-related matters) is not only unlikely but also undesirable (since creative synthesis that drives innovation emerges from transdisciplinary tensions). This is why decisions regarding the direction of user research or, more importantly, the ideas to carry forward from ideation to prototyping are based on aggregated individual preferences (i.e. voting) rather than a rational consensus. If voting turns out to be inconclusive (or divisive) coaches take control of decision-making. Or, as is more often the case, the threat of an authoritarian decision often focuses the group mind.

Reigning in Expertise

Process-oriented methods, in turn, are predicated on an inordinate degree of trust in status, authority and expertise. They ensure appropriate stewardship of processes and procedures. This risks losing sight of what processes are really about: enabling and supporting teams in generating innovative solutions to wicked problems.

Overly expert-oriented processes potentially alienate and marginalise the members of the Design Thinking team. This occurs when experts on the process (i.e. coaches) transfer responsibilities for key tasks, such as data collection, synthesis and decision-making, out of team (where they rightly belong). This can lead to team members losing touch with the design challenge, the work and, most importantly, the users.

The antidote and therapy consists of robustly 'low grid' responses. For one, the ideation phases aims at generating a large quantity of ideas (implying the equality or potential value of the contribution of every team member). Rather than aiming for 'quality' based on authoritative knowledge, coaches insist that teams 'defer judgement'. But teams are not deferring judgement to experts but users. During the test phase, teams set out to elicit critical feedback from the people for whom they are supposed to be designing innovations. The aim of user testing is not so much to defend ideas as to submit the hypotheses and assumptions that inhere in ideas and innovations to critical scrutiny. However, those doing the scrutinising are not experts (in the sense that they wield authoritative and accredited knowledge) but users and stakeholders—experts of their own life-worlds, if you will.

Another effective way of ensuring that experts do not dominate Design Thinking processes is to encourage critical feedback from teams about coaches. Design Thinking processes, if run properly (the rightful role of hierarchical process-orientation), provide teams and coaches with ample opportunity to reflect upon the power relationship that inevitably emerge between coaches and teams. Experience of the D-Schools in both Potsdam and Stanford suggest this is a fluid and rather volatile relationship; it is subject to constant change and is highly sensitive to changing conditions in the project. The question that arise around this relationship—how much responsibility should teams take, when is it legitimate to abdicate responsibility? What constitutes an illegitimate use of power by coaches? How much expertise is necessary?—are subject to ongoing negotiation and renegotiation in successive loops feedback and reflection sessions.

Processes that rely on authority and expertise tend to concentrate power in those that wield authoritative and accredited knowledge. Design Thinking processes counter this tendency to centralise among processes expert (i.e. coaches and teachers) by reproducing egalitarian team constellations and the attendant practices at the level of teaching. At the HPI D-School in Potsdam, teaches and coaches strive to 'teach teams with teams'. The team of coaches adopts the many of the same egalitarian practices that they expect the teams to implement. Like Design Thinking teams, coaching teams check-in in the morning and check-out in the evening. Ideally, coaching teams make decisions as a group (if not always unanimously). Coaching teams make sure to share information and methods. Coaching teams strive to grow the collective knowledge of the community by providing regular skills and knowledge updates. For example, the D-School in Potsdam organises regular "Method Jams" in which the coaching community shares new methods and techniques. Over and above these method jams, the D-School also organises so-called 'teacher's meeting'—semi-social evening events—in which one coach presents a new method or introduced the community to their research or work. Like Design

Thinking teams, coaching teams do not feature a formal hierarchy or seniority. Like design teams, tasks are not distributed according to seniority or specific expertise but to any team members who volunteer for the tasks in question.

Table 6.3 outlines the characteristic vulnerabilities and the suitable antidotes.

Pluralist Practices in Large Organisations

In principle, then, Design Thinking in academic programmes at universities features a plurality of practices. While these practices 'speak' with a distinctive low grid accent, that is they seem to come together in an individualist/egalitarian institutional settlement (6 2003), they would appear sufficiently variegated to promote 'clumsy' responses to wicked design challenges. Thus, applying these (or similar) practices to wicked design challenges in appropriate social spaces and with a rich reservoir of ideas should allow Design Thinking teams to engage in effective team-based integrative thinking.

Yet, to what extent did Design Thinking initiatives install a pluralist set of practices in large organisations?

Output-Oriented Practices

The studies indicate that Design Thinking initiatives introduced a range of output-oriented practices in all three areas outlined in Fig. 6.2: place, team and process. Although not a focus of the studies, research suggests that all initiatives transformed working spaces for Design Thinking teams. Whether equipping fully fledged Design Thinking studios (Dribbisch 2016) or encouraging Design Thinking teams to appropriate and recommission existing work spaces (Köppen 2016; Rhinow 2018), Design Thinking initiatives created physical spaces that allowed for more variability and flexibility.

As we have seen in the two preceding chapters, Design Thinking initiatives also introduced team management practices that valued performance and individual engagement over expertise and status (Köppen 2016; Dribbisch 2016; Rhinow 2018; Carlgren et al. 2014b). In particular, both Köppen and Rhinow point out how the design initiative at the large German software corporation encouraged Design Thinking team members to adopt a 'beginner's mindset' (Köppen 2016; Rhinow 2018). Evidence also suggests that Design Thinking initiatives encouraged pragmatic approaches to knowledge and decision-making: for example, Köppen (2016, p. 157), Rhinow (2018) as well as Dribbisch (2016) point to the introduction of voting and other forms aggregating preferences.

Last, the research also suggests that Design Thinking initiatives introduced output-oriented practices to drive team-based integrative thinking. Output-oriented ideation practices were common to all Design Thinking initiatives studied (Rhinow

Table 6.3 Characteristic vulnerabilities and suitable antidotes

	Trusts	Vulnerabilities	Antidote	Example
Individualism	Competitiveness	Dilettantism	Quality control by experts (hierarchy)	Feedback by expert coaches (hierarchy)
		Divide the team	Sharing information, tasks, contacts, insights, etc. equally in the team (egalitarianism)	Syncing the team/check in; sharing sessions; idea shopping
		Hubris/ overconfidence	Make team experience failure (fatalism)	Setting impossible challenge and project parameters
Egalitarianism	Inherent good in people	Paralysis caused by the inability to make decisions	Move the process on efficiently by focusing on doing (individualism)	Dot-voting; rapid prototyping; rules of ideation
		Infighting and schisms	Effective implementation of scheduling and sequencing of tasks to allow for time to address grievance (hierarchy)	Time-boxing; moderated DT agenda
Hierarchy	Authority and expertise	Alienation of team members	Empower the user rather than the expert (egalitarianism)	User-testing; co-creation; user-research
			Make experts and coaches accountable to teams (egalitarianism)	Feedback from teams to coaches
		Expert dominance of team outputs	Emphasise pragmatic nature knowledge (individualism)	Go for quantity during ideation
			Promote empathy with teams among coaches (egalitarianism)	Reproduce team practices at level of coaching team

2018; Köppen 2016; Carlgren et al. 2014b). In her study of the implementation of Design Thinking in the Singaporean public sector, Katrin Dribbisch (2016) points to the introduction of output-oriented ideation practices. Further, Dribbisch argues that these output-oriented practices have encouraged "…employees to go for radical ideas and be open and not restrictive when thinking about solutions" (Dribbisch 2016, p. 119). What is more, all studies suggest that large organisations point to the introduction of—or at least some degree of dabbling in — prototyping practices. Rhinow (2018) reports that project managers looked favourably on prototyping as a means of ensuring efficiency; members of Design Thinking teams, in turn, appreciated the way prototyping helps make ideas tangible.

Inclusion-Oriented Practices

Like output-oriented practices, studies indicate that Design Thinking initiatives introduced inclusion-oriented patterns of behaviour into large organisations. Köppen (2016) and Rhinow (2018) report how the Design Thinking initiative in the large German software enterprise was based largely on voluntary participation. The initiative encouraged employees interested in learning Design Thinking to apply; this formed the pool of people from which the Design Thinking teams emerged. What is more, as we have seen, Rhinow reports how Design Thinking teams found intrinsic motivation in framing and reframing design challenges: deliberating about purposes and ends generated within the team an inherent drive to solve problems the team—rather than project managers—had redefined as relevant.

As we have seen in the previous sections, inclusion-oriented practices tend to provide the means for self-governance of Design Thinking teams. Köppen's (2016) reveals how Design Thinking teams analysed in her study introduced informal practices to reshape relations between employees. As we have seen, she reports how Design Thinking teams would use practices such as 'check-ins' and 'check-outs' or 'warm-ups' to break down formal distinctions between team members. In this way, Design Thinking teams can create what Eva Köppen (2016) calls "protective spheres" (*Schutzsphären*). The teams are (or should be) fully accountable for the entire Design Thinking process: they have no need for the type of hierarchical oversight by superiors external to the Design Thinking team. As one of Köppen's respondent argues, in Design Thinking teams, decisions feel more legitimate as responsibility and accountability diffuses through the team (Köppen 2016, pp. 159–160). Instead of ego-driven decision-making, coaches interviewed in the study contend, Design Thinking teams relied on more democratic means of decision-making. Here, Design Thinking teams based their decisions of prior deliberation in which everyone had the right (one of Köppen's respondents even speaks of obligation) to contribute regardless of formal qualifications or status (Köppen 2016, p. 158).

But, as we have seen in the previous sections, inclusion-oriented practices are not limited to team governance. The evidence suggests that many inclusion-oriented practices entered organisations via the introduction of user research. In her study of the adoption of Design Thinking in the public sector in Singapore, Dribbisch describes how different divisions of the ministry she studied adopted and integrated stakeholder research. Not only, she argues, did user research give Singaporean citizens a voice in the design of public services, it also enabled civil servants—as policy and service designers—to arrive at a more fundamental understanding of the policy challenges at hand. It was stakeholder research conducted by the a specific unit in the Singaporean ministry into the high volume of appeals that revealed a deep distrust in officers' judgement (Dribbisch 2016). This, Dribbisch contends, enabled policy officers to take an alternative, more comprehensive and holistic approach to solving the problem (Dribbisch 2016). In the large German software enterprise, Köppen contends that user voices imbued helped shift authority from superiors to

Design Thinking teams: Design Thinking teams came to see user voices, she observed, as more authoritative than the opinion of superiors (Köppen 2016, p. 151).

Last, Carlgren et al.'s study of six large organisations suggests that inclusion-oriented practices were instrumental in the implementation of Design Thinking. Here, they argue, the creation and support of bottom-up initiatives among employees generated the requisite sense of ownership, empowerment and, ultimately legitimacy. For many respondents, the researchers report, Design Thinking is best suited to bottom-up initiatives; indeed, the researchers find that implementation worked best when Design Thinking was integrated into actual practices on the 'shop floor'. By the same token, implementation of Design Thinking was successful when programmes managed to co-opt and integrate employees in the diffusion process. Here, participants of introductory workshops were offered further training. These individuals then went on to become part of an ambassador network that diffused the practices of Design Thinking as peers (Carlgren et al. 2012). Carlgren et al. argue that

> ...creation of an ambassador network was seen as a central effort in diffusing and implementing Design Thinking in the organisation—especially the involvement of top management and the internal training and certification programmes for employees, as well as the collaboration with HR (Carlgren et al. 2012, p. 55).

Process-Oriented and Chance-Oriented Practices

Researchers found little explicit evidence that design initiatives implemented practices in the upper two quadrants of the Cultural Map (see Chap. 3). While there is very little in the way of explicit evidence, the studies do point to the implementation of process-oriented practices. In particular, both Köppen's and Rhinow's work alludes, albeit rather obliquely, to the regulatory role of external Design Thinking coaches. Indeed, respondents in Köppen's study of the implementation of Design Thinking in a large German enterprise report that they perceived the Design Thinking coaches—mostly external consultants—as being the new "boss" (Köppen 2016, p. 181). Rhinow points to the somewhat tense relationship between project managers and Design Thinking coaches (Rhinow 2018). Similarly, Köppen contends that some participants perceived the external Design Thinking coaches as superiors (Köppen 2016, p. 179).

The studies provided no evidence—either of a direct or indirect nature—of chance-oriented practices.

How did the implementation of Design Thinking practices affect team-based integrative thinking? How did these practices (or the lack of them) affect the relevant large organisations?

Messiness in Practice: Impacts of Messy Practices on Large Organisations

We can explain the dearth of process- and chance-oriented practices in studies about Design Thinking initiatives in two ways. The first approach points to the thematic focus and objectives of the studies. None of the studies explicitly looked at socio-institutional practices. What is more, researchers did not have (or chose not to have) recourse to a comparative framework such as Cultural Theory. So, even if they were looking for different sets of institutional practices, they may not have had the tools to identify and discern contending practices.

And yet, while this is undoubtedly true, one might still have expected the analyses to unearth some practices geared toward process or chance. This might lead us, with some justification, to conclude that the implementation of Design Thinking in large organisations was imbalanced: the lack of process-oriented and chance-oriented practices would therefore jeopardise the ability for effective team-based integrative thinking. Alternatively, we could, as Katrin Dribbisch does, argue that organisations will inevitably adapt Design Thinking practices—including a selection of practices to suit their specific needs and institutional contexts. But this just begs the questions how much adaptation and selection will still enable Design Thinking teams to engage in effective team-based integrative thinking. Effective, that is, to enable teams to find clumsy responses to wicked design challenges.

The second explanation conceives of Design Thinking initiatives in a wider organisational context. Here, the mini-publics, reservoirs of ideas and plural practices created by Design Thinking initiatives not only aimed at tackling wicked design challenges, they also sought to transform institutional cultures of these organisations. In this sense, then, the Design Thinking teams and their practices set out to change or, at the very least, irritate prevalent organisational cultures. The institutional cultures in the organisations surveyed seemed dominated by reliability- and process-oriented cultures. On this view, Design Thinking reformers in these organisations deployed the ideas and practices of Design Thinking, perhaps unwittingly, to bring about changes in wider institutional environments. This may explain why would-be Design Thinking champions favoured the more provocative output- and inclusion-oriented processes over process-orientation.

It would indeed seem as if Design Thinking initiatives analysed in the studies brought about changes in wider organisational contexts. Or, more precisely, the studies picked up on and thematised these wider institutional aspects. This may go some way in explaining why all studies reported impacts of output- and inclusion-oriented practices on hierarchical practices and structures in the wider organisational environment.

Output- and Inclusion-Oriented Practices as an Antidote to Prevailing Process Orientation

Many of the large organisations examined by the different studies were dominated by vertical structures, a strong bias towards 'reliability' (Martin 2009a) as well as expert-oriented practices. The Design Thinking initiatives examined in the studies sought—either explicitly or implicitly—to counter the perceived deleterious effects of these dominant hierarchical practices. In Carlgren et al.'s (2016) study, at least four of the six large organisations analysed looked to Design Thinking as a means of 'cultural change' or 'mindset change' (Carlgren et al. 2016, pp. 350–351). Similarly, Köppen describes the large German software corporation as vertically segmented organisation that set out software production in a way almost reminiscent of Taylorist processes (Köppen 2016). The organisation, employees told Köppen in interviews, featured a highly specialised division of labour as well as the concomitant hierarchical lines of accountability. Köppen reports that employees felt increasingly isolated by work processes reminiscent of working on conveyor belts. Worse still, employees believed they had no voice: individuals who questioned decisions or working practices were quickly branded as trouble-makers (*Querulanten*) (Köppen 2016, pp. 145–144). Alienation in the corporation, Köppen argues, was evident at three levels: employees felt disconnected from the firm's products, from their colleagues and from users. The Design Thinking initiative, then, was supposed to remedy growing demotivation, disillusionment and alienation among employees. In the Singaporean Ministry, Dribbisch's (Dribbisch 2016) work suggests that the Design Thinking initiative also aimed at not only bringing about innovation in public services (Dribbisch 2016), but also to infuse the entire ministry with new working practices. She notes that the Corporate Planning Department (CPD) embarked on the Design Thinking journey in order to "…educate Ministry staff in the new approach's methodology and enable them to facilitate training courses themselves" (Dribbisch 2016); it would seem, then, that the CPD the practices of Design Thinking were to diffuse through the different departments and units of the Ministry.

How, then, did output- and inclusion-oriented practices impact on wider organisational contexts?

Both Katrin Dribbisch's (2016) and Holger Rhinow's (2018) studies show how output- and inclusion-oriented practices created counterweights to existing, predominantly process-oriented processes. In terms of output-oriented practices, Rhinow (2018) contends that project managers liked the way Design Thinking helped speed up development processes and prevent an "overly academic" approach to problem solving: for example, Rhinow argues, respondents liked the way majority voting on ideas during ideation obviated the need for seemingly endless, circular debate (Rhinow 2018). In Singapore, Dribbisch found that brainstorming and ideation practices found their way into the everyday routines of the civil servants at the Ministry in Singapore (Dribbisch 2016). These output-oriented practices, she contends, encouraged "...employees to go for radical ideas and be open and not restrictive when thinking about solutions..." (Dribbisch 2016).

What is more, existing evidence indicates that the practices of prototyping and user testing significantly impinged on the organisations under scrutiny. Introducing prototyping and user tests, Dribbisch argues, brought about two related changes in the Singaporean Ministry. First, these output-oriented practices enabled more effective communication about policy challenges within project teams as well as across the organisation as a whole. Respondents report that prototyping and testing provided teams with rapid feedback from users. What is more, this enabled teams to argue more effectively and more convincingly to superiors thus improving what she calls "buy-in" from the senior management. Not only did this lead to better outcomes, Singaporean civil servants believed it also saved money (Dribbisch 2016). These output-oriented practices, Dribbisch points out, seem to have generated an environment at the ministry in which experimentation and, more importantly, early failure become part of the service development process. Most importantly, however, output-oriented practices—particularly prototyping—gave rise to what the people at the Stanford d.school call "a bias for action". As a respondent tells Dribbisch:

> I think the other thing about Design Thinking that it is so, I think precious to us, as in the lessons it has taught us is that we spend a lot of time talking and not enough time doing. We spend a lot of time discussing ideas, talking about advantages, disadvantages, a lot of guess work etc., when we will be a lot better off just experimenting and trying.... (Dribbisch 2016)

Rhinow's study (2018) also points to prototyping and user testing as a particularly incisive practice. He reports how project managers see Design Thinking in general and rapid prototyping in particular as a means of increasing efficiency (Rhinow 2018). Over and above efficiency, the studies suggest that prototyping helps teams come to terms with the inherent ambiguity and messiness of wicked design challenges. For example, Rhinow shows how teams in his study developed early prototypes of possible solutions for use as artefacts and 'conversation starters' in interviews with users. This, Rhinow contends, helped the teams and users transform a vague and ambiguous issue into something more tangible as well as manageable (Rhinow 2018).

Similarly, Carlgren et al.'s (2014a) study of Design Thinking programmes in six large enterprises found how prototyping enabled actors within these organisations to better communicate about and more effectively learn from the complex problems at hand:

> There are a lot of things you can learn from quick prototyping, it is kind of interesting too, which is the thing we are trying to explain to [country X]. You don't need to completely design the product to death to really know, to start to learn things (Carlgren et al. 2014a, p. 414).

The existing evidence also suggests that Design Thinking initiatives inclusion-oriented practices to transform predominantly hierarchical and vertical processes in large organisations. As we have seen in the preceding chapters, much of Köppen's argument centres on the impact of inclusion-oriented practices on processes and structures in the large German software corporation. Recall that she recounts how inclusion-oriented team practices created in Design Thinking teams what she called a 'protective sphere' (Köppen 2016, pp. 159–160). These practices not only included check-ins, check-outs and, in particular, warm-ups (see Chaps. 3 and 4) but also encouraged team members to relate to each other in informally by divulging and sharing personal information. In addition to the protective sphere, she argues, inclusion-oriented practices led to a closer emotional bond between team members as well as between team members and users. These emotional bonds, respondents report, led to more constructive conflict within Design Thinking teams. Conflict, no less, that respondents believed led to more effective 'participatory sense-making' in teams (Köppen 2016, p. 175): here, respondents argued, innovation emerges from the constructive conflict between contending points of view.

In Singapore, Dribbisch (2016) argues that the adoption of inclusion-oriented practices in user research complemented and extended existing approaches to policy-making. Specifically, Dribbisch points out that the practice of generating empathy with stakeholders through team-based integrated thinking transformed policy formulation. Whereas before "...policy officers did not really go down to talk to any customer, any user, we just talked on a project like that, based on some cases [...] that happened" (Dribbisch 2016). The introduction of inclusion- and output-oriented practices, however, enabled the policy officers to break out of or, at least, complement a purely expert-based policy formulation process. In this way, Dribbisch argues, policy officers were able to critically reflect the definition of the policy problem at hand. Policy officers, Dribbisch contends,

> ...perceive Design Thinking's value to lie in its ability to come up with a refined problem statement that questions or reframes the initial problem, in contrast to the usual way of immediately jumping at solutions (Dribbisch 2016).

What is more, policy officers report that these inclusion-oriented practices have meant that policy formulation itself is now "...increasingly based on insights from user research" (Dribbisch 2016). This, policy-makers told Dribbisch, contributed to a fundamental change in the organisational culture. Policy formulation using inclusion-oriented practices, they argue, have enabled a better understanding of and renewed focus on citizen needs. As one of Dribbisch's respondents puts it:

> In the past we have policies that caters to our government's needs. In the recent years we have been talking about, coming up with policies that cater to the needs and the real needs of Singaporeans, which is really quite different (Dribbisch 2016).

This, Dribbisch argues, amounts to no less than a "shift in mindset" in which "...understanding customers' and stakeholders' perspectives and their behaviour before coming up with ideas on policy options and designing policies and programmes (solutions) for them" (Dribbisch 2016, p. 58). Rather than relying exclusively on their expertise, inclusion-oriented practices of Design Thinking has enabled these policy-makers to create a "culture of knowing your customers and learning to build effective solutions" (quoted in Dribbisch 2016, p. 89).

In sum, then, the empirical material provides reason to believe that the output-and inclusion-oriented practices introduced by Design Thinking initiatives helped alleviate some of the undesired outcomes of hierarchical organisational cultures.

Dilettantism: Undesired Impacts of Output-Oriented Practices

As we have seen, design initiatives in the large organisations studied seemed to concentrate on the implementation of output- and inclusion-oriented practices. In terms of organisational messiness, placing a strong emphasis on output- and inclusion-oriented practices meant that the mini-publics and the team-based integrative thinking that took place within them had to do without the wisdom of process- and chance-oriented practices. Consequently, the Cultural Theory framework outlined in Chaps. 2 and 3 would suggest that Design Thinking teams were more exposed to the vulnerabilities associated with individualist organisational cultures. We would, then, expect to see the emergence of characteristics tensions centred on dilettantism.

Both Köppen (2016) and Rhinow (2018) point to tensions caused by the pragmatic approach to knowledge. Köppen reports that members of Design Thinking teams saw the injunction to take a 'beginner's mindset' as a decidedly mixed blessing. While it provided a fresh perspective on wicked design challenges, Köppen suggests that the 'beginner's mindset' also devalued expertise in favour of more subjective and opaque skills. For example, respondents remarked that in empathy work, individual personality will trump impersonal knowledge and expertise (Köppen 2016, p. 227). Some of Köppen's respondents felt this pragmatism to be limiting and inhibiting: adopting a beginner's mindset in an organisation traditionally based on expertise, they argued, calls for considerable amount of courage so as not to appear ignorant (Köppen 2016, p. 182). For employees who could not muster this courage, taking a 'beginner's mindset' felt like a demotion. To add insult to injury, diversity in teams exacerbated the relative levelling of expertise. At the large German software enterprise, diversity in teams meant that professionally trained and experienced designers had to collaborate with inexperienced colleagues on tasks the UX designers believed to fall squarely into their professional domain (Köppen 2016, p. 167).

Just as professionals felt undervalued, many individuals felt overwhelmed by tasks for which they believed themselves to be unqualified or unskilled. For example, Rhinow reports that respondents in his study experienced user-research as something daunting. Not only did teams find the gathering of qualitative data challenging, they also struggled with the analysis of this data: Rhinow reports that teams concentrated on too many issues within the 'thick descriptions' and seemed to be unable to find a focus. Similarly, the Singaporean civil servants in Dribbisch's study reported lacking confidence in their ideation and prototyping skills. This led, among other things, to a rather selective application of Design Thinking practices. Dribbisch argues that the practices usually associated with the 'solution space' (Ideation, Testing and Prototyping, see Fig. 1.8) were the first to be sacrificed (Dribbisch 2016). She argues that the ministry's

> ...translation of Design Thinking shows a clear bias towards the empathy phases ('understand' and 'observe') of the d.school's process, as indicated by the fact that its projects often stop at the interviewing stage (Dribbisch 2016).

At a more fundamental level, Katrin Dribbisch (2016) suggests that policy makers in Singapore were suspicious of Design Thinking's fast-paced iterative approach to problem-solving. Unlike the private enterprises, activities of public sector institutions are bound to the notion of fairness. Ministries and organisations delivering public service need to ensure that all citizens have access to similar services not only within the polity but also across different cohorts. This, they argued, makes rapid prototyping, user-testing and iteration less feasible. What is more, Singaporean policy-makers contended, given the complexity of factors that shape the success or failure, testing full-blown policies is tricky (Dribbisch 2016). Here, civil servants did not perceive 'failing often and early' as a viable practice for policy-making.

Resolving these tensions, both Köppen and Rhinow argue, would have required process-oriented interventions. Teams reported that they would have wished for more expertise in qualitative research methods in their teams. By the same token, teams with designated specialists in user research—such as colleagues with a professional UX design background—welcomed the expert guidance when it was available. In other cases, project managers resolved these tensions by setting deadlines (Rhinow 2018). Another project manager points to the importance of Design Thinking coaches: he observes how coaches playfully guide teams that have become unstuck (Rhinow 2018).

In sum, the relative dearth of process-and chance-oriented practices meant that Design Thinking initiatives and Design Thinking teams were left vulnerable to the characteristic dilettantism of output-oriented individualist practices.

Paralysis and Intolerance

The studies also pointed towards evidence of undesired and deleterious impacts of inclusion-oriented practices. In particular, studies point to the characteristic vulnerabilities of egalitarian paralysis and sectarian intolerance.

Rhinow describes a situation in which the Design Thinking team was unable to come to a decision. His interviews reveal that project managers grew increasingly impatient as the Design Thinking projects progressed or, rather, failed to progress. Torn between the open-ended and iterative flow of Design Thinking projects and the hard indicators of conventional project management, Rhinow's interviewees believed that the Design Thinking teams had not achieved expected results and had not even seemed to generate interesting ideas. Design Thinking teams had, in the words of a particular respondent, "got lost in iterations" (Rhinow 2018) and would have needed an exit strategy. In one case, Rhinow reports, a project manager reintroduced elements of classical project management by designating a team member who ensures that the team meets the objectives of the day (Rhinow 2018).

Much of Eva Köppen's book looks at some of the less salubrious effects inclusion-oriented empathy practices. As we have seen in previous chapters, she identifies many instances in which egalitarian practices turned intolerant and even oppressive. Both individuals as well as groups, she argues, became victims of this bullying. At the individual level, she tells of many instances at which Design Thinking teams at the large German software enterprise deployed inclusion-oriented practices to discipline and shame individuals in front of the entire team. For example, Köppen cites the incident in which a Design Thinking team castigated an individual as "not sufficiently flexible" in a "nasty and not very constructive manner" (Köppen 2016, p. 186). In other instances, individuals found themselves under pressure to participate in activities—most prominently warm-ups involving physical contact—that made them feel uncomfortable. At the level of groups, she shows how some employees cast aspersions on the inability or unwillingness of specific constituencies—software developers in this particular case—to yield to and wield inclusion-oriented practices. The inherent inability of these groups to use empathetic practices, so the argument went, disqualifies these groups of people from Design Thinking processes (Köppen 2016).

Köppen's research also suggests that the assumption of the inherent good in people leave inclusion-oriented practices open to strategic (ab)use. She shows how individual members use inclusion-oriented practices in order to manipulate others in the team. She describes how one of her respondents had devised ways of using inclusion-oriented practices to selectively display her skills to the team and the project manager (Köppen 2016, p. 249). What is more, she points to instances in which Design Thinking teams manipulated users during research to elicit (what were perceived to be) beneficial responses (see Chap. 5).

Lessons Learnt

What lessons can we draw from the implementation of Design Thinking practices in large organisations? We can identify four interrelated learnings:

Design Thinking Practices Are 'Messy', But Concentrate on Output and Inclusion

Output- and inclusion-oriented practices are at the heart of Design Thinking. Getting things done quickly in small teams that focus on user experiences is what drives Design Thinking. Here, process- and chance-oriented practices act as a regulative or negative feedback loop to avoid falling prey to the inherent vulnerabilities of individualist and egalitarian practices. And yet, process-oriented practices, such as the policing of rules or maintaining the integrity of the Design Thinking process, are an inextricable part of the overall approach. Advocates of Design Thinking—whether they are would-be organisational reformers or seasoned Design Thinking pundits—regularly underestimate the significance of high-grid practices. This is particularly true for processes that introduce what Christopher Hood (1998) calls "contrived randomness". It is hard enough trying to convince actors in organisations geared toward reliability that failing early and often is a good idea: arguing for planned failure in these organisations seems nothing short of barmy. And yet, these practices are crucial for innovation via effective team-based integrative thinking. *The key lesson here is that would-be reformers need to find ways of integrating high-grid practices in general and chance-oriented practices in particular into Design Thinking processes.*

Design Thinking Programmes at the HPI Schools of Design Thinking Are Probably More 'Messy' Than the Design Thinking Initiatives in the Large Organisations Covered in the Studies

We have seen that the variety of practices in the three HPI Schools of Design Thinking feature practices from all fours provinces of the Cultural Map (see Fig. 3.2). Furthermore, they combine in such a way as to help Design Thinking teams avoid the characteristic vulnerabilities and pitfalls of each set of cultural practices. In the large organisations analysed in the studies, however, evidence suggests that Design Thinking initiatives concentrated on introducing output- and inclusion-oriented practices. As we have seen, this led Design Thinking teams to succumb to culture-specific vulnerabilities and pitfalls. The temptation here is to attribute this depth and breadth of practices to a (somewhat romantic) conception of universities as open-minded places of learning and scholarship. The real reason is a lot more prosaic: the schools of Design Thinking funded by the Hasso-Plattner-Foundation are, by and large, independent of the wider administrative and academic structures in which they are embedded. *It would seem, then, that the messiness required for effective team-based integrative thinking is more likely to emerge in social spaces—that is, mini-publics—that are independent from the vagaries and vicissitudes of the wider organisational context.* This suggests that the more independent and insulated from the wider organisational environment Design Thinking teams are, the more effective team-based integrative thinking is likely to be.

Design Thinking Initiatives in Large Organisations Tend to Be Embedded in Predominantly Hierarchical Institutional Contexts

This is a corollary of the previous learning. If the outputs of Design Thinking teams are to have a sustained and lasting impact on their organisational environments, they need someone to actively transfer, translate and implement these outputs in the wider organisation. While there is some (admittedly scant) evidence of what we might call a 'spontaneous transfer' (Dribbisch 2016) of messy practices into the wider organisation, this would seem to be both an exception and far too sporadic to make much of an impact. *It would seem, then, that the outputs of Design Thinking teams require specific programmes of transfer and implementation if they are to shift organisations towards multi-dexterity and messiness.* Design Thinking teams can plant the seed of messiness within an organisation, but developing a 'messy' garden calls for a specific programme of cultivation.

There May Be a Trade-Off Between Delivering Innovation and Bringing About Cultural Change Within the Wider Organisation

The studies suggest that many of the Design Thinking initiatives aimed at transforming the organisational cultures of their host institutions (Carlgren et al. 2016). As we have seen, the predominance of low-grid practices caused irritation and, consequently, movement in the organisation. In a very real sense, would-be reformers used the methods and mindsets of Design Thinking itself as a programme for transferring messy practices into the institution as a whole. However, we have also seen that provoking organisational irritation is not always conducive to forging effective responses to wicked design challenges. Indeed, evidence suggests that wider organisational irritations often distracted and occasionally even derailed problem-solving processes (c.f. Rhinow 2018). Herein, then, lies a real risk of undermining the legitimacy of Design Thinking practices. *If would-be champions position Design Thinking as an approach for tackling wicked design challenges but then, in pursuit of a 'hidden agenda', set up the mini-publics to cause 'constructive irritation' thereby hobbling effective team-based integrative thinking, then this leaves the Design Thinking project wide open to (justified) criticism.* After all, the new method of innovation caused all sorts of bother without delivering the innovative products and services it promised. The obverse is equally true. Design Thinking initiatives advertised as cultural change programmes that generate products and services so innovative that no one really knows how they could possibly relate to the rest of the institution are not terribly credible.

Conclusion

This chapter has covered a lot of ground. It set out by applying the conceptual framework of institutional messiness introduced in Chap. 3 to the practices of Design Thinking. Taking the practices in the schools of Design Thinking at Stanford, Potsdam and Cape Town as the baseline, we identified four types of practices. First, *output-oriented practices* enable teams to get things done quickly and efficiently in order to move the process forward. Second, *inclusion-oriented practices* provide Design Thinking teams with the means for creating a pluralist, open and egalitarian teams. What is more, these types of processes help teams give an effective voice to users and stakeholders in problem-solving processes. Third, *process-oriented practices* ensure the integrity of the Design Thinking process by enabling teams and coaches to devise and enforce rules. Last, *chance-oriented practices* infuse the Design Thinking process with an element of unpredictability that confronts Design Thinking teams with failure. As we have seen, each type of practice comes equipped with characteristic strengths and weaknesses.

The exposition also showed that Design Thinking at the three schools in Stanford, Potsdam and Cape Town features practices from all four quadrants of the cultural map: in this sense, then, Design Thinking at the schools of Design Thinking is 'messy' (Ney and Verweij 2014a). However, as Table 6.2 suggests, Design Thinking at these universities features a distinctive egalitarian and individualist accent. At the schools of Design Thinking, most practices are oriented towards output and inclusion. This is not to say that rules and 'contrived randomness' are unimportant, but they act in a predominantly regulative role: process- and chance-oriented practices help teams avoid the characteristic pitfalls of individualist and egalitarian ways of tackling wicked design challenges. Overall, then, practices at schools of Design Thinking are sufficiently pluralist to support effective team-based integrative thinking.

The chapter then juxtaposed practices at the schools of Design Thinking with the Design Thinking initiatives in large organisations. Here, the available evidence points to the introduction of a wide range of output- and inclusion-oriented practices. In particular, studies point to the implementation of practices centred on ideation and prototyping as well as practices geared towards team management and user-research. In turn, available studies provide little indication that Design Thinking initiatives implemented process- and chance-oriented practices. Apart from the research designs of the studies covered in this chapter (which did not set out to identify and analyse pluralist practices), part of the reason for this imbalance may lie in way Design Thinking initiatives embedded teams within the wider institutional environment. While the three schools of Design Thinking funded by the Hasso-Plattner Foundation are relatively independent from wider structures and processes of their host institutions, many Design Thinking initiatives planted teams within hierarchical and process-oriented organisational practices. As we have seen, many Design Thinking initiatives, either implicitly or explicitly, intended to transform organisational cultures. Indeed, evidence indicates that all Design Thinking initiatives brought about changes in working practices within the wider institutional environment. Yet, the studies also suggest that prevalent high-grid practices in the wider institutional environment may not help Design Thinking teams from avoiding the characteristic blindspots and pitfalls of individualist and egalitarian practices.

These experiences, then, point to four interdependent lessons:

- Design Thinking practices are potentially messy, but feature a distinctive individualist and egalitarian bias;

- Design Thinking programmes at the schools in Stanford, Potsdam and Cape Town probably feature more pluralist and 'messy' practices than Design Thinking initiatives in the large organisations studied. This may be due to the way Design Thinking initiatives embed teams and projects in the wider institutional environment. The more Design Thinking teams are embedded in the wider institutional environment, the more initiatives will feature types of practices that act as a counterweight to the dominant organisational culture;
- Sustained impact in the wider institutional environment will require a conscious and organised transfer of the outputs of Design Thinking teams into the organisation as a whole. While there is some evidence of practices diffusing 'naturally' to other parts of the organisation, the studies suggest that may be too patchy and haphazard to make much of an impact;
- There may be a trade-off between using Design Thinking as a means of innovation and deploying Design Thinking as a vehicle for transforming organisational cultures. While the methods and mindsets are certainly suitable for both objectives, the evidence seems to indicate that pursing one goal, say innovation, may undermine the basis for pursuing cultural changes in the wider organisational context and vice versa. Design Thinking initiatives that set out to create capabilities for innovation as well as bring about change may end up with neither thereby undermining the legitimacy of the methods and mindsets of Design Thinking.

What does this mean for the management and governance of Design Thinking in large organisations? It is to this question that we turn in the next chapter.

References

6, P. (2003). Institutional viability: A neo-Durkheimian approach. *Innovation: The European Journal of Social Science, 16*(4), 395–415.

Bason, C. (2010). *Leading public sector innovation: Co-creating for a better society*. Bristol, UK: Polity Press.

Buck, J. A., & Villines, S. (2007). *We the people: Consenting to a deeper democracy: A guide to sociocratic principles and methods*. Washington, DC: Sociocracy.info.

Carlgren, L., Elmquist, M., & Rauth, I. (2012). *Implementing design thinking in large organizations*. Proceedings of the IPDM Conference 2012, Manchester.

Carlgren, L., Elmquist, M., & Rauth, I. (2014a). Design thinking: Exploring values and effects from an innovation capability perspective. *The Design Journal, 17*(3), 403–423.

Carlgren, L., Elmquist, M., & Rauth, I. (2014b). Exploring the use of design thinking in large organizations: Towards a research agenda. *Swedish Design Research Journal, 1*(14), 47–56.

Carlgren, L., Elmquist, M., & Rauth, I. (2016). The challenges of using design thinking in industry – Experiences from five large firms. *Creativity and Innovation Management, 25*(3), 344–362.

Cohen, M., March, J., & Olsen, J. (1972). A garbage can model of organisational choice. *Administrative Science Quarterly, 17*, 1–17.

Cross, N. (2011). *Design thinking: Understanding how designers think and work*. New York: Bloomsbury Academic.

De Bono, E. (1989). *Six thinking hats*. Boca Raton, FL: Taylor & Francis.

Doorley, S., & Witthoft, S. (2011). *Make space: How to set the stage for creative collaboration*. Hoboken, NJ: Wiley.

Douglas, M. (1987). *How institutions think*. London: Routledge and Kegan Paul.

Douglas, M., & Ney, S. (1998). *Missing persons: A critique of personhood in the social sciences*. Berkeley, CA: University of California Press.

Dribbisch, K. (2016). Translating innovation: The adoption of design thinking in a Singaporean Ministry.

Hood, C. (1998). *The art of the state: Culture, rhetoric, and public management*. Oxford: Oxford University Press.

Kelley, T. (2001). *The art of innovation*. London: Profile Books.

Köppen, E. (2016). *Empathy by design: Untersuchung einer Empathie-geleiteten Reorganisation der Arbeitsweise*. Konstanz und München: UVK Verlagsgesellschaft mbH.

Löffler, J. (2015, September 1). Unser Unternehmen ist eine Soziokratie. *Der Freitag*.

Martin, R. L. (2009a). *The design of business: Why design thinking is the next competitive advantage*. Boston, MA: Harvard Business Press.

Martin, R. L. (2009b). *The opposable mind: Winning through integrative thinking*. Boston, MA: Harvard Business Press.

Ney, S. (2012). Making sense of the global health crisis: Policy narratives, conflict, and global health governance. *Journal of Health Politics, Policy and Law, 37*(2), 253–295.

Ney, S., & Verweij, M. (2014a). Exploring the contributions of cultural theory for improving public deliberation about complex policy problems. *Policy Studies Journal, 42*(4), 620–643.

Ney, S., & Verweij, M. (2014b). Messy institutions for wicked problems: How to generate clumsy solutions. Available at SSRN 2382191.

Plattner, H., Meinel, C., & Leifer, L. J. (2014). *Design thinking research: Building innovators*. Cham: Springer.

Rhinow, H. (2018). Design thinking Als Lernprozess in Organisationen: Neue Chancen Und Dilemmata Für Die Projektarbeit. Doctoral thesis, University of Potsdam, Potsdam.

Stickdorn, M. (2012). *This is service design thinking: Basics-tools-cases*. Amsterdam: BIS.

Suri, J. F. (2005). *Thoughtless acts?: Observations on intuitive design*. San Francisco, CA: Chronicle books.

Thompson, M., Ellis, R., & Wildavsky, A. (1990). *Cultural theory*. Boulder, CO: Westview Press.

Chapter 7
Leadership, Design Thinking and Messy Institutions

Design thinking not only potentially helps large organisations tackle complex and uncertain problems (Dorst 2015) but can also profoundly transform the institutional complexion of these organisations. If done properly, Design Thinking offers people in large organisations a much wider range of strategies for addressing wicked problems. This cultural change, as seen Chap. 3, is not so much about moving the institution from one culture, say a predominantly hierarchical culture geared towards reliability (Martin 2009b), to another based, for example, on entrepreneurial opportunity-seeking. Instead, organisational change induced by Design Thinking can result in what practitioners and advocates of Design Thinking call a "design-led" organisational culture (Schmiedgen et al. 2015).

But, as we have seen in the preceding chapters, what 'doing Design Thinking properly' may mean is far from obvious. In particular, the review of some of the available evidence suggests that effective implementation and organisation implies new forms of management and leadership. Many commentators argue that the more an organisation integrates the ideas and practices of Design Thinking, the less effective conventional approaches to management and leadership will become (c.f. Martin 2009a; Verganti 2009). This chapter looks at why this may be the case, what leadership of messy and multi-dexterous organisations may involve and what managers need to do to effectively lead teams if design thinkers.

Networks of T-Shaped People: Autonomous, Transversal and Pluralist

Every age, it would seem, develops its own characteristic metaphors to describe the natural and social world around them. The machine dominated and defined the industrial age and it is from this time—roughly the middle of the nineteenth to the middle of the twentieth century—that the concept of the machine bureaucracy emerged (Morgan 1986). Here organisations are a hierarchy of moveable parts that need to fit together precisely according to the engineer's design.

Today, it would seem, the defining image is the network. In the past three decades, commentators have pointed out that our institutions and organisations—indeed our societies as whole—are becoming less like machines and more like networks (Pierre and Peters 2000; Castells 1996; Weick and Sutcliffe 2015). As the organisational scholar, Yiannis Gabriel notes, institutions today are

> ...smaller (as far as number of employees go), flatter, looser, more international, more flexible, less centralised, more likely to be in partnerships with other organisations, less pyramid-like, and more network-like (Gabriel 2008 quoted in Weick and Sutcliffe 2015, p. 10).

Design thinking is as much an outcome as it is a driver of the "networked society" (Castells 1996). The changes that have seen networks and network thinking (Weinberg 2015) permeate our lives have created the fertile social, economic as well as ideational soil for the Design Thinking to flourish. And, adopting the mindset and practices of Design Thinking as outlined in the previous chapters is likely to increase these evolutionary pressures towards networked organisation. For this reason, managers and leaders—whether in the public or the private sector—will have to come to terms with these networks. This implies that leadership and management practices need to adapt to these networked organisational features.

What, then, are these features?

Design Thinkers Are Autonomous and Responsible

Chapters 4 and 5 show us that within Design Thinking spaces, output emerges from team-based integrative thinking. For team-based innovation to be effective, Design Thinking requires diverse teams staffed with so-called 'T-Shaped' people (see Fig. 6.2). More importantly, though, effective creative synthesis requires that these teams be equipped with extensive autonomy over what they do and how they go about doing it. At operational level, teams need control over decisions what users (including extreme users) and stakeholders to seek out, engage and observe. At substantive level, Design Thinking teams need the freedom to radically reframe the wicked problem in the light of insights and inspiration from user research. By extension, teams need the space and the autonomy to develop 'clumsy' (and potentially game changing) innovations; or, conversely, they need to be free to pursue less grandiose goals—incremental improvements—if this is what is needed to most effectively address the challenge at hand.

But autonomy is merely one side of the Design Thinking coin. For autonomy to translate into effective designs, people in design-oriented organisations need to accept a significant degree of responsibility for their activities. For Design Thinking to bring about the organisational changes identified in the previous chapters, Design Thinking teams need to take responsibility for the choices they make before, during and after Design Thinking processes. This includes choices concerning research, reframing, idea development or testing. What is more, Design Thinking teams work best if they inculcate a fundamental sense of responsibility in team members for identifying, framing and tackling the wicked challenges that face an organisation. Whether these Design Thinking teams operate in the private, public or citizen sectors, effective design thinkers take an active part in the organisational debates that define institutional challenges and set institutional agendas.

Substantive and operative autonomy enables individual to recognise how wicked problems relate to the realities of given organisational contexts. Responsibility, in turn, empowers and drives individuals to act on these insights. In this sense, then, autonomy and responsibility transforms employees into institutional entrepreneurs or intrapreneurs that spot opportunities, create innovative solutions and implements these solutions (Ney et al. 2014).

Networks of T-Shaped People Cut Across Organisational Boundaries

Teams of autonomous and entrepreneurial T-Shaped people create organisational spaces that cut across disciplinary, departmental, functional or social boundaries. No surprise there: since wicked problems do not conform to the institutional boundaries that have evolved over time, we would expect effective responses to these challenges to breach these borders in order to fuse different forms of knowledge into innovative solutions.

At structural level, as we have seen, Design Thinking ideas and practices cut across several key boundaries. First, the Design Thinking practices of assembling transdisciplinary teams cuts across the organisational chart—both in a formal as well as an informal sense. Done deftly, as with Citrix, Autodesk or Proctor and Gamble (Schmiedgen et al. 2015; Martin 2009a), this carves out alternative organisational structures across the institutional map. In these spaces, the patterns of transactions between members differ from those in other, perhaps more established provinces of the organisational map. As we have seen in previous chapters, Design Thinking teams are most effective when they feature egalitarian and individualist characteristics alongside more traditional hierarchical patterns of transactions.

Second, these boundaries also include the outer organisational borders in which and, somewhat more problematically, across which Design Thinking teams operate. The networks and organisational spaces Design Thinking sets up reach across organisational boundaries into the wider institutional environment in a number of ways. At one end of the spectrum, as we have seen in the preceding chapters, a Design Thinking team's quest for insights in the life-worlds of users and stakeholders sees design thinkers passing back and forth across the external boundaries of their home organisations. This creates conduits into the organisation for perceptions, ideas and, more importantly, the templates or blue-prints for generates a flow of exchange and communication—sometimes immediate, at other times more remote—across organisational boundaries at what we could call 'unsanctioned and unauthorised crossings'. At the other end of the spectrum, Design Thinking teams set up and engage in co-creation and participative design. Here, Design Thinking teams reach out to include users, customer, citizens or stakeholders in the process of team-based integrative thinking.

In this way, then, the networks created by Design Thinking teams leave the boundaries between the organisation and their environment porous and permeable.

Networks of T-Shaped People Are Pluralist and Diverse

As we have seen in Chap. 2, we can think of team-based integrative thinking as a kind of 'genius hack'. Design thinking teams recreate or simulate what genius entrepreneurs and innovators seem to be able to do in their mind: the integration of contending and contradictory concepts into new and innovative solutions to wicked problems. A key precondition for this process of integrative thinking—the raw material, if you will—is a wide and varied reservoir of contending ideas from which Design Thinking teams can forge innovations.

Design thinking teams introduce this diversity and pluralism in organisations along two different pathways. First, a good Design Thinking team consists of a diverse and pluralist group of T-shaped people. This diversity refers as much to the expertise and knowledge (i.e. the stem of the 'T') each team member contributes to the team as it does to the more general capabilities and interests of individual team members (i.e. bar of the 'T'). Good Design Thinking teams bring together a combination of specialisations that lie somewhat awkwardly across boundaries, be they organisational, functional or disciplinary. Empathy with users and stakeholders, as we have seen, requires more that formal skills and expertise. This is why Design Thinking teams profit immensely from members that can draw on experiences from lifeworlds that differ greatly from one another. Significantly, setting up pluralist Design Thinking teams mobilises the variety of formal skills and expertise signified by functional and departmental provinces on the organisational chart. Beyond the 'requisite variety' of disciplinary, functional or departmental diversity, Design Thinking teams also allow the differences that people in organisations usually play down or may even hide in an effort to 'fit in' to surface as individual assets for tackling wicked problems. By emphasising the value of diversity in tackling wicked problems, Design Thinking teams provide a forum and a voice for ideas, perspectives and frames that usually tend to lie dormant in organisations (see also Chap. 5).

Second, creative synthesis requires these teams of diverse design thinkers to go out an delve into the life-worlds of users and stakeholders. Using the methods and approaches of the qualitative social sciences, design teams go out "hunting and gathering" for material to inspire integrative thinking and creative reframing (Plattner et al. 2014). This not only blurs the boundaries between the organisation and the institutional environment (as we discussed in the previous section), these conduits can also widen and deepen diversity and pluralism in the organisation. For one, Design Thinking teams bring back new, foreign and probably strange ideas and perspectives from their expeditions into the life-worlds of users and stakeholders. This, in turn, enriches and deepens the reservoir of ideas, perspectives and frames available for creative synthesis. More importantly, it also increases the plurality of voices in organisational deliberation about wicked problems. During the process of creative reframing, Design Thinking teams become advocates for the views, perspectives and frames of users. The degree of advocacy in organisations varies. Design thinking teams become advocates for user and stakeholder needs by adopting, working with and, inevitably, defending personas based on insights from fieldwork. In co-creation and co-design, the advocates are actual customers, users and stakeholders that are part of the Design Thinking team. In either case, the exploration of Design Thinking teams not only increases the pool of ideas, perspectives and frames, it also give rise to organisational constituencies that will advocate contending positions in institutional deliberation and debate.

In sum and as we have seen in Chaps. 4, 5, and 6, setting up diverse teams of T-shaped people is likely to increase the plurality and diversity of an organisation. The value that Design Thinking mindsets and practices place on diversity is likely not only to mobilise the 'formal' or explicit pluralism within an organisation, it may also encourage the emergence of latent and informal diversity within institutions. In addition to mobilising the diversity present in large organisations, Design Thinking teams invite user and stakeholder views into the organisation.

Leadership Challenges and Opportunities

What leadership challenges do autonomous and responsible T-Shaped people, transversal socio-institutional spaces, increased pluralism and diversity give rise to? How can leaders of Design Thinking teams respond to these challenges?

Coming to terms with more autonomous, transversal and pluralist institutional networks requires that leaders of design-based organisations focus on three broad areas of activity. First, since networks are inhabited with autonomous teams of T-Shaped individuals, managers need to find ways of *enabling collaboration*. Second, transversality and pluralism lay down the gauntlet for leaders to *make sense of ambiguities*. Third, in networks of diverse and pluralist T-Shaped design thinkers, leadership must find ways to *encourage constructive conflict*.

We will discuss each in turn.

Enabling Collaboration

If Design Thinking teams are to innovate, they need considerable autonomy in what they choose to do and how they choose to do it. Yet, granting this level of autonomy to teams is likely to change the complexion of organisations predominantly geared toward 'reliability' (Martin 2009b) or 'exploitation' (March 1991). Drawing on the work of the political scientist Hal Colebatch, we can think of this change as a shift in the orientation from a 'vertical' to a more 'horizontal' mode of organising (Colebatch 2009).

In 'vertical' organisation, modelled on "authorised decision-making", things get done by command and control. Here, the top of the organisation—the proper locus of requisite expertise and authority—sets goals, objectives and policies which are then passed down to the 'bottom' or the 'frontline' for implementation. The paradigmatic cases—Max Weber's vision of a line bureaucracy, Henry Ford's production process or Taylor's scientific managers—break down challenges into their component parts and assigns each of these parts to specialised departments. Managers need not only to envisage the output, they also need to define and oversee the different activities to ensure that each component part fits seamlessly to make up a product (or problem solution). In short, the top defines the problems, breaks down the tasks, hands these tasks to specialist departments and makes sure that each department does its assigned task as efficiently as possible.

The practices of effective Design Thinking teams, however, are likely to sit rather awkwardly in vertical management regimes. Take, as an example, the way Design Thinking teams relate to the design challenge. Unlike vertical management practices, it is the team (rather than the management or leadership) that comes to 'own' the challenge; indeed, an integral part of the creative reframing consist of the team appropriating the design challenge (Kolko 2010). Further, rather than working on a specialised aspects of problems, Design Thinking teams tackle challenges holistically. They do not to develop part of a solution and 'throw it over the wall' to the next department; instead, Design Thinking teams will actively seek to breach this wall. What is more, the solution evolves as team members move back and forth across these boundaries.

In this way, then, the autonomy of Design Thinking teams creates what Colebatch calls 'horizontal' relationships within organisations (Colebatch 2009). Unlike vertical forms of organisation, horizontal forms of 'structured interaction' offer management far fewer direct levers of control. As we saw in Chap. 6, management tools such as rigid reporting and control practices would, at best, considerably slow down team-based integrative thinking. At worst, attempts by management of determining what is and what is not relevant to the design challenge risk alienating members of the Design Thinking team. Indeed, the tighter the controls leaders wish to impose, the less effective creative synthesis in the teams is likely to be. This is precisely what happens, Schmiedgen et al. argue, when leaders apply inappropriate measures—meaning performance indicators designed to measure 'exploitation' rather than 'exploration'—to the activities, outputs and outcomes of Design Thinking teams: their research suggests that measuring fledgeling Design Thinking activities in terms of financial indicators "...might stifle any display of innovation behaviour right from the beginning..." (Schmiedgen et al. 2015).

In organisations featuring horizontal relations, things get done by encouraging collaboration. Specifically, design-led horizontal management revolves around defining broad outcomes (e.g. the reduction of the digital divide), assembling and assigning teams, creating a fertile environment for the team to operate and, most importantly, negotiating with the team as well as with the organisation as a whole as the project unfolds. This collaboration takes place at three interdependent levels:

- at the level of individual Design Thinking teams;
- at the level of several Design Thinking teams;
- at the level of managing, coordinating, and mediating between Design Thinking teams and other organisational units.

At the team level, leadership enables collaboration by creating and sustaining environments—both material and immaterial—for Design Thinking teams to operate effectively. Sustaining collaborative environments means that managers support Design Thinking teams. As we saw in Chap. 4, 5 and 6, not only do managers need to protect social spaces for Design Thinking teams, they also require sound judgement of what Design Thinking teams need at any particular point in the Design Thinking process. Sound judgement, in turn, depends on leaders' ability to read and interpret of the outputs (i.e. the innovations and insights) that emerge from Design Thinking teams. This implies that managers be capable of understanding and gauging the development and progress of Design Thinking teams. In this way, coaches and managers can strategically tailor suitable interventions from the reservoir of diverse (i.e. messy) practices.

At the level of several Design Thinking teams, coordination is also about enabling collaboration. With several Design Thinking teams, managers need to strike a balance between encouraging competition while simultaneously ensuring cooperation between Design Thinking teams. A key task for leaders and managers here is to set-up spaces and processes for cooperation. Furthermore, managers need to support teams with the identification of areas, themes and times when cooperation between Design Thinking teams is meaningful. Of course, good leadership of Design Thinking teams also involves laying out and, more importantly, policing rules that regulate the interaction between teams.

At the organisational level, enabling collaboration calls for advocacy. Here, leaders need to mediate a wide variety of different organisational structures (as well as ideas and practices). In pluralist and networked organisations, this involves brokering, enabling and motivating effective coalitions of institutional actors. Good leadership is as much about sustaining these coalitions as it is about setting them up. Leadership tasks here include supporting actors in identifying wicked challenges (and messy opportunities), formulating goals and visions as well as setting agendas. However, given the pluralist character of messy organisations, leadership becomes a question of helping coalitions devise challenges and agendas that inspire collaboration across organisational units. What is more, autonomous and responsible design thinkers look to managers to install the requisite organisational structures and practices that enable cooperation across pluralist organisational units.

At all three levels, effective leadership of collaboration is based on a constructive conversation between different, possibly contending institutional constituencies.

Since innovations in Design Thinking result from 'team-based integrative thinking', negotiation and facilitation becomes a key task for design-based leadership. At the team-level, Chap. 6 has shown that team members need to maintain an ongoing critical yet supportive conversation about the state and development of the team. At the level of several Design Thinking teams, leadership depends on functioning channels of communication between competing and cooperating Design Thinking teams as well as between teams and management. Last, institutional coalition-building between pluralist and autonomous organisational units also requires an ongoing debate that needs to be set-up and nurtured very carefully. The key here is that these conversations in the deliberative arenas remain open-ended and geared towards institutional learning.

Making Sense of Ambiguity

Experimentation is, by definition, an open-ended process. Additionally, as we saw in the previous section, autonomous Design Thinking teams largely elude conventional vertical controls. Whatever else it does, the integrating of Design Thinking into an organisation is unlikely to increase predictability (Cross 2011; Schmiedgen et al. 2015). While this is, of course, as it should be, this unpredictability and ambiguity gives rise to management challenges at two levels.

First, in terms of organisational structures, Design Thinking ideas and practices potentially generate variegated and ever-changing institutional landscapes within and beyond organisations. By reaching beyond organisations into wider institutional environments, Design Thinking teams create pathways into (and out of) organisations. But these institutional environments themselves have become increasingly networked and interdependent. This means that the institutional landscapes in which large organisations find themselves are increasingly rugged and variegated terrains. Large firms and enterprises no longer operate in markets consisting solely of other enterprises and customers. Similarly, large public organisations no longer deal only with other public organisations and citizens (Rhodes 1997; Pierre and Peters 2000; Ney 2009). In both cases, large organisations—enterprises as well as large public institutions—are opening portals to highly variegated institutional environments populated with enterprises, SME's, and start-ups, but also NGOs and social entrepreneurs. Most importantly, individuals are no longer just consumers (to firms) or citizens (to public service providers) but will act out both roles, it would seem, indiscriminately. Increasingly, people want to engage with large enterprises as concerned citizens, that is as bearers of political and civil rights. By the same token, public sector organisations—particularly service providers—are finding themselves increasingly confronted with people (more often than not disgruntled) demanding to be treated and valued as customers. By moving back and forth across organisational boundaries, Design Thinking teams import this complexity, unpredictability and ambiguity from the environment into the organisation.

Second, at the substantive level, Design Thinking is a method for tackling wicked problems through redefinition and reframing. In fact, problem-solving in Design Thinking is predicated on recasting the initial design challenge (see Chaps. 2 and 3). Reframing relies on insights gleaned from the lifeworlds of users and stakeholders. These insights are then refracted through the different "perceptual lenses" that each member brings to the team (Allison 1971). For this reason, perceptions of challenges, problems and potential solution spaces can evolve in entirely unpredictable directions as Design Thinking teams frame and reframe challenges (Dorst 2015; Cross 2011).

How are managers and leaders to handle this ambiguity? We can think of the outputs of Design Thinking teams—prototypes, innovations or insights—as signals or messages that teams bring back from the complex institutional environments and lifeworlds. Leaders and managers listen to these messages in the socio-institutional spaces they create in the organisation. These messages tell us about user and stakeholder needs, patterns of behaviour, contending perceptions and beliefs, as well as challenges and opportunities for innovation. But these messages are 'coded': if Design Thinking teams are doing their job, their outputs are not ready-made solutions that comfortably slot into existing organisational structures, ideas and practices. Decoding these messages means that managers and leaders need to work through the potential ramifications of design-driven insights for wider organisational structures, goals and practices. Much like Design Thinking teams during creative synthesis, then, managers need to *make sense* of the insights and innovations that surface from Design Thinking teams.

The outcomes of sense-making are rarely obvious and are difficult to predict. They may affect the very foundations of an organisation (which, in a way, is the point of promoting disruptive innovations). For example, a large logistics company asked a student team at the D-School in Potsdam to tackle the problem of delivering post and parcels in a future of increasingly pedestrianised urban centres. The team's solution was as disruptive as it was simple: they suggested encouraging city dwellers to deliver packages as they go about their everyday business along the paths and routes that they carve through urban spaces. A senior executive is reputed to have remarked that this idea would fundamentally transform the character of the company: instead of being in the business of delivering packages, it would now manage, incentivise and oversee the network of citizens-deliverers (see Box 3.1). Similarly, Christian Bason recounts how horizontal design teams helped reorient the very basic operating assumptions of the Danish tax office (Bason 2010). Traditionally, tax authorities in Denmark (as well as, it is probably safe to say, much of the rest of Europe) assume that people are basically dishonest. This is why, so the argument goes, we need strong institutions to coerce dishonest citizens to pay taxes (a view of human nature that strongly resonates with hierarchical institutions, see Chap. 3). Instead, design-led innovators suggested that the tax office reverse its assumptions: most citizens actually see the sense in contributing to society (by paying taxes) and only a very few people will try to avoid contributing. This simple reframing of the issue has had profound implications not only for the way the Danish tax office conducts their business but also for the identity of the institution itself (Bason 2010).

Now, the tax office has made it easier for the law-abiding citizens to pay taxes and can concentrate their efforts (and resources) to apprehend and prosecute the few that evade taxes (Bason 2010).

The outputs of Design Thinking teams, then, tell stories that contain valuable insights about organisations and their place in the wider institutional environment. Insights, no less, that would otherwise probably not be readily available to these organisations. However, turning these insights and innovations into workable institutional solutions means that leadership needs to listen carefully to these stories and reflect on what they are hearing. Unfortunately, the structures and practices of most large organisations militate against this type of careful listening and reflection. For people working in large organisations, ambiguity and unpredictability tend to be acutely uncomfortable. Institutions generate immense pressures on people to banish—rather than embrace—ambiguity and uncertainty. In part, time-budgets to satisfy the needs of what the Germans call the *Tagesgeschäft*—the daily struggle to keep operations ticking over efficiently—curtails the appetite for exploring ambiguity with few predictable outcomes. In short, managers in large organisations often simply do not have the time or the patience to listen for signals and insights in the stories of Design Thinking teams.

But listening to these messages is only the necessary condition. Managers and leaders also need to be able to *make sense* of what they are hearing. Again, the set-up in many large organisations is often not very conducive to this type of reflection. Large institutions do not provide actors with the cognitive and normative resources—meaning a plurality of frames—to explore *contending* implications of the stories that Design Thinking teams tell organisations. As a result, even if they are listening, organisational actors are under pressure to transform ambiguity—with all its potential opportunities—into operable certainties. This is done by forcing innovations and insights into readily available and well-worn (indeed, often worn-out) interpretative templates.

Yet, reducing ambiguities to one of the "contradictory certitudes" (Thompson and Ney 2000) on the Cultural Map (see Chap. 4) exposes sense-making to the frame-specific blind-spots and vulnerabilities identified in previous chapters. Hierarchical frames will rely on authoritative expertise and discount other, possibly more relevant insights. "How does this reflect what our R&D department tells us and how does it fit into our standard operating procedures?" they are likely to ask. Individualist frames will look for a tangible bottom-line in messages and dismiss other insights as frivolously fanciful. "How is this going to make us money?", output-oriented actors will ask. Egalitarian perceptual lenses will foreground issues of equity and justice to the detriment of more pragmatic messages in the stories. "How does this idea promote equality and strengthen social cohesion at the workplace?". Fatalist frames, essentially a "council of despair" (Verweij 2011), dismiss any message as random noise. "How is this different from any of the other ideas (that have, inevitably, failed)?". These are, of course, very good and important questions to ask of an insight or innovation. However, relying on any single question introduces a particular bias that creates awareness for certain signals but dulls the (collective) senses to others.

The impacts of reducing uncomfortable (but pluralist) ambiguities to familiar (but selective) certainty this way can be profound. Karl Weick and Kathleen Sutcliffe argue that organisations eager to assimilate ambiguous messages into dominant organisational cultures are unlikely to pick up what they refer to as "weak signals of failure" (Weick and Sutcliffe 2015). The two organisational scholars show how an inability to perceive these weak signals coupled with an eagerness explain away those signals that are perceived potentially leads to catastrophic outcomes for so-called *High-Reliability Organisations* (such as aircraft carriers or firefighters). However, they suggest that much the same is true for other types of organisations. Leaders who do not or cannot listen and that are quick to integrate messages into existing frames may very well miss opportunities for solving wicked problems.

Preventing mistakes and seizing these opportunities, then, involves using the deliberative arenas and ongoing organisational conversations to elicit, listen to and make sense of the ambiguous messages that Design Thinking teams bring home. This, in turn, will require managers to cultivate *a mindset of patience* as well as *a set of reflective practices*. First, leaders of design-oriented organisations will need to develop the ability to endure ambiguity and uncertainty as design projects unfold characterises (Cross 2011). This patience with uncertainty, this willingness to leave potential pathways suspended but available, the design researcher Nigel Cross contends, is a characteristic of leading designers (Cross 2011). What is more, Schmiedgen et al. have shown that managers in successful design-driven organisations—often with a background in design—understand this ambiguity and uncertainty to be part of the innovation process (Schmiedgen et al. 2015). Second, inculcating a 'reluctance to simplify' not only involves preventing would-be leaders from forcing messages into familiar frames but also providing them with a "requisite variety" of alternative frames and interpretative templates (Weick and Sutcliffe 2015). An effective way of ensuring this type of frame reflexivity is to encourage critical, frame-based debates within organisational conversations and deliberative arenas.

How, then, can leaders promote this critical debate?

Encouraging Constructive Conflict

Design thinking practices can potentially set up profoundly pluralist organisations, something that we have called 'messy institutions' (see Chap. 3). Not only do messy institutions embrace the diversity of people and ideas, they demand that the diversity of frames be applied and reapplied to wicked design challenges. If done properly, this generates a wide and rich reservoir of diverse ideas and practices (see Chap. 5). Design thinking teams turn to this reservoir for inspiration when engaging in team-based integrative thinking.

However, ideas and frames within the reservoir are fundamentally incompatible with one another. As we saw in Chap. 3, they originate in and are designed to support fundamentally incommensurate patterns of social relations. Recall that these frames are cognitive as well as normative resources that enable individuals to make sense of wicked challenges (see Chap. 2). They help organisational actors construct plausible, yet inherently selective, accounts of what is and, more importantly, what ought to be going on. What is more, since these frames emerge from contending ways of organising, they socially construct the world in contradistinction to one another.

Team-based integrative thinking (Martin 2009a) involves bringing these contending frames to bear on wicked problems using the Design Thinking process (see Chap. 6). Invariably, this means that—sooner or later—contending frames will create tensions within and possibly, beyond, Design Thinking teams. This, of course, is a good thing. Tensions that emerge from applying contending frames to wicked problems are the very stuff of team-based integrative thinking (see also Cross 2011). Tensions are the gateways and conduits of creative synthesis. They are the channels through which Design Thinking teams become aware of and can reflect on the inbuilt blind-spots and vulnerabilities of frame-based perception. At the same time, the articulation of tensions—through disagreement and conflict in deliberative processes—is an inextricable part of integrative thinking because it points to the potential sites of creative synthesis: it is at points of conflicts (and potential deadlock) that reframing and innovation can keep problem-solving processes moving.

Yet, important as it is, frame-based conflict is a fragile resource. These types of conflicts have no resolution, if resolution means "result" or "solution" or a finding on which contending parties can agree. For one, as we have seen, the different cognitive and normative resources provided by organisational cultures lead to conflicting accounts of wicked problems. These accounts help actors tell persuasive stories that identify causalities, point to responsibilities and apportion blame in very different ways. Accounts of wicked problems (and their solutions) rely on facts and knowledge, albeit, as we have seen, on a selection of 'relevant' or 'salient' facts. Furnishing further or other facts—no matter how objective, rational or scientific—cannot resolve a frame-based dispute. This is because, as the sociologists Martin Rein and Donald Schön argue, individuals use frames to guide the selection of facts and help determine 'relevance' and 'salience' for the particular wicked problem at hand (Rein and Schön 1994). Actors use these frames to construct very different stories about wicked problems. In this sense, then, frames not only guide us in determining what facts are relevant but what is to count as a facts at all (Rein and Schön 1994). For this reason, then, conflicts about wicked problems are not amenable to resolution by recourse to authoritative knowledge—indeed, insistence on the objectivity and authority of facts is likely to fan the flames of contention.

While frame-based tensions drive creative synthesis, there is also a very real risk that frame-based conflict about wicked problems become what Martin Rein and Donald Schön have called 'intractable' (Rein and Schön 1994). This means, the scholars tell us, that frame-based conflicts become "...enduring, relatively immune to resolution by reference to evidence, and seldom finally resolved" (Rein and Schön 1994). Intractable controversies render debate and deliberation little more than a "dialogue of the deaf" in which contending parties look to defend their values and their ways-of-life (Sabatier and Jenkins-Smith 1993).

Sadly, examples for intractable policy controversies abound. In the public sphere, where, of course, intractable policy controversies are a matter of public record, we need only to look at debates on immigration or education in Europe and abortion or gun control in the USA. These debates feature persistent and divisive conflict which seems to lead to stronger polarisation of positions in the controversy. Often, controversies are punctuated by executive decisions—say the financial crisis of 2008 or the Euro crisis in the summer of 2015—that manage to shunt the issue off the political agenda for a while (Baumgartner and Jones 1993). Invariably, however, these issues resurface, often with renewed vigour, deeper trenches and more venom.

The private sector is not all that different. As we saw in the previous section, frame-based conflicts about wicked problems no longer respect sectoral boundaries. The private sector has become an active player in public debates about messy policy challenges such as transport, the environment or even social issues. Likewise, civil society and the public sector are making claims in what would seem, at first glance, to be issues internal to companies. For example, the events concerning the suspicions of fraud on environmental automobile tests at the German car manufacturer Volkswagen demonstrate how internal processes and the culture of control has had uncontrollable repercussions outside the company.

Once frame-based conflict deteriorates into intractability, it can no longer support creative synthesis. Team-based integrative thinking is about learning from the application of contending frames to wicked problems (c.f. Dorst 2015; Martin 2009b). As we saw in the previous section, this depends on ability of actors to listen to conflicting arguments and critically reflect their own assumptions in the light of what they have heard (Weick and Sutcliffe 2015). When institutions engage in this type of collective cogitation, we can, following the political scientist Hugh Heclo, think of them as 'puzzling' (Heclo 1974). Here, puzzling is an open-ended inquiry in which contending parties are not primary pursuing their interests and defending their core values. Puzzling, figuring out what the institution ought to do next, is an integral part of 'experimentation' within an organisation (March 1991).

Intractable conflicts, however, evolve when actors believe cherished values and their ways-of-life to be at risk (Fuller and Myers 1941; Douglas 1992). Here, debate and deliberation no longer aim at exploring wicked problems to find new, possibly innovative solutions. Instead, parties to an intractable policy controversy mobilise available rhetorical resources to apportion blame for the wicked problem to contending parties and claim credit themselves for solving it (Rein and Schön 1994; Ney 2009; Pierson 1996; Stone 1997). Here, information, facts and knowledge are little more than a weapon in the rhetorical arsenal to be strategically deployed for maximum impact. And that impact is the defence of existing organisational structures, ideas and practices. In contrast to 'puzzling', Heclo called this strategic organisational activity 'powering'. Since powering is about strategically and rationally deploying resources to pursue (clearly perceived and ranked) objectives, it contributes to the 'exploitation' activities of an organisation.

Enabling constructive conflict, then, involves ensuring that frame-based tensions and debates do not deteriorate into an 'intractable policy controversies'. This, in turn, requires that managers and leaders nurture 'puzzling' and discourage 'powering' when working on wicked problems. But what causes powering? Perhaps somewhat counterintuitively, narrowing the scope of conflict by limiting exploration to certain persons or groups in an organisations (say, the tinkers from engineering, the creative types from the design department or the boffins from R&D) is likely to spark strategic behaviour and powering. While excluding from problem-solving the people who typically ask uncomfortable and awkward questions may make for a smooth and consensual discussion, it also could set off a vicious cycle of polarisation and powering. As we have seen, relying solely on any particular frame risks designing the characteristic weaknesses and vulnerabilities of this perspective into innovations. What is more, the perceptual lenses of contending (and excluded) organisational cultures would have enabled people in the design process to identify and correct these vulnerabilities. As solutions fail to live up to expectations (or, depending on one's perceptual lenses, perform exactly as expected), the debate is likely to become increasingly polarised. On the one hand, excluded constituencies will look to apportion blame ("if you had only asked, we could have told you long ago that this solution is unworkable"). On the other hand, the parties responsible for the solution will seek to defend their accomplishments ("Why didn't you then? And anyway, these 'problems' you keep pointing out are minor issues and, over all, this solution is a great success"). The more the positions polarise, the less the incentive for any party in the dispute to adopt a constructive approach to deliberation: the rational strategy for the excluded is to point out vulnerabilities and weaknesses thus encouraging those responsible for the innovation to defend their solution and play down concerns. Significantly, the more the debate polarises, the 'louder' the excluded parties are likely to become. This, then, kicks off the vicious spiral that, if left unchecked, leads to intractable controversies.

Preventing polarisation and powering, then, means ensuring that sense-making in ongoing organisational conversations can draw on the insights from a 'requisite variety' of frames (Weick and Sutcliffe 2015; Thompson et al. 1990). For leaders and managers of these deliberative spaces, this means two things. First, the deliberative spaces in which sense-making about the insights and outputs of Design Thinking teams takes place need to be open to this 'requisite variety' of perspectives and frames. In other words, these need to reflect a 'messy' conversation including frames and perspectives from each province of the Cultural Map (see Chap. 3). Second, managers and leaders need to ensure that these perspectives engage constructively in sense-making and debate. This means setting up processes and procedures that ensure responsiveness.

In sum, dealing with the management challenges that emerge when integrating Design Thinking practices into an organisation involves three types of activities. First, since the autonomy of Design Thinking teams undercuts more conventional 'vertical' form of control, would-be leaders need to find ways of enabling and supporting collaboration between T-shaped people, their teams as well as between Design Thinking teams and other actors in the institutional environment. Second, leaders can tackle the inherent ambiguity that seems to emerge from Design Thinking teams by engaging in reflexive and 'messy' sense-making. Just like Design Thinking teams listen closely to and observe users and stakeholders, leaders can only make sense of Design Thinking outputs if they listen and reflect on the stories that emerge from Design Thinking teams. Sense-making can lead to sound judgement if it avoids the inherent weaknesses and vulnerabilities of any particular frame; in short, like members of Design Thinking teams, managers and leaders need to practice 'messy' frame reflection. Third, protecting the fragile resource of constructive conflict involves avoiding organisational paralysis of polarisation without curtailing the reservoir of ideas and frames.

Each of these activities involves both setting-up and protecting the suitable environments (for collaboration, messy sense-making and constructive conflict) as well as sustaining an ongoing conversation or deliberation within the institution. Environments that enable collaboration between autonomous yet responsible T-Shape people include physical and virtual spaces (see Chap. 4) as well as the processes that help Design Thinking teams innovate (see Chap. 6).

Engaging with Design Thinking

Setting-up and, more importantly, sustaining the suitable spaces for collaboration, sense-making and constructive conflict requires that managers or Design Thinking Guardians engage with and immerse into Design Thinking at three interrelated levels. First, at the individual level, understanding and making sense of what emerges from Design Thinking teams, managers and leaders be knowledgeable about Design Thinking. Second, effective leadership of Design Thinking teams involves actually applying Design Thinking practices at leadership level.

We will discuss each in turn.

Experiencing Design Thinking

Effective management of Design Thinking teams presupposes ability to empathise with teams at any stage of the Design Thinking process. This includes an awareness of the methods and mindsets of Design Thinking and how they work. However, leaders not only have to make sense of what outputs emerge from Design Thinking teams. Sustaining Design Thinking environments within institutions also implies that leaders are capable of understanding and making sense of what *is emergent* in Design Thinking teams. Over and above making sense and interpreting the artefacts and insights that Design Thinking teams produce, effective leadership rests on an appreciation of the pathways, possibilities and potential outcomes implicit in ambiguity of the visions and insights that Design Thinking teams bring home. What is more, this appreciation needs to be credible, not least to critically challenge and inspire these teams, as well as plausible, in order to communicate these visions to other people in the organisation. This, as Schmiedgen et al. argue, is more likely the more managers have themselves experienced Design Thinking and worked in a Design Thinking team (Schmiedgen et al. 2015).

This goes far beyond the fairly standard injunction that efforts to reform or change an organisation needs to secure commitment and support from management. Schmiedgen et al. point out that instances of successful implementation all featured management that "...either have design capabilities or they acknowledge and know how to lead Design Thinking teams" (Schmiedgen et al. 2015). In these companies, they continue, "...it is natural that the CEO also has to live mindset: 'You have to experience it in order to understand it. We can talk about it. But you actually have to do it...'" (Schmiedgen et al. 2015). The research team suggests that where sense-making leads, infrastructural support (most notably funding) for design teams will follow. Conversely, cases in which of Design Thinking failed to take hold in organisations tend to feature lonely Design Thinking pioneers that "...often struggled to explain the value of Design Thinking to their leadership, which was not willing to experience it themselves" (Schmiedgen et al. 2015). Successful integration and adoption of Design Thinking into large organisations, then, rests on the commitment of managers and leaders to become T-Shaped themselves and immerse in the practices and mindsets of Design Thinking.

Hands-on Management

If you want to be a manager of Design Thinking teams, Annie Kerguenne of the HPI School of Design Thinking suggests "getting your hands dirty". At the HPI School of Design Thinking, a key principle is to 'teach teams with teams'. Here, the team of teachers uses methods of Design Thinking to develop teaching content for the students. What is more, the teaching and coaching team also applies similar team-building processes and methods to secure cohesion to those they teach students. By the same token, in Schmiedgen et al.'s study of the implementation of Design Thinking in organisations, it was the successful cases in which "...it was the task of management to provide directions and project visions, to facilitate brainstorming or synthesis sessions and to coordinate the different team roles" (Schmiedgen et al. 2015). For these organisations, "Design Thinking *is* management" (Schmiedgen et al. 2015).

For management to get their hands dirty with Design Thinking means three things. For one, reproducing the practices and ideas of Design Thinking teams implies opening management teams to a plurality of frames. This may mean that management teams be composed of transdisciplinary T-Shaped persons or that leadership finds ways of making these frames and perspectives available for institutional sense-making (or, ideally, both). This prevents leadership teams from unduly simplifying the stories that Design Thinking teams tell (Weick and Sutcliffe 2015). Messy frame reflection, then, enables management teams to explore the implications of Design Thinking innovations and insights without falling prey to the vulnerabilities and blindspots of individual frames. Further, management teams need, in one form or another, to adopt the 'messy' practices of participation, deliberation and decision-making that guide Design Thinking teams to innovation (discussed in Chap. 6, see also Grint 2010). For one, the typology of frames enables management teams to engage in reflexive interpretation of artefacts, insights and innovations that emerge from Design Thinking teams. What is more, applying a judicious—meaning 'messy'—combination of methods and procedures to management processes will ensure that things get done competently (hierarchy), efficiently (market) and yet without excluding any voices (egalitarianism) or being above exploiting a windfall (fatalism).

Tailoring Design Thinking

Last, the management of Design Thinking teams also requires conceptual engagement with the methods and mindsets of Design Thinking. As Schmiedgen et al. suggest, organisations are more likely to benefit from Design Thinking the closer they integrate Design Thinking teams into the organisational structure (Schmiedgen et al. 2015). Perhaps unsurprisingly, then, the researchers find that people working in organisations that embrace Design Thinking at their core or as an intrinsic practice can readily point to both the impacts on as well as the benefits of Design Thinking for their institutions. Conversely, wherever Design Thinking is peripheral or contained in a specific department, organisational actors are far more equivocal concerning the organisational impacts, let alone benefits of Design Thinking.

Key to the successful integration of Design Thinking within an organisation, Schmiedgen et al. surmise, is the way organisational actors appropriate Design Thinking and adapt the practices to the particular institutional circumstances (Schmiedgen et al. 2015). Organisations that deploy Design Thinking successfully—be it for product and service innovation, institutional development or strategic decision-making—usually have adapted the methods and mindsets in all three dimensions with respect to the particular institutional context as well as the wider organisational environment. This can start as modestly as coining a new name for the Design Thinking practices (e.g. Jantrix at the German pharmaceutical business Jansen-Cilag or the Design for Delight programme at Intuit Labs). Alternatively, organisations may allow new ways of appropriating spaces for Design Thinking to evolve. For example, the Open Lab in Stockholm—an innovation lab geared towards developing ideas for the public and citizen sectors—has designed whiteboards on moveable racks each project team. Teams also store their materials in chests at the base of the scaffolding. This, then, allows the lab to maximise its relatively limited space.

Significantly, organisations also adapt methods and processes. The evolution of methods and tools occurs in three interrelated ways. First, organisations tailor Design Thinking though *selection*. By putting together a specific toolbox by selecting from the 'library' of Design Thinking methods and tools, managers of Design Thinking teams in organisations customise the practices to the strengths (and weaknesses) of people in the organisation. As we saw in Chap. 6, this may mean emphasising methods and approaches familiar to people in the organisations that nonetheless enable the experience, exploration and application of the mindsets of Design Thinking. For example design thinkers in a very large former public utility in Germany—a rather hierarchical organisation—rely extensively on templates to enable team-based integrative thinking (i.e. filling in forms). Another way of selecting methods is to look for overlaps with existing creativity and productivity practices. For example, organisations in operating in ICT and software production may want to look for and exploit existing synergies with methods from approaches such as Scrum, Agile or Lean. Second, organisations appropriate Design Thinking practices by changing or tweaking the methods to better suit their organisational environments. Tweaks or hacks may encompass the entire Design Thinking process. Organisational actors realign basic exercises to ensure relevance with organisational aims and missions. Tweaking and hacking can also includes the Design Thinking process itself. Last, organisations (or, more precisely, people in organisations) devise, develop and test new tools and methods.

Finally, integrating Design Thinking in an organisations also requires adapting practices for putting together, sustaining and managing design teams. In a very real sense, the building, fostering and management of Design Thinking teams are key management activities for strategically integrating Design Thinking in organisations. Here, managers and would-be leaders of Design Thinking teams need to adopt a two-pronged strategy. One the one hand, Design Thinking teams—their composition, their activities and their management—are well placed to address and overcome perceived problems and weaknesses in the organisational culture. Often, these include issues such as a silo-mentality that undermines effective collaboration and innovation or vertical structures that encourage a "deference to authority" therefore preventing decisions, as Weick and Sutcliffe phrase it, "migrating to the expertise" (Weick and Sutcliffe 2015). Managers and leaders, then, ought to ensure that Design Thinking teams address these issues. On the other hand, the introduction of structures, ideas and practices radically juxtaposed to existing institutional ways-of-life may alienate the very organisational actors needed to make Design Thinking a success. In particular, as we saw in Chap. 3, Design Thinking teams are about mobilising the inherent *plurality of competence* inherent in large organisations. Alienating carriers of key competences through team constellations and practices that fail to engage these organisational actors is likely to be counter-productive.

Striking a balance between team practices that engage but also challenge prevalent organisational cultures points to a wider issue. Schmiedgen et al.'s work implies that, if they are not to languish in some remote organisational backwater, the ideas and practices of Design Thinking need to connect to the existing institutional ways-of-life (Schmiedgen et al. 2015). Customisation of Design Thinking, therefore, has to *engage* with existing cultural practices. Engagement here means that managers and leaders identify existing practices and ideas that contribute and strengthen Design Thinking teams. Yet, at the same time, tailoring the methods and mindsets of Design Thinking should not end with the assimilation or submission of Design Thinking to dominant institutional ideas and practices. The reproduction of perceived organisational ailments—such as a silo-mentality, an inability to collaborate or a deference to authority rather than expertise—in Design Thinking teams is probably as clear an indication as any that Design Thinking is not working. The adaptation of Design Thinking, then, needs to find ways of *challenging* existing institutional cultures, or at least the aspects of these cultures that get in the way of tackling wicked problems by creative synthesis. And a crafty way of identifying and addressing these issues is in a user-centric manner: which means finding out about peoples' experiences—both bad and good— in the organisation.

Conclusion

If Design Thinking is to make a lasting impression on innovation and problem-solving in organisations, it is important to integrate the mindsets and practices of Design Thinking into organisational cultures. As Schmiedgen et al. (2015) as well as the preceding chapters show isolating Design Thinking from the goings-on in the rest of the organisation is unlikely to yield desired innovative benefit (Schmiedgen et al. 2015). However, integrating Design Thinking brings about changes to organisations that give rise to specific leadership and management challenges.

Design thinking is a potential catalysts for the emergence of autonomous, transversal and pluralist networks within and beyond organisations. As we have seen, for Design Thinking to generate innovations, teams need considerable autonomy at both operational and substantive level. Further, Design Thinking teams cut across boundaries; this applies both to boundaries within organisations (e.g. departmental or functional boundaries) as well as borders between the organisation and its institutional environment. Last, Design Thinking teams increase the diversity and pluralism of ideas within organisations, both by mobilising diversity within the organisation as well as bringing in new ideas from the life-worlds of users and stakeholders.

These characteristics give rise to specific management and leadership challenges. First, networks consisting of autonomous teams of T-Shaped design thinkers are likely to elude conventional methods of vertical control. As we saw, the autonomy of Design Thinking teams shifts the orientation of an organisation away from vertical models of command and control towards more horizontal approaches of cooperation and negotiation. In networks of autonomous Design Thinking teams, managers and leaders need to *enable collaboration* if the want to get anything done. Leadership in networked organisations means setting up and maintaining spaces—both actual and virtual—that make effective cooperation possible within Design Thinking teams, between different Design Thinking teams as well as between Design Thinking teams and other units in the organisation. These spaces or deliberative arenas need to support and sustain an ongoing organisational conversation about how best to tackle the wicked problems the organisation faces. Second, design-driven and networked organisations are likely to generate more rather than less ambiguity about how best to respond to complex and uncertain challenges. Managers and leaders—the Design Thinking Guardians—need to *make sense of ambiguity* inherent in the messages and stories that Design Thinking teams bring home. As we have seen, leaders need to resist the considerable organisational pressures for banishing uncertainty by either not listening carefully or by hastily subsuming messages in existing (but not always appropriate) interpretative templates. Inculcating what Weick and Sutcliffe call the 'reluctance to simplify', calls for the cultivation of *patience* as well as the ability to engage in *critical frame reflection* (Weick and Sutcliffe 2015). Third, growing the diversity of ideas and perspectives in an organisation increases the likelihood of conflict. While tensions drive team-based integrative thinking, frame-based conflict is a fragile resource. Based on fundamentally incompatible framings, deliberation about wicked problems risk deteriorating into a so-called 'intractable controversy'. Here, strategic rhetorical strategies—something we (following Hugh Heclo) have called 'powering'—displace organisational learning and exploration—something we have called 'puzzling'. Managers and leaders of networked Design Thinking teams, then, need to *encourage constructive conflict* by enabling and managing a 'messy' conversation in collaborative spaces. 'Institutional messiness', as we have seen in previous chapters, means not only including but actively engaging contending frames and perspectives in problem-solving.

However, enabling collaboration, making sense of ambiguity as well as encouraging constructive conflict require that leaders actively engage with the ideas and practices of Design Thinking at three level. First, at the individual levels, effective management of Design Thinking teams presupposes a practical knowledge of Design Thinking. Second, making sense of Design Thinking outputs and insights means that managers need 'to get their hands dirty'; effective management involves applying Design Thinking practices to the leadership of networked teams itself. Just as we at the D-School "teach teams with teams", managers may need to start "leading teams with teams". Third, effective implementation of Design Thinking in an organisation will imply a considerable degree conceptual engagement with the methods and mindsets of Design Thinking. As we have seen, organisations that can adapt one or more of the three dimensions of Design Thinking (space, teams and practices) to their specific circumstances are more likely to sustainably integrate Design Thinking in their organisations.

References

Allison, G. T. (1971). *The essence of decision: Explaining the Cuban missile crisis*. Cambridge, MA: Little Brown.
Bason, C. (2010). *Leading public sector innovation: Co-creating for a better society*. Bristol, UK: Polity Press.
Baumgartner, F. R., & Jones, B. D. (1993). *Agendas and instability in American politics*. Chicago, IL: University of Chicago Press.
Castells, M. (1996). *The rise of the network society*. Malden, MA: Blackwell.
Colebatch, H. K. (2009). *Policy*. Maidenhead: Open University Press.
Cross, N. (2011). *Design thinking: Understanding how designers think and work*. New York: Bloomsbury Academic.

References

Dorst, K. (2015). *Frame innovation*. Boston, MA: MIT Press.
Douglas, M. (1992). *Risk and blame: Essays on cultural theory*. London: Routledge.
Fuller, R. C., & Myers, R. R. (1941). The natural history of social problems. *American Sociological Review, 6*(3), 320–329.
Gabriel, Y. (2008). *Organizing words: A critical thesaurus for social and organization studies*. Oxford: Oxford University Press.
Grint, K. (2010). *Leadership: A very short introduction*. Oxford: Oxford University Press.
Heclo, H. (1974). *Modern social politics in Britain and Sweden: From relief to income maintenance*. London: Yale University Press.
Kolko, J. (2010). *Exposing the magic of design: A practitioner's guide to the methods and theory of synthesis*. Oxford: Oxford University Press.
March, J. G. (1991). Exploration and exploitation in organizational learning. *Organization Science, 2*(1), 71–87.
Martin, R. L. (2009a). *The design of business: Why design thinking is the next competitive advantage*. Boston, MA: Harvard Business Press.
Martin, R. L. (2009b). *The opposable mind: Winning through integrative thinking*. Boston, MA: Harvard Business Press.
Morgan, G. (1986). *Images of organisation*. London: Sage.
Ney, S. (2009). *Resolving messy policy issues*. London: Earthscan.
Ney, S., Beckmann, M., Gräbnitz, D., & Mirkovic, R. (2014). Social entrepreneurs and social change: Tracing impacts of social entrepreneurship through ideas, structures and practices. *International Journal of Entrepreneurial Venturing, 6*(1), 51–68.
Pierre, J., & Peters, B. G. (2000). *Governance, politics, and the state*. London: Palgrave.
Pierson, P. (1996). The new politics of the welfare state. *World Politics, 48*, 143–179.
Plattner, H., Meinel, C., & Leifer, L. J. (2014). *Design thinking research: Building innovators*. Cham: Springer.
Rein, M., & Schön, D. (1994). *Frame reflection: Towards the resolution of intractable policy controversies*. New York: Basic Books.
Rhodes, R. A. W. (1997). *Understanding governance: Policy networks, governance, reflexivity and accountability*. Buckingham: Open University Press.
Sabatier, P. A., & Jenkins-Smith, H. (1993). *Policy change and learning: An advocacy coalition approach*. Boulder, CO: Westview Press.
Schmiedgen, J., Rhinow, H., Köppen, E., & Meinel, C. (2015). *Parts without a whole? The current state of design thinking practice in organisations* (Technical Report No 97). Potsdam: Verlag der Universität Potsdam.
Stone, D. (1997). *Policy paradox: The art of political decision making*. London: W.W. Norton & Company.
Thompson, M., & Ney, S. (2000). Cultural discourses in the global climate change debate. In E. Jochem, J. Sathaye, & D. Bouille (Eds.), *Society, behaviour and climate change mitigation* (pp. 65–92). Dordrecht: Kluwer.
Thompson, M., Ellis, R., & Wildavsky, A. (1990). *Cultural theory*. Boulder, CO: Westview Press.
Verganti, R. (2009). *Design-driven innovation: Changing the rules of competition by radically innovating what things mean*. Boston, MA: Harvard Business Press.
Verweij, M. (2011). *Clumsy solutions for a wicked world: How to improve global governance*. Basingstoke: Palgrave Macmillan.
Weick, K. E. A., & Sutcliffe, K. M. (2015). *Managing the unexpected: Sustained performance in a complex world* (3rd ed.). Hoboken, NJ: Wiley.
Weinberg, U. (2015). *Network thinking: Was Kommt Nach Dem Brockhaus Denken?* Hamburg: Murmann.

Chapter 8
Conclusion

How does design thinking shape large organisations? Answering this question has meant doing two things. First, in Chaps. 2 and 3, we set out a conceptual framework for understanding the way Design Thinking impacts upon and shapes large organisations. This framework describes the ever-changing relationship between wicked problems, innovation, and organisational cultures. Second, we then applied this framework to actual Design Thinking initiatives in large public and private sector organisations. In Chaps. 4–6, we looked at how Design Thinking initiatives brought about institutional change at the level of structures, ideas and practices.

We will review each in turn.

The Conceptual Framework: Wicked Problems, Innovation and Messy Institutions

In the last decade, interest in Design Thinking has soared. People in a wide range of organisations in both the public and private sector are wondering whether the methods and mindsets of Design Thinking can help them (Liedtka and Bennett 2013; Carlgren et al. 2016).

Help them do what, though? What makes Design Thinking so attractive to people in large organisations?

The answer is innovation. And not just any type of innovation. Design thinking seems to promise a pathway to so-called 'disruptive' innovations; the 'breakthroughs' in technology, services or organisation that wash away conventional ways of doing things. These innovations cause tidal waves that rearrange institutions, markets, and, most importantly, people's perceptions and practices.

Significantly, these types of innovation leave competitors in their wake, treading water at best. Today, innovative capability not only has become synonymous with success but also with the very survival of an organisational. People in businesses feel they need innovations to maintain an edge in increasingly competitive global markets: if we don't innovate today, someone else might disrupt our markets tomorrow. The same is true for the public sector, albeit with somewhat more sinister implications. People designing and delivering public services feel their current tools are increasingly ineffective: if we are unable find responses to the many public policy challenges, people may turn to far less palatable solutions. For many, Design Thinking looks like a recipe for creating the 'next big thing'. Small wonder that businesses and public service providers are curious about Design Thinking.

However, we suspect that there is considerably more to Design Thinking than merely allaying businesses' ever-present fear of missing 'the next big thing' or of ensuring the popularity of the government of the day. Indeed, for us Design Thinking is about empowering people to effectively tackle problems. Specifically, Design Thinking helps teams to deal with particularly complex and uncertain challenges also known as "wicked problems" (Rittel and Webber 1973). Problems and challenges are wicked if there are many possible and plausible but no obviously correct or right solutions. What is more, since wicked problems are dynamic, what seemed like a workable solution yesterday may no longer be as effective today. Wicked challenges include health care, globalisation, digital transformation, climate change or poverty. Wicked problems increasingly smudge the boundary between business challenges and public policy problems.

How are we to deal with these wicked challenges? Since wicked problems are highly complex and uncertain, it is unwise to rely on a single perspective, paradigm or discipline to provide a definitive solution. Paradigms or frames that help us make sense of the world are inherently selective: this is how frames and models allow us to focus on what is salient. Yet, complexity means that 'selecting' or 'reducing' is never free of risk. Making sense of issues is always at danger of missing a potentially crucial factor that lurks in the perceptual blindspot of our preferred paradigms.

Actors can avoid these dangers by bringing different and contending paradigms to bear on these wicked challenges. Instead of embarking on a futile quest for the one single paradigm to explain and thereby solve wicked problems, it makes far more sense to mobilise the valuable insights that each frame, paradigm or discipline has to offer. On this view, tackling wicked problems is all about integrating different, often contradictory paradigms. This is what Roger Martin calls "integrative thinking": the ability to forge innovative solutions to wicked problems from opposing conceptions on how best to deal with them. Martin "integrative thinking" as being a something that characterises individual entrepreneurs: in his book, he associates this capability with particularly inventive individuals such as the founder of AIG, the Four Seasons Hotel franchise or the Cirque de Soleil (Martin 2009).

We, in turn, believe that "integrative thinking" is at the heart of how Design Thinking teams tackle wicked challenges. As we argued in Chap. 2, Design Thinking teams bring a wide range of perceptions, ideas and potential solutions to bear on wicked design challenges. This happens during the process called 'creative synthesis'. This plurality of perceptions and ideas emerges from both the diversity of the Design Thinking teams as well as from the insights obtained through user research. By integrating these different ideas, workarounds and potential solutions, Design Thinking teams reframe the initial design challenge. In this way, they define and open up new solution spaces. So, far from being a 'management fad', the methods and mindsets of Design Thinking potentially enable people to deal with wicked problems.

Why, then, have large organisations not embraced 'team-based integrative' thinking? Or, in terms of innovation, why do large organisations not grasp and exploit 'the next big thing'? Why do successful organisations find themselves relegated to the sidelines of markets and domains believed to be under their control? How do relatively small start-ups (or, if you will, up-starts) manage to outmanoeuvre large and powerful organisation?

The reasons large organisations cannot act upon, let alone develop, path-breaking innovations are rooted in the very set-up of these institutions. In large organisations, success is a function of running their business—be it commercial, policy-making or public service provision—in a way that ensures, as Roger Martin would put it, 'reliability' (Martin 2009). Reliability in operations ensures, as James March (March 1991) tells us, effective 'exploitation' of available resources. Recognising and developing 'break-through' innovations, however, requires an organisational set-up that revolves around "validity" (Martin 2009); rather than focusing on the integrity and reliability of processes, institutions in this mode engage with meaning and substance of organisational activity. Since these types of institutions make possible "exploration" (March 1991), they are well equipped to look out for and occupy new fields of opportunity.

What is to be done? The simple answer, of course, is to transform these institutional set-ups, or organisational cultures, so that they support "exploration" based on "validity". At the same time, however, changes to organisations need to be careful not to erode capabilities for "reliability" and "exploitation". Yet, like many simple answers, this is very tricky to put into practice.

First, the fundamental set-up of organisations militates against this type of transformation. As we argued in Chap. 3, we can think of organisations as the dynamic interplay of three elements: structures, ideas and practices. Organisational structures emerge from the pattern of transactions between members of the organisation that make up the social relations; the ideas are norms, perceptions and beliefs that help regulate and legitimate what goes on in organisations; practices consist of those patterns of behaviour that successfully reproduce social relations. Not any arbitrary combination of structures, ideas and practices results in a functioning organisation: viable institutions combine all three elements in a way that mutually reinforces one another. Organisations geared towards reliability and exploitation may not be terribly innovative, but they are viable.

Viability implies resilience. Tinkering with any of the institutional elements is unlikely to yield more and more effective innovative capabilities. At best, reforms targeted at one or two of the institutional dimensions may trigger a response from what one might call the 'organisational immune system': the organisation will ingest and assimilate the changes so that they reinforce put the dominant organisational culture. At worst, these types at reforms can impede the operations of the institution. In this case, transformation provides neither reliability nor validity; reforms simply damage the organisation. So, for reforms to bring about cultural transformation, they need to take place at all three institutional dimensions (albeit not at the same time). This type of reform programme is never likely to be easy, straightforward or even promising. Small wonder that many organisational actors do not have the stomach for real cultural transformation.

Second, even if, against considerable odds, these reforms successfully change organisational cultures, this merely changes the hue but not the essence of the problem. A programme of organisational change may shift an institution from, say, a collection of hierarchically structured silos (that reliably produces what it was set up to produce) to a more entrepreneurial organisation (that explores and finds new fields of opportunity). However, this may simply exchange one set of strengths and weaknesses for another: the transformation may buy innovative capabilities at the cost of the ability to exploit these innovations. This is because any viable organisation must also be able to help its members perceive, understand and affect some aspects of the complex and uncertain challenges they face. This implies that it may make more sense to set up organisations so that they can draw on the strengths of both reliability and validity. Organisations capable of both exploitation and exploration are what Charles O'Reilly and Michael Tushman call 'ambidextrous organisations' (O'Reilly and Tushman 2013).

However, as we discussed in Chap. 3, there is yet another complication. What if we need more than two organisational cultures to tackle wicked problems? What if there were a relevant set of organisational capabilities not covered by either reliability-based or validity-based organisations? What is needed, then, is a typology of organisational cultures; a typology such as the Cultural Theory framework derived from the work of the British social anthropologist the late Dame Mary Douglas. As we have seen, this framework provides us with a fourfold typology of organisational cultures (see Fig. 8.1).

Two of these cultures correspond to reliability-based and validity-based organisations: the high grid/high group hierarchies and the low grid/low group markets (respectively).

The Cultural Map points to two further organisational cultures. Each of these cultures features a viable combination of structures, ideas and practices. This is why each of these cultures offers valuable insights into wicked problems; each of these cultures provides practical strategies to help tackle and mitigate wicked problems. Just like reliability-based and validity-based organisations focus of different, often incompatible aspects of wicked problems, so too do inclusion-based egalitarian and chance-based fatalist organisations. But each organisational culture provides the cognitive tools for understanding as well as strategies for dealing with vital aspects of wicked problems (see Box 3.1).

Consequently, if large organisations are to find innovative strategies for dealing with the wicked design challenges they face, then they will have to find ways of mobilising and integrating these contending organisational cultures. In other words,

The Conceptual Framework: Wicked Problems, Innovation and Messy Institutions

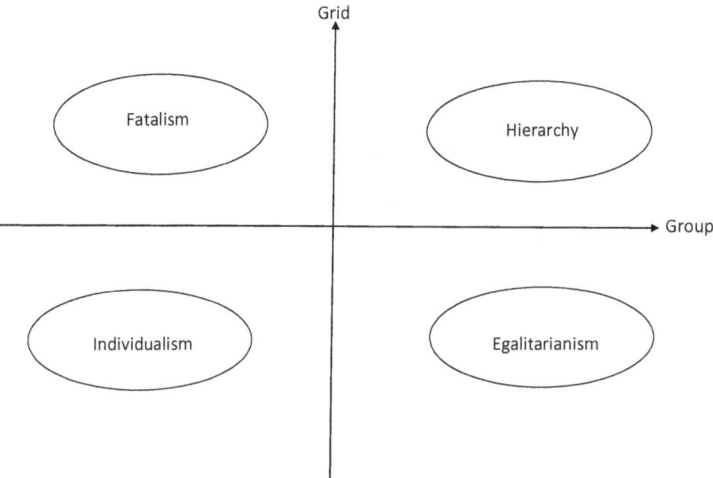

Fig. 8.1 The Cultural Map. Source: Thompson et al. (1990)

Fig. 8.2 Janus and Vishnu. Source: http://moziru.com/explore/Gods%20clipart%20janus/; http://www.wordzz.com/lord-vishnu-images-1/

effective team-based 'integrative thinking' will require a far wider cultural plurality than 'validity' and 'reliability'. Rather than merely ambidextrous, effective innovative capability may call for 'multi-dextrous' organisations: instead of the two-faced Roman god Janus (O'Reilly and Tushman 2013), we may have to invoke the many-armed Hindu god Lord Vishnu (see Fig. 8.2). We called these types of 'multi-dextrous' organisations *messy institutions*. These types of organisations give their members access to a wide range of cultural strategies for setting-up, sustaining and adapting in 'team-based integrative thinking'.

In principle, then, Design Thinking could potentially inhabit a pivotal position in any process of organisational transformation. One the one hand, Design Thinking is one of a very select group of methods that tackles wicked problems in terms of messy institutions (Ney and Verweij 2014b, pp. 12–13). The methods and mindsets of Design Thinking incorporate elements of all four contending organisational cultures. On the other hand, Design Thinking can also drive the process of making large organisations more 'messy', i.e. providing organisations with a plurality of different strategies for engaging in 'team-based integrative thinking'. For one, Design Thinking touches all three organisational dimensions: it affects structures, ideas and practices in large organisations. Moreover, Design Thinking can introduce a rich and, more importantly, sufficiently broad diversity of contending structures, ideas and practices into large organisations.

So, how have actual transformation programmes revolving around the methods and mindsets of Design Thinking fared? In the second part of the book, we used the framework and concept of 'messy institutions' to assess the impact of Design Thinking initiatives on large organisations in the private and public sector.

Design Thinking in Practice

In Chaps. 4–6, the book critically reviewed some of the existing empirical evidence on the implementation of Design Thinking in large private and public sector organisations. We relied on the institutional model introduced in Chap. 3 to structure our argument. If Design Thinking is to transform large organisations, we contend, it would need to affect them at the level of structures, ideas and practices. For this reason, we looked at different programmes of Design Thinking reforms—which we have called 'Design Thinking initiatives'—in terms of how they brought about changes in these dimensions. In other words, we have refracted and reordered the available evidence through a three-way prism. How have Design Thinking initiatives affected *social relations* in large organisations (Chap. 4)? How have they shaped the *pool of available ideas* (Chap. 5)? And, last but certainly not least, how have different reform attempts changed *practices* in large organisations (Chap. 6)?

As we have seen, the outcomes and impacts of these pioneering initiatives have been a mixed bag. On the one hand, the methods, practices and mindsets of Design Thinking definitely show potential to contribute to and even drive the transformation towards a multi-dextrous organization: reforms have generated and extended organisational capabilities for deploying team-based integrative thinking to tackle wicked design challenges. On the other hand, the available evidence also suggests that creating Design Thinking teams and setting them onto projects alone is unlikely to generate the necessary momentum needed to bring about multi-dexterity and messiness within large organisations.

Design Thinking in Practice 175

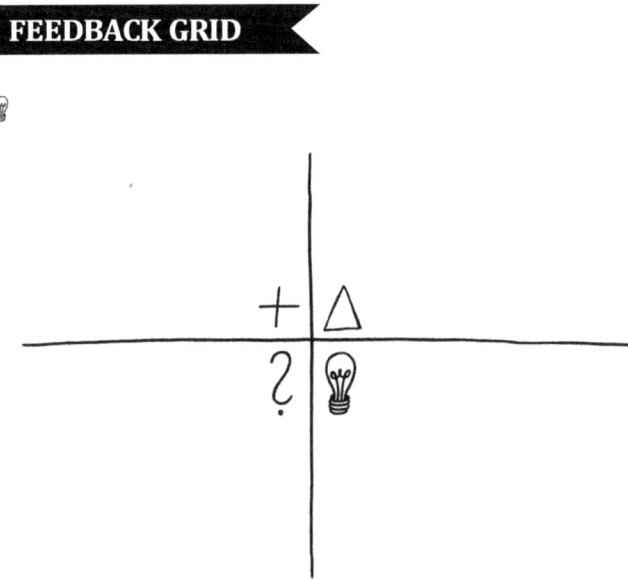

Fig. 8.3 The feedback grid. This grid offers a framework to cluster and work with feedback from testing in four categories: what worked well (plus), what should be changed (delta), questions (question mark) and new ideas (bulb). Source: ©HPI Academy 2018

The Design Thinking initiatives covered in Chaps. 4–6 were prototypes of implementation programmes; no one really knew what to expect. As we have seen, apart from very general objectives couched terminology full of buzzwords—such as 'agile', 'innovation capability', 'flexibility', 'disruption', 'ambidexterity' or 'breakthrough innovation', to name but a few—the expected outcomes remained rather nebulous (Köppen 2016; Dribbisch 2016; Rhinow 2018). A key function of prototypes is to find out what concrete changes contributed to the overall transformation would-be reformers want to see. This also means, of course, looking for the things that do not ultimately contribute to the transformation process. In other words, prototypes help us understand how better to achieve the overall objectives of change processes by pinpointing what does not work. In what follows, then, we apply the tool favoured by teams at the HPI School of Design Thinking in Potsdam for collecting and analysing feedback from testing prototypes: the feedback grid. As Fig. 8.3 shows, teams collect and collate feedback in terms of *what worked, what didn't work, new ideas and insights* as well as *open questions*.

What Worked?

Chapters 4–6 discuss how Design Thinking initiatives brought about changes in large organisations in all three institutional dimensions.

Recall that—according to the framework put forward in Chap. 3—sustainable institutional transformation not only requires change in all three dimensions (albeit not necessarily at the same time), but also that this changes generates viable institutions. Not any arbitrary combination of structures, ideas and practices yields a functioning institution. Moreover, effectively dealing with wicked design challenges calls for more than merely shifting organisations from one province of the Cultural Map (see Fig. 8.1 above) to another; say from hierarchical reliability (or process-orientation) to a more entrepreneurial validity (or outcome-orientation). Tackling wicked problems calls for the expansion of strategic options. Organisations need to become more than just entrepreneurial but need to equip themselves with the cognitive (and normative) tools of a wide plurality of different institutional logics: in order to switch strategies nimbly, organisations need to become "messy".

This suggests two evaluative questions:

- Did Design Thinking initiatives bring about change in the relevant institutional dimension?
- Did this change promote 'messiness' in the large organisations?

Structures

The Design Thinking initiatives covered in Chaps. 4–6 partly managed to reconfigure patterns of transactions and social relations in parts large organisations. In particular, the evidence suggests that these initiatives carved *new social spaces* out of vertically structured and departmentalised organisations in both the private and public sectors. As we saw in Chap. 4, these social spaces spanned departmental as well as hierarchical divisions within the businesses and ministries in which they were implemented.

These new social spaces replaced *vertical* forms of accountability with more *horizontal* ways of holding people to account. Instead of coordinating interaction between team members in terms of status, authority and expertise (Colebatch 2009), members of newly formed Design Thinking teams needed to secure the cooperation of their colleagues through negotiation, argument and the forging of a common purpose. As we have seen, the Design Thinking initiatives brought about these shifts by creating small teams spanning different departments. These teams featured no formal internal distinction either in terms of position or in terms of expertise or specialist skills (Köppen 2016). Promotion of informal modes of interaction as well as the injunction to "take a beginner's mindset" helped dissolve established vertical modes of interaction (Rauth et al. 2014; Köppen 2016; Rhinow 2018).

The studies also show how Design Thinking initiatives protected Design Thinking teams from hierarchical control in the wider organisational environment. All studies report of efforts to endow Design Thinking teams with effective capabilities for self-governance and autonomy. Internally, all initiatives analysed encouraged Design Thinking teams to develop, implement and police their own team-management tools. More importantly, Design Thinking initiatives attempted to provide teams with the autonomy to explore and (more importantly, reframe) the wicked design challenges they were given.

In conjunction, then, new forms of accountability and autonomy (both organisational and thematic) gave rise—at least in part—to what we have called "mini-publics". In these social spaces, self-governance (internal) and autonomy (external) set out the conditions that enabled effective team-based integrated thinking. Specifically, 'mini-publics' encouraged a form of deliberation with two key characteristics. First, Design Thinking teams featured deliberation in which team members contribute to problem-solving by formulating their own reasoned and evidence-based arguments. Here, the evidence-base consists of both the diverse expertise and experience of each team member as well as, more importantly, user experiences. Second, effective team-based integrative thinking requires a debate in which each team member is open to adapt and change their reasoned opinion in light of a 'better argument' (Habermas 1987).

In sum, the available evidence indicates that Design Thinking initiatives created spaces in which

- Design Thinking team members related to each other in terms of horizontal forms of accountability;
- Design Thinking teams were (relatively) autonomous in pursuing the best response to wicked design challenges;
- Deliberation in Design Thinking teams was based on argument aimed to explore the problem-space. Team members formed these arguments from the insights of user-research.

Ideas

Effective team-based integrated thinking is predicated on a wide pool of contending ideas. Recall that sustainable responses to complex and uncertain design challenges feature a flexible and creative integration of insights from contending frames in to something we can call "clumsy solutions" (2006). This means that Design Thinking teams need access to as wide a reservoir of ideas and concepts as is possible.

The available evidence indicates that Design Thinking initiatives expanded and enriched the reservoir of available ideas in two ways. First, the initiatives studied expanded the pool of ideas by mobilising the diversity inherent in the sizeable populations of employees that work in these large organisations. Design thinking initiatives created an awareness within corporations of the benefits of diversity and plurality for innovation. Further, these initiatives also encouraged individuals in Design Thinking teams to draw on their individual perceptions, backgrounds, experiences and preferences as sources of valuable contributions to team-based integrated thinking. As a result, Design Thinking initiatives also generated acceptance of a wider gamut of personalities and, more importantly, the ideas and practices that go along with these personalities.

Second, Design Thinking initiatives further deepened and widened the reservoir of ideas in large organisations by encouraging teams to go "hunting and gathering" for user perceptions, experiences and ideas (Plattner et al. 2014). Here, the methods of qualitative social scientific research—in particular ethnography—enabled Design Thinking teams in large organisations to hunt for and gather user and stakeholder perceptions. Apart from furnishing Design Thinking teams with the 'raw material' for team-based integrative thinking, user research also provided stakeholders with a voice, albeit vicariously, in design processes of large businesses and ministries. Design Thinking teams and the stakeholder research they engaged in became causeways for ideas and perceptions into large organisations.

Here, the public sector case in Singapore is particularly illuminating. For the ministry in question, stakeholder research introduced by the Design Thinking initiative was one of the few means for civil servants to identify citizen perceptions and needs. Given a restrictive public sphere with limited opportunity for voicing opinions, let alone grievances, many Singaporeans are left only with the options of loyalty and exit (Hirschman 1972). In this way, then, user research becomes an effective means of including citizen ideas and perception in policy formulation and the design of public services.

The studies also point to the impacts of contending ideas on deliberation and problem-solving. For one, evidence suggests that the expansion of the reservoir of ideas improved the quality of debate and nature of team-based integrated thinking. Studies show how insights gleaned from user and stakeholder research encouraged Design Thinking teams to confront, examine and explore their prior, mostly unquestioned assumptions about wicked design challenges. Moreover, studies also report that these deliberative processes led to the design of better—meaning more user-centred—products and services (Carlgren et al. 2014). It would seem, then, that in addition to the normative benefits of expanding the pool of ideas (i.e. giving users an effective voice in problem-solving processes), 'hunting and gathering' of Design Thinking teams also generated functional benefits (i.e. better products and services).

Practices

The Design Thinking initiatives introduced a range of practices that both complemented and challenged existing ways of doing things. The studies suggest that Design Thinking initiatives focussed on implementing output-and inclusion-oriented practices; practices, then, that helped teams efficiently create outputs and that strengthened inclusion either within teams or in user research.[1] On the one hand, practices such as time-boxing, dot voting, or rapid prototyping ensured that teams produced outputs quickly so that they could 'fail early to succeed later'. On the other hand, empathy-based approaches such as team check-ins and check-outs, warm-ups

---

[1]Following the 'grid/group' terminology of Cultural Theory, we have labelled these types of practices as 'low grid', supporting as they do, market and egalitarian organisational cultures.

or the search for extreme users helped teams ensure the widest possible inclusion of team members and stakeholder groups.

In many of the organisations, these 'low grid' practices provided an effective counterpart to dominant cultural orientations towards process, reliability and exploitation. Output-oriented practices—in particular rapid prototyping and user testing—allowed Design Thinking teams to learn from user insights and experiences. Inclusion-oriented practices, in turn, offered employees respite from what many perceived to be alienating working conditions. Design Thinking teams became, to use Eva Köppen's term, "protective spheres" that shielded Design Thinking team members from the impersonal control of hierarchical oversight (Köppen 2016). In addition to giving stakeholders a voice in design processes, user research also evolved into a new, somewhat objective standard in deliberation: this, studies suggest, contributed to the emancipation of individual Design Thinking team members vis-a-vis the wider organisational hierarchy. The upshot of these changes, the studies indicate, is that these practices helped bring about a shift in mindsets (Carlgren et al. 2016). In almost all cases, researchers report a heightened awareness of user and stakeholder input as well as an increased appreciation of diversity within teams (Carlgren et al. 2016).

In sum, the Design Thinking initiatives covered in this book brought about changes in all three institutional dimensions. In terms of structures, Design Thinking initiatives created self-governing spaces in which teams autonomously explored wicked design challenges. At the level of ideas, Design Thinking initiatives expanded and enriched the reservoir of contending ideas and perceptions. Not only did this provide stakeholders with an effective voice in design processes, it also improved the quality of deliberation and, evidence suggests, led to better outputs in the form of product and service innovations. Last, studies show that Design Thinking initiatives expanded the scope of institutional practices. Overall, then, these changes offered actors in large organisations a wider palette of institutional strategies for tackling wicked design challenges. In this sense, then, reforms helped move large organisations towards messiness.

What Didn't Work

As one would expect from prototypes, the Design Thinking initiatives covered in this book were not all unqualified successes. What problems, tensions and turbulences did the Design Thinking initiatives gave rise to? Again, we can review the more problematic impacts of Design Thinking on large organisations in terms of structures, ideas and practices.

Structures

Some of the new self-governing and autonomous spaces caused significant turbulence within their host organisations. Not only did these new spaces sit awkwardly across existing boundaries and management structures, they also chafed against established informal structures of professionalism and accrued status. Of course, fundamental cultural change is unlikely to occur without some degree of discomfort. And yet, the evidence in some of the studies—in particular Köppen (2016) and Rhinow (2018)—describe how the new mini-publics and their horizontal forms of accountability ran roughshod over individual and professional sensibilities. Their research reports of how individuals found themselves overwhelmed by tasks, such as qualitative user and stakeholder research, for which they felt both unqualified and unsuited. At another level, professionals looked on the new social spaces with considerable scepticism. Some felt threatened by the fact that expertise and acquired specialist skills did not necessarily convey status in the new mini-publics. Indeed, it seemed to these actors that any type of expertise was up for grabs; after all, members were encouraged to 'take a beginner's mindset' to everything. Consequently, certain professionals, in particular designers, felt that new spaces usurped their rightful role as design experts in problem-solving processes.

More importantly, project managers responsible for Design Thinking teams felt displaced by the autonomy of the new mini-publics. Rhinow (2018) describes how project managers were torn between the imperative to report to their superiors and the feeling of having lost control of mini-publics. As a result, project managers devised effective ways of wresting back control. One set of strategies involved breaking up the holistic flow of the Design Thinking process by dividing teams and assigning separate takes according to imputed capabilities (such as user-research and synthesis). Another strategy limited the autonomy of mini-publics by setting agendas and limiting the scope of issues that Design Thinking teams could explore. A third set of strategies manipulated the practices of Design Thinking itself to reassert control over teams. This included the deployment empathy tools to order pursue individual, power-oriented objectives. Others manipulated methods—such as brainstorming—until teams produced ideas deemed appropriate by project managers.

Ideas

While the Design Thinking initiatives expanded and deepened the reservoir of contending ideas, there is reason to believe that this pool was probably not sufficiently 'messy' to support effective team-based integrative thinking. None of the studies explicitly looked at the degree of diversity in the reservoir of ideas. This should probably not come as a surprise: none of the studies actually sets out to measure the diversity of the 'primeval soup' of ideas (Kingdon 1984). However, the research ought to make us suspicious of the breadth of the ideational spectrum available to Design Thinking teams for two distinct reasons.

First, user and stakeholder research in large institution was fraught with difficulties. As we saw in Chap. 5, studies show that many employees experienced considerable difficulties interacting with users and stakeholders. Köppen and Rhinow, in particular, point out that the perceived lack of skill in user research led to the marginalisation of individuals within Design Thinking teams; this was the case both for individuals ostensibly lacking empathy skills or for individual members of professions believed intrinsically incapable of conducting qualitative research. Over and above the imputed shortfall of qualitative research capabilities, the studies also pointed to actual instances of poor quality research. In part, this may be due to the expressed lack of confidence in research abilities (Dribbisch 2016; Rhinow 2018). In part, and more significantly, the studies found a more fundamental misunderstanding of social scientific methods. This, they argue, led Design Thinking team members to lose patience with the research methods. In practice, this meant that Design Thinking teams would strategically manipulate methods to align research findings with commercial objectives (Köppen 2016). As we saw in Chap. 5, this undermined the value of exploratory and open-ended user research.

Second, the studies further revealed that a wider reservoir at ideas was viewed with considerable suspicion by incumbent project managers. Extending the pool of ideas and concepts had widened the scope of legitimate conflict within organisations: user views, perceptions and experiences became a powerful source of argumentative authority for members of Design Thinking teams. An authority, no less, that would trump appeals to expertise and status. As we have seen, this did not leave project managers favourably disposed towards the Design Thinking initiatives.

Practices

Arguably, the Design Thinking initiatives did not introduce a sufficiently variegated range of practices to ensure a multi-dextrous approach to tackling wicked design challenges. The typology of organisational cultures introduced in Chap. 3 suggests four distinct families of practices:

- *output-oriented* practices that support individualist social relations;
- *inclusion-oriented* practices that emerge from and reinforce egalitarian structures;
- *process-oriented* practices that reproduce hierarchies;
- *chance-oriented* practices associated with isolation.

Design thinking draws most of its power and innovative drive from output-and inclusion-oriented practices.[2] In turn, practices that ensure the integrity of processes

---

[2]This emphasis on so-called 'low grid' practices explains much of Design Thinking's allure for large and, more often than not, lumbering organisations. These types of practices promise to instil

(hierarchy) and that introduce "contrived randomness" (isolation) (Hood 1998) are relatively sparse. However, these practices act as important regulatory mechanisms.

Chapter 6 discusses how Design Thinking initiatives curtailed practices both in breadth and in length. In terms of breadth, research findings indicate that the implementation of Design Thinking practices concentrated on an output- and inclusion-oriented practices to the apparent detriment of process- and chance-oriented practices. As we have seen above, these low grid practices both inspired and irritated the large organisations studied. While in many cases irritation may have been an intended element of organisational change, it did distract from the ostensible main purpose of the Design Thinking teams: innovation.

In terms of length, the study of Design Thinking initiatives in the public sector describes how civil servants adapted the Design Thinking process by omitting phases. In particular, it would seem as if Singaporean civil servants found stakeholder research and team-building aspects of Design Thinking most useful. In turn, the same civil servants deemed the more generative practices associated with the solution space—ideation and, specifically, prototyping—far less congenial to either policy-making or to the available skill sets in the ministry. However, instead of adapting and appropriating practices, such as prototyping, to the needs of policy-making, civil servants chose to omit these phases from the process.

Whether lacking in depth or curtailed in length, studies suggest that partially messy practices left Design Thinking teams vulnerable to the characteristic pitfalls and blindspots of cultural practices. Without the regulative force of process- and output-oriented practices, the focus on output-orientation exposed teams to the risk of *dilettantism*. As Chap. 6 shows, the pragmatic approach to knowledge enabled Design Thinking teams to explore and tackle wicked design challenges. However, the relative dearth of process-oriented practices meant that the enthusiasm of 'taking a beginner's mindset' remained unchecked by expert opinion. As we have seen, teams committed mistakes as brief consultation with experts could have easily avoided. For example, Köppen and Rhinow report how Design Thinking teams committed basic errors during fieldwork that detracted from the quality of their output. Similarly, the available evidence points to instances in which unchecked egalitarian practices led to *paralysis* and *intolerance*. Studies, in particular Rhinow (2018), point to tendencies towards sclerosis and paralysis in decision-making. Köppen describes how individual team members, in the absence of formal means of distinction and sanction, strategically manipulated empathy tools to secure their own charismatic leadership position within teams. Moreover, as we have seen, the research also brought to light rather unsavoury patterns of behaviour associated with egalitarian teams; members of some Design Thinking teams created a 'wall of virtue' to exclude individuals and professionals perceived to be inherently incapable of empathy. To make matters worse, Köppen identifies instances in which individuals

---

the spirit of can-do individualism, practiced more in the breach than in observance in most large enterprises and corporations.

felt coerced and bullied into team-activities that made them feel deeply uncomfortable.

Last, there is little evidence for the diffusion of new practices throughout the large organisations studied. The research suggests that actors within the wider organisation sporadically picked up and applied selected practices. In particular, Dribbisch (2016) describes how several departments in the Singaporean ministry adopted practices such as user interviews or brainstorming. Here, the research suggests that practices complemented (rather than transformed) existing work modes. While the studies suggest that these practices helped change some mindsets and ideas, there is little evidence to suggest that Design Thinking initiatives led to a sustained and pervasive transformation of organisational cultures. In short, practices diffused into the organisation in a haphazard and selective manner.

New Ideas and Insights

What new insights have emerged from the analysis of Design Thinking initiatives? We can tentatively point to five sets of learnings.

Simply Replacing Organisational Cultures Is Unlikely to Work

The experience with the Design Thinking initiatives suggests that 'tidy' (i.e. non-messy) organisational reforms are not terribly effective. This is true whether change aims for innovation or for organisational transformation. While simply shifting organisations across the Cultural Map (see Fig. 8.1) can bring about desired impacts, the available evidence also suggests that these desired benefits—say, a increase in innovative efficiency or more cohesive teams—will come at a price: the blind spots and weaknesses characteristic of the particular organisational culture.

The available evidence seems to point to instances in which Design Thinking initiatives generated imbalanced transformations. Köppen and Rhinow describe how Design Thinking initiatives led to turbulent and painful changes within the organisation they studied. As we have seen, for many employees, Design Thinking felt more like a reallocation of power than a universal liberation. Rather than expanding the scope of strategic choices, it would seem that Design Thinking initiatives had merely replaced one set of social controls—namely vertical and hierarchical—with another—horizontal and egalitarian. In this case, Design Thinking initiatives had redrawn (rather than dissolved) the lines of status and authority. Instead of empowering the entire team to build robust structures and practices for self-governance, Design Thinking initiatives had merely shifted the focus of alienation from one group to another.

This gives rise to two related challenges. First, alienating key organisational constituencies—such as designers and software developers in an enterprise that designs software—is probably not the most effective way to win the 'hearts and minds' needed for successful organisational transformation. As the Nobel Laureate Albert Hirschman (1972) argues, people who feel they have no voice will probably vote with their feet. Or, worse still, withdraw into apathy (fatalism, on the Cultural Map). And while some may see this as inevitable blood-letting (a dubious therapy abandoned by medicine centuries ago), this would exacerbate the second, far more serious problem. If organisations are to tackle wicked challenges, they will need to mobilise a wide plurality of perceptions and approaches. Not least to recognise and avoid pitfalls that lurk in the cognitive blind spots of organisational cultures.

This may mean, as we have seen, not throwing out the messy baby with the hierarchical bath water. Horizontal forms of accountability are useful only to the extent that they enable flexibility in selecting, devising and, if necessary, switching organisational strategies. Design thinking initiatives, then, need to expand the spectrum of available organisational strategies, including vertical, expert-oriented and hierarchical structures, ideas and practices.

The New Management: Interfaces, Ambiguity and Conflict

The implementation of Design Thinking in large organisations shifts the focus of management away from processes towards interfaces between different types of organisational spaces. Design Thinking teams, replete with new forms of internal accountability and external argumentative legitimation, create within large organisations regions of horizontal decision-making. Recall that horizontal relations mean that organisational constituencies coordinate their activities through negotiation and cooperation. Management, as scholars of governance point out, is increasingly about "rowing less and steering more" (Pierre and Peters 2000). Specifically, this means that managers can no longer directly control what goes on in autonomous mini-publics (without, that is, undermining their innovative capacity); rather, they need to minimise friction at the interfaces of this new institutional landscape.

Where, then, do Design Thinking initiatives give rise to new interfaces?

First, at organisational level, Design Thinking teams create new (and potentially irritating) interfaces between self-governing Design Thinking teams and the rest of the organisation. Part of the protective tasks of 'Design Thinking Guardians' will be to ensure that what passes across this boundary is actionable for the receiving system. Here, interface management means making sure that demands from the wider organisational environment inspire and encourage, but do not cripple or obstruct, self-governance. Conversely, management of the internal boundary would also involve 'translating' outputs and demands from Design Thinking teams into a form that is acceptable or, at least, comprehensible for the rest of the organisation. Furthermore, the management of this interface will significantly impinge on the diffusion of ideas and practices of Design Thinking throughout the institution.

A second somewhat more complex set of new interfaces emerge between Design Thinking teams, the organisation and the world of users and stakeholders.

Management of this interface involves safeguarding the flow of external ideas, perceptions and concepts into the organisation without triggering a destructive response from the 'organisational immune system'. What is more, managers here need to support teams in constructing effective causeways for external ideas, concepts and perceptions into the institution; causeways may consist of direct approaches—such as co-creation—to more vicarious pathways—such as the collection and synthesis of qualitative data.

Last, Design Thinking initiatives give rise to new interfaces between different Design Thinking teams themselves. Dealing with these interfaces means finding incentives and means for encouraging cooperation between self-governing and autonomous Design Thinking teams. The challenge here will be to bring about cooperation without (unduly) restricting the autonomy of Design Thinking Teams. In effect, management becomes an exercise in governance: managers need to set broad goals, develop incentives that reward autonomous teams, and evaluate the outputs of Design Thinking teams against the broader objectives.

Design Thinking Teams Are Vulnerable and Need Protection

Design Thinking teams in large organisations need protection. As we have seen, autonomous and self-governing social spaces throw down the gauntlet to the powers that be. Conventional management wisdom advises would-be reformers to ensure senior management support or, to use the jargon, 'buy-in'. However, as important the support of senior management may be, the research reviewed shows that significant peril for Design Thinking teams lurks at operational level. Project managers can scupper Design Thinking teams by manipulating operative parameters both within teams as well as between teams and the wider organisation.

If Design Thinking teams are to autonomously explore the problem-space, then their structures and practices of self-governance require active protection from these potential threats. Protection, no less, that extends beyond the, no doubt important, general legitimation provided by senior management endorsement. This type at protection will need to react to developments as the ramifications of Design Thinking for the organisation unfold. In addition to the necessary condition of senior management support, then, Design Thinking teams need a *guardian* to provide ongoing tactical and strategic support.

Design Thinking Requires Active Dissemination

Another key finding is that Design Thinking teams alone do not necessarily cause structures, ideas and practices of Design Thinking to diffuse throughout large organisations. The research suggests that cultural transformation not only requires effective Design Thinking teams but also a programme to help identify, diffuse and, if necessary, adapt ideas and practices to the organisational context.

This will involve transporting practices into the organisation in two distinct modes. First, dissemination programmes would need to create a broad level of literacy of Design Thinking in the organisation. Literacy means that organisational actors not only are able to recognise but also to critically engage with the activities and outputs at Design Thinking teams. For many employees in the organisation, this may be the only exposure to Design Thinking they will ever need. Second, dissemination also requires the continuous expansion and deepening of Design Thinking-specific skills. If, for example, user research, prototyping or brainstorming are to become part of available institutional strategies, Design Thinking initiatives will need to build capabilities throughout the organisation. This not only implies continuous learning but also will mean that organisations invest in the continuous development and adaptation of Design Thinking practices.

In addition, this raises the issue of the quality of training and teaching of Design Thinking-relevant skills. As the studies have shown, continuous learning and acquisition of skills—such as interviewing, the analysis of qualitative data or prototyping—proved to be a significant bottle-neck for effective diffusion of Design Thinking throughout the large organisations studied (Dribbisch 2016). Therefore, access to high quality training is not only imperative for the duration of the Design Thinking initiative but, for Design Thinking to make a significant impact on large organisations, people need continuous access to education and training. This, then, suggests that there may be a need to establish, maintain and develop comparable standards for training and teaching Design Thinking.

Innovation and Organisational Transformation May Pull in Opposite Directions

The comparative work of Lisa Carlgren and her colleagues shows that Design Thinking initiatives do not always pursue the same types of objectives. While some Design Thinking initiatives explicitly aimed to build and extend innovative capabilities, others sought to reform the prevalent organisational culture as a whole. Undoubtedly the two objectives are interrelated: innovation capacity is predicated on a shift of organisational culture towards messy institutions. Similarly, effective team-based integrative thinking provides blueprints for organisational structures, ideas and practices that can help bring about a messy transformation.

In practice, however, these two objectives may get in each other's way, at least in the short-term. Design Thinking teams may not be able to pursue both objectives at the same time. The evidence suggests that when Design Thinking initiatives set up relatively self-contained, autonomous and internally diverse Design Thinking teams, they successfully engage in team-based integrative thinking to generate innovation. There impact of these types of teams, however, remains relatively localised. The evidence suggests that often their connection to the rest of the institution was rather tenuous (c.f. Schmiedgen et al. 2015). In extreme cases, the rest of the organisations does not understand or see the relevance of innovations that emerge from these teams. Conversely, teams exposed to the wider organisational environment that worked with ideas and practices that sat awkwardly to prevalent organisational cultures were far more effective in highlighting issues of institutional interest. However, successfully irritating the wider organisational environment distracted from team-based integrative thinking.

Organisational irritation sidetracks innovation in at least two ways. First, as we have seen, irritation tends to draw unwelcome attention from actors that perceive Design Thinking to be a threat. Since Design Thinking teams are vulnerable at operational level, these players can easily derail innovation thereby undermining the legitimacy of the Design Thinking initiative. This is the case whether senior management buys in or not. Second, even if the wider institutional environment welcomes the changes that Design Thinking teams introduce, the 'translation' of practices and outputs from the Design Thinking team into the organisation takes time and effort. If there is no Design Thinking Guardian to manage this particular interface, the effort of translation is likely to distract the team from integrative thinking and innovation (Rhinow 2018). As the Singaporean example suggests, if the tasks associated with translation and transfer become too onerous, organisational actors will edit the structures, ideas and practices of Design Thinking. As the preceding chapters have shown, people in large organisations either emphasise and focus on some elements or background simply omit others in order to fit Design Thinking to their organisational realities. This, weakens the regulatory functions of messiness and leaves teams them vulnerable to characteristic inherent weaknesses of dominant organisational cultures. The real danger here is that Design Thinking initiatives may end up promoting neither innovation nor organisational change.

Open Questions

What, then, are the new questions that emerge from our exploration of the implementation prototypes?

The review of the selected studies has shown that the methods and mindsets at Design Thinking have the potential to transform organisations into 'messy institutions'. These types of organisations have a wide array of contending (and even contradictory) institutional strategies at their disposal: they are multi-dextrous and, thereby, her more flexible in responding to wicked design challenges.

In this context, three main questions emerge for future inquiry.

How Best to Gauge and Operationalise Messiness

Despite pointing towards the potential of Design Thinking for messiness at all three institutional levels, existing studies could not tell us much about the degree of plurality the Design Thinking initiatives actually managed to implement in large organisations. In terms of structure, there was some indication that Design Thinking teams made use of different governance patterns, but it is far from clear whether the mini-publics made deft use of all available sets of social relations. Similarly, the studies provide reasons to believe that both the diversity of Design Thinking teams and user research expanded and enriched the pool of ideas in these large organisations. At the same time, however, we know very little about the degree or depth of diversity of ideas in these reservoirs. Last, reviewing the studies using Cultural Theory's typology of organisational cultures, our exposition suggests that the implementation of Design Thinking practices in the large organisations may not have been sufficiently pluralist (or messy) to prevent Design Thinking teams from succumbing to the characteristic pitfalls of particular organisational cultures.

It is important to stress that these are not omissions or errors of the studies reviewed in the previous chapters. Neither the objectives nor the theoretical approaches of the studies were designed for gauging messiness. And yet, assessing the extent Design Thinking initiatives extend the plurality of structures, ideas and practices in large organisations is not only crucial for evaluating the reform endeavours ex-post, it may also play an important role in the design and ongoing management of Design Thinking initiatives.

Future research, then, will need to do two things. First, it could revisit existing and instigate new studies of Design Thinking initiatives that, among other things, measure the extent to which Design Thinking initiatives installed and then mobilised a requisite plurality of structures, ideas and practices in large organisations. Studies of this kind would provide valuable insights into the effective and, more importantly, ineffective measures for bringing about organisational messiness. Moreover, if these studies were to be comparative (like, say, Carlgren et al.'s work), they would provide valuable data about the efficacy of measures in different organisational contexts. Second, and as corollary, such research would also yield indicators and measures of messiness that could serve in the set-up of future Design Thinking initiatives.

How to Best Protect Design Thinking Teams in Large Organisations?

The discussion in Chap. 5 highlighted the potentially exposed and vulnerable position of Design Thinking team in large organisations. If left unprotected, Design Thinking teams are open to manipulation at operational level; and, as we have seen, there is little that top management can do to prevent the scuppering of Design Thinking teams. This implies that Design Thinking teams in large institutions need some form at protection located at project management level; we have tentatively called this position a '*Design Thinking Guardian*'.

The precise shape or form this protection should take is far less clear. Research and experimentation will need to identify both the general and specific tasks at Design Thinking Guardians. This will involve a systematic and (ideally) comparative analysis of the barriers and risks that Design Thinking teams face in different phases of the Design Thinking initiative. Here, research should aim to outline a typology of risks for different institutional contexts. Further, the research project could compile existing and devise new strategies for overcoming the barriers and dealing with the risks.

In addition to the potential dangers and strategies, research will also need to look into the kind characteristics and skills individuals require to protect teams. Research across different organisations, sectors and regions could ascertain what types of individuals equipped with what types of skills are best suited to defend Design Thinking Teams from organisational pressures. What is more, research will need to map the institutional regions and provinces in which 'Design Thinking Guardians' need to operation to protect and promote the ideas and practices of Design Thinking. This, then, would provide a catalogue of tactical and strategic tools that could support both the training and the ongoing work of *'Design Thinking Guardians'*.

How to Ensure That Design Thinking's Structures, Ideas and Practices Diffuse Through the Organisation?

The structures, ideas and practices of Design Thinking do not diffuse automatically throughout large organisations. As we have seen, even if Design Thinking initiatives successfully install Design Thinking teams, impacts were often rather limited and localised. This begs the question of how Design Thinking reformers in organisations can devise and implement strategies for diffusing the benefits of Design Thinking throughout large organisations?

Although no systematic study on diffusion strategies of Design Thinking exists (at least none that we are aware of), early indications—mostly anecdotal evidence gleaned from participants of the professional education programmes at the HPI Academy—indicate the would-be Design Thinking reformers develop strikingly divergent strategies for ostensibly the same aims. For example, a sizeable division of a large global engineering enterprise developed and implemented central diffusion strategy located in a specific department. Senior management explicitly endorsed and participated in the implementation of this strategy. Conversely, the diffusion strategy in a German public sector bank was predicated on keeping senior management out of the implementation process: members of the board of directors were asked to sign agreements that ensured their non-interference in the practical implementation. This suggests, then, that not all strategies are likely to be appropriate for diffusion in all organisational contests.

For this reason, research could draw on both a comparative and experimental approach. A comparative research design would help identify and delimit the range of existing dissemination strategies. Further, the comparison of different types of organisations would also provide insights into the efficacy and contextual fit of dissemination approaches. However, this inquiry should not be limited to researchers in academia alone. Large organisations would also profit from research aimed to design, test and, evaluate different strategies. Ownership of this research would typically reside in the core team responsible for the diffusion and development of Design Thinking within the organisation. Unlike external actors, such as D-Schools, design consultancies or other types at agencies, these internal centres of Design Thinking competence have more immediate access to and a more intimate understanding of the local organisational cultures.

Over and above comparative analysis of existing strategies, this question also calls for a more generative and experimental approach. There is also need for designing, testing and refining new tools and strategies or diffusing Design Thinking throughout organisations. A crucial issue and as yet unsolved question is how different organisations can ensure that the knowledge and skills of Design Thinking disseminated are of the highest possible quality. At the same time, organisations need to adapt these Design Thinking skills to the organisational realities of each institutional context. This is why, ideally, these generative and experimental activities ought to be situated within a network of diverse actors including (but certainly not limited to) schools of Design Thinking (and other sites of research and learning), businesses (large and small), public sector institutions (both in policy-making and service provision) as well as civil society organisations. Such a diverse network would allow the design, testing and comparison of different dissemination approaches.

Among other things, a key objective of such a research endeavour would be to devise practicable standards of training and teaching of Design Thinking-relevant skills. The success of diffusion and dissemination strategies is inextricably tied to the quality of training and teaching throughout the dissemination process. This would apply both to external training resources that accompanies the early stages of a Design Thinking initiative as well as to internal teaching capabilities for later in the diffusion process. Research—both comparative and generative—could set out to develop teaching and training standards that help organisational actors acquire high quality skills that, at the same time, are relevant to their specific organisational environment.

The preceding chapters have shown how the methods and practices of Design Thinking can shape large organisations. To do this, we first outlined a framework that allows us to conceptualise the potential impacts of Design Thinking on large organisations. The logic that brings about innovation in Design Thinking, we argued, not only effectively equips organisations for tackling complex and uncertain design challenges, it also provides an outline or blueprint for the transformation of organisations. Team-based integrative thinking that draws on the rich experiences of users not only allows organisations to formulate 'clumsy solutions' to wicked problems, it also points the way towards transforming organisations into 'multi-dextrous' or 'messy' institutions. Instead of simply infusing 'entrepreneurship' into 'bureaucratic' organisations—thereby exchanging one set of weaknesses for another—Design Thinking potentially enables organisations to draw on and mobilise a wide range ideas and practices to tackle wicked problems.

The methods and mindsets of Design Thinking do this by generating transformational sparks within the three fundamental institutional dimension: structures, ideas and practices. In all three dimensions, a deft implementation of the methods and mindsets of Design Thinking will not only supply organisational actors with the a requisite diversity of potential governance structures (hierarchies when reliability is needed, markets for efficient allocations, egalitarian groups for creating solidarity, and isolation for contemplation and regrouping) but also provide them with a wide variety of ideas as well as a set of pluralist practices for forging clumsy solutions and switching strategies when necessary.

The book also used this framework to analyse cases—or, if you will, prototypes—of what we have called Design Thinking initiatives: programmes aiming to implement the structures, ideas and practices of Design Thinking. We found that, while these Design Thinking initiatives brought about change in all three institutional dimensions, this change did not always install and foster a sufficiently wide range of structures, ideas and practices to ensure 'messy' team-based integrative thinking.

What is more, it would seem that a sustainable implementation of Design Thinking in large organisations will also require new approaches to leadership and management. In particular, 'Design Thinking Guardians' will need to start identify and developing tools for managing the interfaces between Design Thinking teams and the rest of the organisation. Further, Design Thinking leadership will need to find ways of living with and leveraging the inherent ambiguity that real work with wicked design challenges will inevitably give rise to. Last, effective Design Thinking Guardians will foster and manage constructive conflict within messy institutions.

In an article for the Harvard Business Review in 2015, the design theorist Jon Kolko wrote that Design Thinking was 'coming of age'. For him, this meant that people are successfully applying the methods and mindsets of Design Thinking to issues and problems beyond mere product design. Here, Kolko points to social innovation and development issues. But the term 'coming of age' more often than not implies of a 'rite of passage', of becoming part of a larger society. In this sense, our book has looked at Design Thinking's 'rite of passage' as it tries to find its place in and make its mark on the wider institutional landscape. We hope that we have been able to help make out a path, point to dangers and pitfalls along this path, and equip Design Thinking (and the Design Thinking community) with ideas and concepts that will make this passage safe and, more importantly, successful.

References

Carlgren, L., Elmquist, M., & Rauth, I. (2014). Exploring the use of design thinking in large organizations: Towards a research agenda. *Swedish Design Research Journal, 1*(14), 47–56.

Carlgren, L., Elmquist, M., & Rauth, I. (2016). The challenges of using design thinking in industry – Experiences from five large firms. *Creativity and Innovation Management, 25*(3), 344–362.

Colebatch, H. K. (2009). *Policy*. Maidenhead: Open University Press.

Dribbisch, K. (2016). Translating innovation: The adoption of design thinking in a Singaporean Ministry.

Habermas, J. (1987). *Theorie des Kommunikativen Handelns Bd.2 (vierte Auflage)*. Frankfurt am Main: Suhrkamp.

Hirschman, O. (1972). *Exit, voice, and loyalty: Response to decline in firms, organizations, and states*. Cambridge, MA: Harvard University Press.

Hood, C. (1998). *The art of the state: Culture, rhetoric, and public management*. Oxford: Oxford University Press.

Kingdon, J. W. (1984). *Agendas, alternatives and public policies*. Boston, MA: Little Brown.

Köppen, E. (2016). *Empathy by design: Untersuchung einer Empathie-geleiteten Reorganisation der Arbeitsweise*. Konstanz und München: UVK Verlagsgesellschaft mbH.

Liedtka, J., & Bennett, K. B. (2013). *Solving problems with design thinking: 10 stories of what works*. New York: Columbia University Press.

March, J. G. (1991). Exploration and exploitation in organizational learning. *Organization Science, 2*(1), 71–87.

Martin, R. L. (2009). *The opposable mind: Winning through integrative thinking*. Boston, MA: Harvard Business Press.

Ney, S., & Verweij, M. (2014b). Messy institutions for wicked problems: How to generate clumsy solutions. Available at SSRN 2382191.

O'Reilly, C., & Tushman, M. (2013). Organizational ambidexterity: Past, present and future. *The Academy of Management Perspectives, 27*(4), 324–338. https://doi.org/10.5465/amp.2013.0025.

Pierre, J., & Peters, B. G. (2000). *Governance, politics, and the state*. London: Palgrave.

Plattner, H., Meinel, C., & Leifer, L. J. (2014). *Design thinking research: Building innovators*. Cham: Springer.

Rauth, I., Carlgren, L., & Elmquist, M. (2014). Making it happen: Legitimizing design thinking in large organizations. *Design Management Journal, 9*(1), 47–60.

Rhinow, H. (2018). Design thinking Als Lernprozess in Organisationen: Neue Chancen Und Dilemmata Für Die Projektarbeit. Doctoral thesis, University of Potsdam, Potsdam.

Rittel, H., & Webber, M. (1973). Dilemmas in a general theory of planning. *Policy Sciences, 4*, 155–169.

Schmiedgen, J., Rhinow, H., Köppen, E., & Meinel, C. (2015). *Parts without a whole? The current state of design thinking practice in organisations* (Technical Report No 97). Potsdam: Verlag der Universität Potsdam.

Thompson, M., Ellis, R., & Wildavsky, A. (1990). *Cultural theory*. Boulder, CO: Westview Press.

CPSIA information can be obtained
at www.ICGtesting.com
Printed in the USA
LVHW082002190819
628159LV00009B/115/P